154
CROCHET WAVE PATTERNS

LEISURE ARTS, INC.
Little Rock, Arkansas

154 CROCHET WAVE PATTERNS

The shortest distance between a skein of yarn and creative happiness is—a row of waves. Or chevrons. Or ripples. That's because any one of these 154 stitch patterns will bring you hours of relaxation as you crochet afghans, bedspreads, dishcloths, placemats—whatever pleases you most. Since you choose the yarn weight and the size of the crochet hook, there's no limit to the textures you'll create. We used worsted weight yarn and a size H crochet hook to create the photo models, but you may decide to use lightweight yarns for baby blankets and table runners. Chunky yarns work well for rugs or potholders. Or try novelty yarns with metallic sparkles or fuzzy fibers to crochet one-of-a-kind scarves.

Round out your Darla Sims stitch collection by visiting your local retailer or leisurearts.com to find Leisure Arts leaflet 3903, *280 Crochet Shell Patterns*.

EDITORIAL STAFF

Managing Editor: Susan White Sullivan

Executive Director of Product Development:
   Cheryl Nodine Gunnells

Director of Designer Relations: Debra Nettles

Director of Knit and Crochet Publications:
   Cheryl Johnson

Director of Special Projects: Susan Wiles

Senior Director of Prepress: Mark Hawkins

Art Publications Director: Rhonda Hodge Shelby

Technical Writer: Linda Luder

Contributing Technical Editor: Donna Jones

Graphic Artists: Angela Ormsby Stark
   and Amy Temple

Editorial Writer: Susan McManus Johnson

Imaging Technician: Mark R. Potter

Contributing Photographers: Jerry Davis
   and Ken West

Systems Administrator: Becky Riddle

Publishing Systems Assistants: Clint Hanson
   and John Rose

BUSINESS STAFF

Chief Operating Officer: Tom Siebenmorgen

Vice President, Sales and Marketing: Pam Stebbins

Director of Sales and Services: Margaret Reinold

Vice President, Operations: Jim Dittrich

Comptroller, Operations: Rob Thieme

Retail Customer Service Managers: Stan Raynor

Print Production Manager: Fred F. Pruss

Swatches made and instructions tested by Janet Akins.

ISBN-13 978-1-60140-558-6
ISBN-10 1-60140-558-8

LEISURE ARTS, INC.
Little Rock, Arkansas

PLANNING AN AFGHAN

When planning an afghan, decide what size afghan you'd like to make, then select your favorite yarn and pattern stitch and make a swatch. Measure the width of one repeat in the swatch to determine the number of pattern repeats necessary to make your afghan the desired width.

For example, if you want to use pattern stitch #7 Bobbin' Along, on page 10, to make an afghan that is 45" (114.5 cm) wide and your pattern repeat measures 3" (7.5 cm), you'll divide 45 by 3 to determine the number of pattern repeats you need for the desired width (45 divided by 3 = 15 pattern repeats). It takes 16 chains to work one repeat so you'll need 240 chains to work 15 pattern repeats (16 x 15 = 240). Then add any additional chains that are necessary to work the first row of the pattern (240 + 4 = 244 chains).

one repeat

1 LULLABY LACE

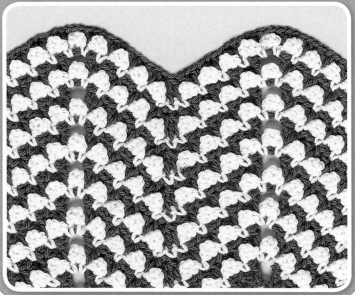

Note: Uses MC and CC in the following sequence: ★ 1 Row **each** MC, CC; repeat from ★ for stripe sequence.

With MC, chain a multiple of 28 + 4 chs.

To decrease (uses next 3 sts), YO, insert hook in next st, YO and pull up a loop, YO and draw through 2 loops on hook, YO, skip next ch, insert hook in next st, YO and pull up a loop, YO and draw through 2 loops on hook, YO and draw through all 3 loops on hook **(counts as one dc)**.

To double decrease (uses next 3 sts), ★ YO, insert hook in **next** st, YO and pull up a loop, YO and draw through 2 loops on hook; repeat from ★ 2 times **more**, YO and draw through all 4 loops on hook **(counts as one dc)**.

Row 1 (Right side)**:** Dc in fourth ch from hook, [skip next 2 chs, (dc, ch 1, dc) in next ch] 4 times, ch 3, skip next ch, (dc, ch 1, dc) in next ch, [skip next 2 chs, (dc, ch 1, dc) in next ch] 3 times, ★ skip next 2 chs, double decrease, [skip next 2 chs, (dc, ch 1, dc) in next ch] 4 times, ch 3, skip next ch, (dc, ch 1, dc) in next ch, [skip next 2 chs, (dc, ch 1, dc) in next ch] 3 times; repeat from ★ across to last 5 chs, skip next 2 chs, decrease; finish off.

Note: Loop a short piece of yarn around any stitch to mark Row 1 as **right** side.

To work Cluster, ch 3, dc in third ch from hook.

Row 2: With **wrong** side facing, join CC with sc in first dc *(see Joining With Sc, page 158)*; ch 1, (sc in next ch-1 sp, work Cluster) 4 times, (sc, work Cluster) twice in next ch-3 sp, sc in next ch-1 sp, (work Cluster, sc in next ch-1 sp) 3 times, ★ skip next dc, sc in next dc, (sc in next ch-1 sp, work Cluster) 4 times, (sc, work Cluster) twice in next ch-3 sp, sc in next ch-1 sp, (work Cluster, sc in next ch-1 sp) 3 times; repeat from ★ across to last 2 dc, ch 1, skip next dc, sc in last dc; finish off.

Row 3: With **right** side facing, join MC with slip st in first sc; ch 2, dc in next sc, [skip next Cluster, (dc, ch 1, dc) in next sc] 4 times, ch 3, [skip next Cluster, (dc, ch 1, dc) in next sc] 4 times, ★ skip next Cluster, double decrease, [skip next Cluster, (dc, ch 1, dc) in next sc] 4 times, ch 3, [skip next Cluster, (dc, ch 1, dc) in next sc] 4 times; repeat from ★ across to last Cluster, skip last Cluster, decrease; finish off.

Repeat Rows 2 and 3 for pattern.

2 TILE WORKS

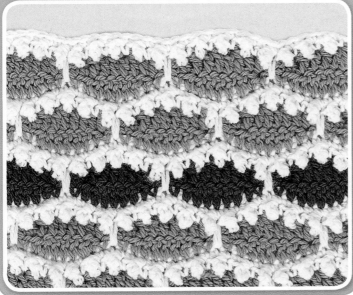

Note: Uses Colors A, B, C, and D in the following sequence: 1 Row Color A, ★ 2 rows **each** Color B, Color A, Color C, Color A, Color D, Color A, Color C, Color A; repeat from ★ for stripe sequence.

With Color A, chain a multiple of 10 chs.

Row 1 (Right side)**:** Sc in second ch from hook and in each ch across; finish off.

Note: Loop a short piece of yarn around any stitch to mark Row 1 as **right** side.

Row 2: With **wrong** side facing, join Color B with sc in first sc **(see Joining With Sc, page 158)**; hdc in next sc, dc in next 5 sc, hdc in next sc, sc in next sc, ★ ch 1, skip next sc, sc in next sc, hdc in next sc, dc in next 5 sc, hdc in next sc, sc in next sc; repeat from ★ across.

Row 3: Ch 1, turn; sc in first sc, hdc in next hdc, dc in next 5 dc, hdc in next hdc, sc in next sc, ★ ch 1, skip next ch, sc in next sc, hdc in next hdc, dc in next 5 dc, hdc in next hdc, sc in next sc; repeat from ★ across; finish off.

To treble crochet (abbreviated tr), YO twice, insert hook in st indicated, YO and pull up a loop, (YO and draw through 2 loops on hook) 3 times.

To work Long Single Crochet (abbreviated LSC), working **around** previous 2 rows **(Fig. 6, page 159)**, sc in skipped sc 2 rows **below** next ch.

Row 4: With **wrong** side facing, join Color A with sc in first sc; sc in next hdc, tr in next dc, (sc in next st pushing tr to **right** side, tr in next st) 3 times, work LSC pushing tr to **right** side, tr in next sc, ★ (sc in next st pushing tr to **right** side, tr in next st) 4 times, work LSC pushing tr to **right** side, tr in next sc; repeat from ★ across to last 8 sts, (sc in next st pushing tr to **right** side, tr in next st) 3 times, sc in last 2 sts.

Row 5: Ch 1, turn; sc in each st across; finish off.

Row 6: With **wrong** side facing, join Color C with slip st in first sc; ch 3 **(counts as first dc, now and throughout)**, dc in next sc, hdc in next sc, sc in next sc, ch 1, skip next sc, sc in next sc, hdc in next sc, ★ dc in next 5 sc, hdc in next sc, sc in next sc, ch 1, skip next sc, sc in next sc, hdc in next sc; repeat from ★ across to last 2 sc, dc in last 2 dc.

Row 7: Ch 3, turn; dc in next dc, hdc in next hdc, sc in next sc, ch 1, skip next ch, sc in next sc, hdc in next hdc, ★ dc in next 5 dc, hdc in next hdc, sc in next sc, ch 1, skip next ch, sc in next sc, hdc in next hdc; repeat from ★ across to last 2 dc, dc in last 2 dc; finish off.

Row 8: With **wrong** side facing, join Color A with sc in first dc; tr in next dc, sc in next hdc pushing tr to **right** side, tr in next sc, work LSC pushing tr to **right** side, tr in next sc, ★ (sc in next st pushing tr to **right** side, tr in next st) 4 times, work LSC pushing tr to **right** side, tr in next sc; repeat from ★ across to last 3 sts, sc in next hdc pushing tr to **right** side, tr in next dc, sc in last dc pushing tr to **right** side.

Row 9: Ch 1, turn; sc in each st across; finish off.

Rows 10 and 11: With Color D, repeat Rows 2 and 3.

Rows 12-17: Repeat Rows 4-9.

Repeat Rows 2-17 for pattern.

3 CLOUDS ON THE MOUNTAINS

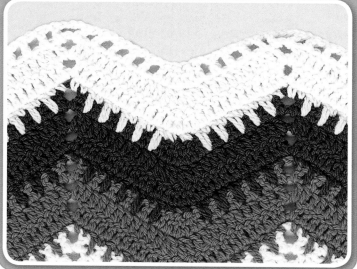

Note: Uses Colors A, B, and C in the following sequence: ★ 4 Rows **each** Color A, Color B, Color C; repeat from ★ for stripe sequence.

With Color A, chain a multiple of 27 + 24 chs.

To dc decrease (uses next 2 sts), ★ YO, insert hook in **next** st, YO and pull up a loop, YO and draw through 2 loops on hook; repeat from ★ once **more**, YO and draw through all 3 loops on hook **(counts as one dc)**.

Row 1 (Right side)**:** Working in back ridges of beginning ch **(Fig. 1, page 159)**, dc in third ch from hook and in next 9 chs, (dc, ch 3, dc) in next ch, ★ dc in next 11 chs, skip next 4 chs, dc in next 11 chs, (dc, ch 3, dc) in next ch; repeat from ★ across to last 11 chs, dc in next 9 chs, dc decrease.

Note: Loop a short piece of yarn around any stitch to mark Row 1 as **right** side.

Rows 2 and 3: Ch 2, turn; skip first st, dc in next 10 sts, (dc, ch 3, dc) in next ch-3 sp, ★ dc in next 10 sts, dc decrease twice, dc in next 10 sts, (dc, ch 3, dc) in next ch-3 sp; repeat from ★ across to last 11 sts, dc in next 9 sts, dc decrease.

Row 4: Ch 2, turn; skip first dc, (dc in next dc, ch 1, skip next dc) 5 times, (dc, ch 3, dc) in next ch-3 sp, ★ (ch 1, skip next dc, dc in next dc) 5 times, dc decrease twice, (dc in next dc, ch 1, skip next dc) 5 times, (dc, ch 3, dc) in next ch-3 sp; repeat from ★ across to last 11 sts, ch 1, skip next dc, (dc in next dc, ch 1, skip next dc) 4 times, dc decrease; finish off.

To work Long Double Crochet (abbreviated LDC), working **around** previous row **(Fig. 6, page 159)**, dc in skipped dc one row **below** next ch.

To sc decrease, pull up a loop in each of next 2 sts, YO and draw through all 3 loops on hook **(counts as one sc)**.

Row 5: With **right** side facing, join Color B with slip st in first dc; (work LDC, sc in next dc) 5 times, (sc, ch 3, sc) in next ch-3 sp, ★ (sc in next dc, work LDC) 5 times, sc decrease twice, (work LDC, sc in next dc) 5 times, (sc, ch 3, sc) in next ch-3 sp; repeat from ★ across to last 6 dc, sc in next dc, (work LDC, sc in next dc) 4 times, YO, working **around** previous row, insert hook in skipped dc one row **below** next ch, YO and pull up a loop (3 loops on hook), YO and draw through 2 loops on hook, pull up a loop in last dc, YO and draw through all 3 loops on hook.

Rows 6-8: Repeat Rows 2-4.

Rows 9-12: With Color C, repeat Rows 5-8.

Row 13: With Color A, repeat Row 5.

Repeat Rows 2-13 for pattern.

4 POPCORN PIZAZZ

Chain a multiple of 24 + 5 chs.

To decrease (uses next 3 dc/chs), ★ YO, insert hook in **next** st/ch, YO and pull up a loop, YO and draw through 2 loops on hook; repeat from ★ 2 times **more**, YO and draw through all 4 loops on hook **(counts as one dc)**.

To double crochet 5 together (abbreviated dc5tog), ★ YO, insert hook in **next** st/ch, YO and pull up a loop, YO and draw through 2 loops on hook; repeat from ★ 4 times **more**, YO and draw through all 6 loops on hook **(counts as one dc)**.

Row 1 (Right side)**:** Decrease beginning in fourth ch from hook **(3 skipped chs count as first dc)**, dc in next 9 chs, 5 dc in next ch, dc in next 9 chs, ★ dc5tog, dc in next 9 chs, 5 dc in next ch, dc in next 9 chs; repeat from ★ across to last 4 chs, decrease, dc in last ch.

Note: Loop a short piece of yarn around any stitch to mark Row 1 as **right** side.

Row 2: Ch 3 **(counts as first dc, now and throughout)**, turn; decrease, dc in next 9 dc, 5 dc in next dc, dc in next 9 dc, ★ dc5tog, dc in next 9 dc, 5 dc in next dc, dc in next 9 dc; repeat from ★ across to last 4 dc, decrease, dc in last dc.

Row 3: Ch 3, turn; decrease, ch 1, skip next dc, (dc in next dc, ch 1, skip next dc) 4 times, 5 dc in next dc, ch 1, (skip next dc, dc in next dc, ch 1) 4 times, ★ skip next dc, dc5tog, ch 1, skip next dc, (dc in next dc, ch 1, skip next dc) 4 times, 5 dc in next dc, ch 1, (skip next dc, dc in next dc, ch 1) 4 times; repeat from ★ across to last 5 dc, skip next dc, decrease, dc in last dc.

Row 4: Ch 3, turn; decrease, dc in next ch-1 sp, (dc in next dc and in next ch-1 sp) 3 times, dc in next 2 dc, 5 dc in next dc, dc in next 2 dc and in next ch-1 sp, (dc in next dc and in next ch-1 sp) 3 times, ★ dc5tog, dc in next ch-1 sp, (dc in next dc and in next ch-1 sp) 3 times, dc in next 2 dc, 5 dc in next dc, dc in next 2 dc and in next ch-1 sp, (dc in next dc and in next ch-1 sp) 3 times; repeat from ★ across to last 3 dc, decrease, dc in last dc.

To work Popcorn (uses one dc), 5 dc in dc indicated, drop loop from hook, insert hook from **front** to **back** in first dc of 5-dc group, hook dropped loop and draw through st.

Row 5: Ch 3, turn; decrease, ch 2, skip next dc, (work Popcorn in next dc, ch 2, skip next dc) 4 times, work (Popcorn, ch 3, Popcorn) in next dc, ch 2, (skip next dc, work Popcorn in next dc, ch 2) 4 times, ★ skip next dc, dc5tog, ch 2, skip next dc, (work Popcorn in next dc, ch 2, skip next dc) 4 times, work (Popcorn, ch 3, Popcorn) in next dc, ch 2, (skip next dc, work Popcorn in next dc, ch 2) 4 times; repeat from ★ across to last 5 dc, skip next dc, decrease, dc in last dc.

Row 6: Ch 3, turn; 2 dc in each of next 5 ch-2 sps, 5 dc in next ch-3 sp, ★ 2 dc in each of next 4 ch-2 sps, dc in next ch-2 sp and in next dc, dc in next ch-2 sp, 2 dc in each of next 4 ch-2 sps, 5 dc in next ch-3 sp; repeat from ★ across to last 5 ch-2 sps, 2 dc in each of last 5 ch-2 sps, skip next dc, dc in last dc.

Repeat Rows 3-6 for pattern.

5 HARMONY

Note: Uses Colors A, B, and C in the following sequence: 3 Rows Color A, ★ 1 row Color B, 2 rows Color C, 1 row Color B, 2 rows Color A; repeat from ★ for stripe sequence.

With Color A, chain a multiple of 24 + 2 chs.

To sc decrease, pull up a loop in each of next 2 sts, YO and draw through all 3 loops on hook **(counts as one sc)**.

To double sc decrease, pull up a loop in each of next 3 sts, YO and draw through all 4 loops on hook **(counts as one sc)**.

Row 1 (Right side)**:** Sc decrease beginning in second ch from hook, sc in next 10 chs, 3 sc in next ch, sc in next 10 chs, ★ double sc decrease, sc in next 10 chs, 3 sc in next ch, sc in next 10 chs; repeat from ★ across to last 2 chs, sc decrease.

Note: Loop a short piece of yarn around any stitch to mark Row 1 as **right** side.

To dc decrease (uses next 2 sts)**,** ★ YO, insert hook in **next** st, YO and pull up a loop, YO and draw through 2 loops on hook; repeat from ★ once **more**, YO and draw through all 3 loops on hook **(counts as one dc).**

To double dc decrease (uses next 3 sts)**,** ★ YO, insert hook in **next** st, YO and pull up a loop, YO and draw through 2 loops on hook; repeat from ★ 2 times **more**, YO and draw through all 4 loops on hook **(counts as one dc).**

Rows 2 and 3: Ch 2, turn; skip first st, dc in next 11 sts, 3 dc in next st, dc in next 10 sts, ★ double dc decrease, dc in next 10 sts, 3 dc in next st, dc in next 10 sts; repeat from ★ across to last 2 sts, dc decrease.

Finish off.

Row 4: With **wrong** side facing, join Color B with slip st in first dc; ch 2, dc in next 11 dc, 3 dc in next dc, dc in next 10 dc, ★ double dc decrease, dc in next 10 dc, 3 dc in next dc, dc in next 10 dc; repeat from ★ across to last 2 dc, dc decrease; finish off.

To work Cluster (uses next dc)**,** ★ YO, insert hook from **front** to **back** around post of dc indicated **(Fig. 4, page 159)**, YO and pull up a loop, YO and draw through 2 loops on hook; repeat from ★ 2 times **more**, YO and draw through all 4 loops on hook.

Row 5: With **right** side facing, join Color C with slip st in first dc; ch 1, sc decrease beginning in same st as joining, work Cluster around next dc, (sc in next 3 dc, work Cluster around next dc) twice, sc in next dc, 3 sc in next dc, sc in next dc, work Cluster around next dc, (sc in next 3 dc, work Cluster around next dc) twice, ★ double sc decrease, work Cluster around next dc, (sc in next 3 dc, work Cluster around next dc) twice, sc in next dc, 3 sc in next dc, sc in next dc, work Cluster around next dc, (sc in next 3 dc, work Cluster around next dc) twice; repeat from ★ across to last 2 dc, sc decrease.

Row 6: Ch 1, turn; sc decrease beginning in first sc, sc in next 10 sts, 3 sc in next sc, sc in next 10 sts, ★ double sc decrease, sc in next 10 sts, 3 sc in next sc, sc in next 10 sts; repeat from ★ across to last 2 sts, sc decrease; finish off.

Row 7: With **right** side facing, join Color B with slip st in first sc; ch 2, dc in next 11 sc, 3 dc in next sc, dc in next 10 sc, ★ double dc decrease, dc in next 10 sc, 3 dc in next sc, dc in next 10 sc; repeat from ★ across to last 2 sts, dc decrease; finish off.

Row 8: With **wrong** side facing, join Color A with slip st in first dc; ch 2, dc in next 11 dc, 3 dc in next dc, dc in next 10 dc, ★ double dc decrease, dc in next 10 dc, 3 dc in next dc, dc in next 10 dc; repeat from ★ across to last 2 dc, dc decrease.

Repeat Rows 3-8 for pattern.

6 LITTLE RELIEF CHEVRONS

Note: Uses MC and CC in the following sequence: ★ 2 Rows **each** MC, CC; repeat from ★ for stripe sequence.

With MC, chain a multiple of 4 chs.

Row 1 (Right side)**:** Sc in second ch from hook and in next 2 chs, ★ ch 1, skip next ch, sc in next 3 chs; repeat from ★ across.

Note: Loop a short piece of yarn around any stitch to mark Row 1 as **right** side.

Row 2: Ch 3 **(counts as first dc, now and throughout)**, turn; dc in next sc and in each sc and each ch-1 sp across; finish off.

To treble crochet (abbreviated tr), YO twice, insert hook in st indicated, YO and pull up a loop (4 loops on hook), (YO and draw through 2 loops on hook) 3 times.

Row 3: With **right** side facing, join CC with sc in first dc *(see Joining With Sc, page 158)*; working in **front** of previous row *(Fig. 6, page 159)*, tr in first skipped st on row **below**, skip next dc (behind tr just made), sc in next dc, ch 1, skip next dc, sc in next dc, ★ YO twice, working in **front** of previous row, insert hook in **same** skipped st on row **below** as previous st, YO and pull up a loop, (YO and draw through 2 loops on hook) twice, YO twice, insert hook in **next** skipped st on row **below**, YO and pull up a loop, (YO and draw through 2 loops on hook) twice, YO and draw through all 3 loops on hook, skip next dc (behind st just made), sc in next dc, ch 1, skip next dc, sc in next dc; repeat from ★ across to last 2 dc, working in **front** of previous row, tr in same skipped st on row **below** as previous st, skip next dc (behind tr just made), sc in last dc.

Row 4: Ch 3, turn; dc in next tr and in each st and each ch-1 sp across; finish off.

Repeat Rows 3 and 4 for pattern, working in stripe sequence.

7 BOBBIN' ALONG

Note: Uses Colors A, B, and C in the following sequence: ★ 1 Row **each** Color A, Color B, Color C, Color B; repeat from ★ for stripe sequence.

With Color A, chain a multiple of 16 + 4 chs.

To dc decrease (uses next 3 sts), ★ YO, insert hook in **next** st, YO and pull up a loop, YO and draw through 2 loops on hook; repeat from ★ 2 times **more**, YO and draw through all 4 loops on hook **(counts as one dc)**.

Row 1 (Right side)**:** Dc in fourth ch from hook **(3 skipped chs count as first dc)** and in next 6 chs, dc decrease, dc in next 6 chs, ★ 3 dc in next ch, dc in next 6 chs, dc decrease, dc in next 6 chs; repeat from ★ across to last ch, 2 dc in last ch; finish off.

Note: Loop a short piece of yarn around any stitch to mark Row 1 as **right** side.

To treble crochet (abbreviated tr), YO twice, insert hook in next st, YO and pull up a loop (4 loops on hook), (YO and draw through 2 loops on hook) 3 times.

To sc decrease, pull up a loop in each of next 3 dc, YO and draw through all 4 loops on hook **(counts as one sc)**.

Row 2: With **wrong** side facing, join Color B with sc in first dc *(see Joining With Sc, page 158)*; tr in same st, (sc in next dc pushing tr to **right** side, tr in next dc) 3 times, sc decrease pushing tr to **right** side, (tr in next dc, sc in next dc pushing tr to **right** side) 3 times, ★ (tr, sc, tr) in next dc, (sc in next dc pushing tr to **right** side, tr in next dc) 3 times, sc decrease pushing tr to **right** side, (tr in next dc, sc in next dc pushing tr to **right** side) 3 times; repeat from ★ across to last dc, (tr, sc) in last dc; finish off.

Row 3: With **right** side facing, join Color C with slip st in first sc; ch 3 **(counts as first dc, now and throughout)**, dc in same st as joining and in next 6 sts, dc decrease, dc in next 6 sts, ★ 3 dc in next st, dc in next 6 sts, dc decrease, dc in next 6 sts; repeat from ★ across to last sc, 2 dc in last sc; finish off.

Row 4: With **wrong** side facing, join Color B with sc in first dc; tr in same st, (sc in next dc pushing tr to **right** side, tr in next dc) 3 times, sc decrease pushing tr to **right** side, (tr in next dc, sc in next dc pushing tr to **right** side) 3 times, ★ (tr, sc, tr) in next dc, (sc in next dc pushing tr to **right** side, tr in next dc) 3 times, sc decrease pushing tr to **right** side, (tr in next dc, sc in next dc pushing tr to **right** side) 3 times; repeat from ★ across to last dc, (tr, sc) in last dc; finish off.

Row 5: With **right** side facing, join Color A with slip st in first sc; ch 3, dc in same st as joining and in next 6 sts, dc decrease, dc in next 6 sts, ★ 3 dc in next st, dc in next 6 sts, dc decrease, dc in next 6 sts; repeat from ★ across to last sc, 2 dc in last sc; finish off.

Repeat Rows 2-5 for pattern.

8 EYE CANDY

Note: Uses MC, and Colors A, B, C, and D in the following sequence: ★ 1 Row **each** MC, Color A, MC, Color B, MC, Color C, MC, Color D; repeat from ★ for stripe sequence.

With MC, chain a multiple of 15 + 1 ch.

Row 1 (Right side)**:** Dc in third ch from hook, ch 1, skip next ch, (dc in next ch, ch 1, skip next ch) twice, (dc, ch 3, dc) in next ch, ★ ch 1, skip next ch, (dc in next ch, ch 1, skip next ch) twice, YO, † insert hook in **next** ch, YO and pull up a loop, YO and draw through 2 loops on hook †, YO, skip next 2 chs, repeat from † to † once, YO and draw through all 3 loops on hook, ch 1, skip next ch, (dc in next ch, ch 1, skip next ch) twice, (dc, ch 3, dc) in next ch; repeat from ★ across to last 7 chs, ch 1, skip next ch, (dc in next ch, ch 1, skip next ch) twice, [YO, insert hook in **next** ch, YO and pull up a loop, YO and draw through 2 loops on hook] twice, YO and draw through all 3 loops on hook; finish off.

Note: Loop a short piece of yarn around any stitch to mark Row 1 as **right** side.

To work Cluster (uses one st), ★ YO, insert hook in st indicated, YO and pull up a loop, YO and draw through 2 loops on hook; repeat from ★ 3 times **more**, YO and draw through all 5 loops on hook, pushing Cluster to **right** side.

Row 2: With **wrong** side facing, join Color A with sc in first st *(see Joining With Sc, page 158)*; skip next ch, sc in next dc, (ch 1, skip next ch, sc in next dc) twice, (sc, ch 2, sc) in next ch-3 sp, sc in next dc, (ch 1, skip next ch, sc in next dc) twice, ★ skip next ch, work Cluster in next st, skip next ch, sc in next dc, (ch 1, skip next ch, sc in next dc) twice, (sc, ch 2, sc) in next ch-3 sp, sc in next dc, (ch 1, skip next ch, sc in next dc) twice; repeat from ★ across to last 2 sts, skip next ch, sc in last dc; finish off.

To decrease (uses next 2 sc), ★ YO, insert hook in **next** sc, YO and pull up a loop, YO and draw through 2 loops on hook; repeat from ★ once **more**, YO and draw through all 3 loops on hook.

To double decrease (uses next 3 sts), ★ YO, insert hook in **next** st, YO and pull up a loop, YO and draw through 2 loops on hook; repeat from ★ 2 times **more**, YO and draw through all 4 loops on hook.

Row 3: With **right** side facing, join MC with slip st in first sc; ch 2, (dc in next sc, ch 1, skip next st) 3 times, (dc, ch 3, dc) in next ch-2 sp, ch 1, skip next sc, (dc in next sc, ch 1, skip next ch) twice, ★ double decrease, ch 1, skip next ch, (dc in next sc, ch 1, skip next st) twice, (dc, ch 3, dc) in next ch-2 sp, ch 1, skip next sc, (dc in next sc, ch 1, skip next ch) twice; repeat from ★ across to last 2 sc, decrease; finish off.

Repeat Rows 2 and 3 for pattern, working in stripe sequence.

9 SYMMETRICAL WAVES

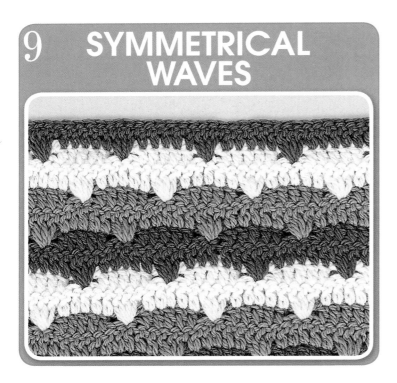

Note: Uses Colors A, B, and C in the following sequence: 1 Row Color A, ★ 2 rows **each** Color B, Color C, Color A; repeat from ★ for stripe sequence.

With Color A, chain a multiple of 8 + 3 chs.

Row 1 (Right side)**:** Dc in fourth ch from hook **(3 skipped chs count as first dc)** and in next ch, ch 3, ★ skip next 3 chs, dc in next 5 chs, ch 3; repeat from ★ across to last 6 chs, skip next 3 chs, dc in last 3 chs; finish off.

Note: Loop a short piece of yarn around any stitch to mark Row 1 as **right** side.

Row 2: With **wrong** side facing, join Color B with slip st in first dc; ch 3 **(counts as first dc, now and throughout)**, dc in next 2 dc, working **around** previous row **(Fig. 6, page 159)**, 3 dc in center skipped ch one row **below**, ★ dc in next 5 dc, working **around** previous row, 3 dc in center skipped ch one row **below**; repeat from ★ across to last 3 dc, dc in last 3 dc.

Row 3: Ch 3, turn; dc in next 6 dc, ch 3, ★ skip next 3 dc, dc in next 5 dc, ch 3; repeat from ★ across to last 10 dc, skip next 3 dc, dc in last 7 dc; finish off.

Row 4: With **wrong** side facing, join Color C with slip st in first dc; ch 3, dc in next 6 dc, working **around** previous row, 3 dc in center skipped dc one row **below**, ★ dc in next 5 dc, working **around** previous row, 3 dc in center skipped dc one row **below**; repeat from ★ across to last 7 dc, dc in last 7 dc.

Row 5: Ch 3, turn; dc in next 2 dc, ch 3, ★ skip next 3 dc, dc in next 5 dc, ch 3; repeat from ★ across to last 6 dc, skip next 3 dc, dc in last 3 dc; finish off.

Row 6: With **wrong** side facing, join Color A with slip st in first dc; ch 3, dc in next 2 dc, working **around** previous row, 3 dc in center skipped dc one row **below**, ★ dc in next 5 dc, working **around** previous row, 3 dc in center skipped dc one row **below**; repeat from ★ across to last 3 dc, dc in last 3 dc.

Row 7: Ch 3, turn; dc in next 6 dc, ch 3, ★ skip next 3 dc, dc in next 5 dc, ch 3; repeat from ★ across to last 10 dc, skip next 3 dc, dc in last 7 dc; finish off.

Repeat Rows 4-7 for pattern, working in stripe sequence.

10 CELEBRATION

To work Long Double Crochet (abbreviated LDC), working in **front** of previous 3 rows *(Fig. 6, page 159)*, YO, insert hook in center sc of 3-sc group on fourth row **below**, YO and pull up a loop even with loop on hook (3 loops on hook), (YO and draw through 2 loops on hook) twice. Skip sc **behind** LDC just made.

Row 5: With **right** side facing, join Color B with sc in first sc *(see Joining With Sc, page 158)*; skip next sc, sc in next 2 sc, work LDC, sc in next 3 sc, 3 sc in next sc, sc in next 3 sc, work LDC in same st as last LDC, ★ sc in next 3 sc, skip next 2 sc, sc in next 3 sc, work LDC, sc in next 3 sc, 3 sc in next sc, sc in next 3 sc, work LDC in same st as last LDC; repeat from ★ across to last 4 sc, sc in next 2 sc, skip next sc, sc in last sc.

Rows 6-8: Ch 1, turn; sc in first sc, skip next sc, sc in next 6 sts, 3 sc in next sc, ★ sc in next 7 sts, skip next 2 sc, sc in next 7 sts, 3 sc in next sc; repeat from ★ across to last 8 sts, sc in next 6 sts, skip next sc, sc in last sc; at end of last row, finish off.

Repeat Rows 5-8 for pattern, working in stripe sequence.

Optional: Measure the length of the piece and add 10" (25.5 cm). Cut 4 strands of Color B this total measurement and weave through center sc every 4 rows; tie a knot at the top and bottom. Repeat for each "point" on piece.

Note: Uses Colors A, B, and C in the following sequence: ★ 4 Rows **each** Color A, Color B, Color C, Color B; repeat from ★ for stripe sequence.

With Color A, chain a multiple of 17 plus 16 chs.

Row 1 (Right side)**:** Working in back ridges of beginning ch *(Fig. 1, page 159)*, sc in second ch from hook and in next 6 chs, 3 sc in next ch, sc in next 7 chs, ★ skip next 2 chs, sc in next 7 chs, 3 sc in next ch, sc in next 7 chs; repeat from ★ across.

Note: Loop a short piece of yarn around any stitch to mark Row 1 as **right** side.

Rows 2-4: Ch 1, turn; sc in first sc, skip next sc, sc in next 6 sc, 3 sc in next sc, ★ sc in next 7 sc, skip next 2 sc, sc in next 7 sc, 3 sc in next sc; repeat from ★ across to last 8 sc, sc in next 6 sc, skip next sc, sc in last sc; at end of last row, finish off.

11 POPCORN-EDGED DIAMONDS

Chain a multiple of 21 chs.

Row 1: Dc in fourth ch from hook **(3 skipped chs count as first dc)** and in next 7 chs, (dc, ch 3, dc) in next ch, ★ dc in next 8 chs, [YO, insert hook in **next** ch, YO and pull up a loop, YO and draw through 2 loops on hook] 4 times, YO and draw through all 5 loops on hook, dc in next 8 chs, (dc, ch 3, dc) in next ch; repeat from ★ across to last 9 chs, dc in last 9 chs.

To work Popcorn (uses one sp), 5 dc in sp indicated, drop loop from hook, insert hook from **front** to **back** in first dc of 5-dc group, hook dropped loop and draw through st.

Row 2 (Right side)**:** Ch 1, turn; sc in first dc, skip next dc, sc in next 8 dc, (sc, work Popcorn, sc) in next ch-3 sp, ★ sc in next 9 dc, skip next st, sc in next 9 dc, (sc, work Popcorn, sc) in next ch-3 sp; repeat from ★ across to last 10 dc, sc in next 8 dc, skip next dc, sc in last dc.

Note: Loop a short piece of yarn around any stitch to mark Row 2 as **right** side.

To decrease (uses next 4 sts), YO, insert hook in next st, YO and pull up a loop, YO and draw through 2 loops on hook, YO, skip next 2 sc, insert hook in next st, YO and pull up a loop, YO and draw through 2 loops on hook, YO and draw through all 3 loops on hook **(counts as one dc)**.

Row 3: Ch 3 **(counts as first dc, now and throughout)**, turn; skip first 2 sc, dc in next 7 sc, ch 1, skip next sc, (dc, ch 3, dc) in next Popcorn, ch 1, skip next sc, dc in next 7 sc, ★ decrease, dc in next 7 sc, ch 1, skip next sc, (dc, ch 3, dc) in next Popcorn, ch 1, skip next sc, dc in next 7 sc; repeat from ★ across to last 2 sc, skip next sc, dc in last sc.

Row 4: Ch 1, turn; sc in first dc, skip next dc, sc in next 6 dc, work Popcorn in next ch-1 sp, sc in next dc, 3 sc in next ch-3 sp, sc in next dc, work Popcorn in next ch-1 sp, ★ sc in next 7 dc, skip next dc, sc in next 7 dc, work Popcorn in next ch-1 sp, sc in next dc, 3 sc in next ch-3 sp, sc in next dc, work Popcorn in next ch-1 sp; repeat from ★ across to last 8 dc, sc in next 6 dc, skip next dc, sc in last dc.

Row 5: Ch 3, turn; skip first 2 sc, dc in next 5 sc, ch 1, skip next Popcorn, dc in next sc, ch 1, skip next sc, (dc, ch 3, dc) in next sc, ch 1, skip next sc, dc in next sc, ch 1, skip next Popcorn, dc in next 5 sc, ★ decrease, dc in next 5 sc, ch 1, skip next Popcorn, dc in next sc, ch 1, skip next sc, (dc, ch 3, dc) in next sc, ch 1, skip next sc, dc in next sc, ch 1, skip next Popcorn, dc in next 5 sc; repeat from ★ across to last 2 sc, skip next sc, dc in last sc.

Row 6: Ch 1, turn; sc in first dc, skip next dc, sc in next 4 dc, work Popcorn in next ch-1 sp, sc in next dc and in next ch-1 sp, sc in next dc, 3 sc in next ch-3 sp, sc in next dc and in next ch-1 sp, sc in next dc, work Popcorn in next ch-1 sp, ★ sc in next 5 dc, skip next dc, sc in next 5 dc, work Popcorn in next ch-1 sp, sc in next dc and in next ch-1 sp, sc in next dc, 3 sc in next ch-3 sp, sc in next dc and in next ch-1 sp, sc in next dc, work Popcorn in next ch-1 sp; repeat from ★ across to last 6 dc, sc in next 4 dc, skip next dc, sc in last dc.

Row 7: Ch 3, turn; skip first 2 sc, dc in next 3 sc, ch 1, skip next Popcorn, (dc in next sc, ch 1, skip next sc) twice, (dc, ch 3, dc) in next sc, ch 1, (skip next sc, dc in next sc, ch 1) twice, skip next Popcorn, dc in next 3 sc, ★ decrease, dc in next 3 sc, ch 1, skip next Popcorn, (dc in next sc, ch 1, skip next sc) twice, (dc, ch 3, dc) in next sc, ch 1, (skip next sc, dc in next sc, ch 1) twice, skip next Popcorn, dc in next 3 sc; repeat from ★ across to last 2 sc, skip next sc, dc in last sc.

Row 8: Ch 1, turn; sc in first dc, skip next dc, sc in next 2 dc, work Popcorn in next ch-1 sp, (sc in next dc and in next ch-1 sp) twice, sc in next dc, 3 sc in next ch-3 sp, (sc in next dc and in next ch-1 sp) twice, sc in next dc, work Popcorn in next ch-1 sp, ★ sc in next 3 dc, skip next dc, sc in next 3 dc, work Popcorn in next ch-1 sp, (sc in next dc and in next ch-1 sp) twice, sc in next dc, 3 sc in next ch-3 sp, (sc in next dc and in next ch-1 sp) twice, sc in next dc, work Popcorn in next ch-1 sp; repeat from ★ across to last 4 dc, sc in next 2 dc, skip next dc, sc in last dc.

Row 9: Ch 3, turn; skip first 2 sc, dc in next sc, ch 1, skip next Popcorn, (dc in next sc, ch 1, skip next sc) 3 times, (dc, ch 3, dc) in next sc, ch 1, (skip next sc, dc in next sc, ch 1) 3 times, skip next Popcorn, dc in next sc, ★ decrease, dc in next sc, ch 1, skip next Popcorn, (dc in next sc, ch 1, skip next sc) 3 times, (dc, ch 3, dc) in next sc, ch 1, (skip next sc, dc in next sc, ch 1) 3 times, skip next Popcorn, dc in next sc; repeat from ★ across to last 2 sc, skip next sc, dc in last sc.

Row 10: Ch 1, turn; sc in first dc, skip next dc, work Popcorn in next ch-1 sp, (sc in next dc and in next ch-1 sp) 3 times, sc in next dc, 3 sc in next ch-3 sp, (sc in next dc and in next ch-1 sp) 3 times, sc in next dc, work Popcorn in next ch-1 sp, ★ sc in next dc, skip next dc, sc in next dc, work Popcorn in next ch-1 sp, (sc in next dc and in next ch-1 sp) 3 times, sc in next dc, 3 sc in next ch-3 sp, (sc in next dc and in next ch-1 sp) 3 times, sc in next dc, work Popcorn in next ch-1 sp; repeat from ★ across to last 2 dc, skip next dc, sc in last dc.

Row 11: Ch 3, turn; skip next Popcorn, dc in next 8 sc, (dc, ch 3, dc) in next sc, dc in next 8 sc, ★ decrease, dc in next 8 sc, (dc, ch 3, dc) in next sc, dc in next 8 sc; repeat from ★ across to last 2 sts, skip next Popcorn, dc in last sc.

Repeat Rows 2-11 for pattern.

12 LACY CROSS STITCH

Note: Uses Colors A, B, and C in the following sequence: ★ 1 Row **each** Color A, Color B, Color C, Color B; repeat from ★ for stripe sequence.

With Color A, chain a multiple of 39 + 1 ch.

Row 1 (Right side)**:** Dc in third ch from hook, skip next 2 chs, (3 dc in next ch, skip next 2 chs) 5 times, (3 dc, ch 1, 3 dc) in next ch, (skip next 2 chs, 3 dc in next ch) 5 times, ★ YO, skip next 2 chs, insert hook in next ch, YO and pull up a loop, YO and draw through 2 loops on hook, [YO, insert hook in **next** ch, YO and pull up a loop, YO and draw through 2 loops on hook] 3 times, YO and draw through all 5 loops on hook, skip next 2 chs, (3 dc in next ch, skip next 2 chs) 5 times, (3 dc, ch 1, 3 dc) in next ch, (skip next 2 chs, 3 dc in next ch) 5 times; repeat from ★ across to last 4 chs, YO, skip next 2 chs, insert hook in next ch, YO and pull up a loop, YO and draw through 2 loops on hook, YO, insert hook in last ch, YO and pull up a loop, YO and draw through 2 loops on hook, YO and draw through all 3 loops on hook; finish off.

Note: Loop a short piece of yarn around any stitch to mark Row 1 as **right** side.

To treble crochet (abbreviated tr), YO twice, insert hook in st or sp indicated, YO and pull up a loop (4 loops on hook), (YO and draw through 2 loops on hook) 3 times.

To work Cross St, skip next 3 dc, tr in sp **before** next dc *(Fig. 5, page 159)*, ch 2, working **behind** tr just made, tr in sp **before** first skipped dc.

Row 2: With **right** side facing, join Color B with slip st in first dc; ch 2, work 6 Cross Sts, (tr, ch 2, tr) in same ch-1 sp, ★ work 6 Cross Sts, skip next st, tr in sp **before** next dc, working **behind** tr just made, tr in sp **before** skipped st, work 6 Cross Sts, (tr, ch 2, tr) in same ch-1 sp; repeat from ★ across to last 19 sts, work 5 Cross Sts, skip next 3 dc, tr in sp **before** last dc, ch 2, working **behind** tr just made, tr in sp **before** first skipped dc to last step (2 loops on hook), YO, insert hook in last st, YO and pull up a loop (4 loops on hook), YO and draw through 2 loops on hook, YO and draw through last 3 loops on hook; finish off.

Row 3: With **right** side facing, join Color C with slip st in first tr; ch 2, dc in next ch-2 sp, 3 dc in each of next 5 ch-2 sps, (3 dc, ch 1, 3 dc) in next ch-2 sp, 3 dc in each of next 5 ch-2 sps, ★ YO, insert hook in next ch-2 sp, YO and pull up a loop, YO and draw through 2 loops on hook, YO, skip next 2 tr, insert hook in next tr, YO and pull up a loop, YO and draw through 2 loops on hook, YO, insert hook in next ch-2 sp, YO and pull up a loop, YO and draw through 2 loops on hook, YO and draw through all 4 loops on hook, 3 dc in each of next 5 ch-2 sps, (3 dc, ch 1, 3 dc) in next ch-2 sp, 3 dc in each of next 5 ch-2 sps; repeat from ★ across to last ch-2 sp, YO, insert hook in last ch-2 sp, YO and pull up a loop, YO and draw through 2 loops on hook, YO, insert hook in last st, YO and pull up a loop, YO and draw through 2 loops on hook, YO and draw through all 3 loops on hook; finish off.

Repeat Rows 2 and 3 for pattern, working in stripe sequence.

13 INVERTED SHELL WAVES

Chain a multiple of 12 chs.

Row 1: Dc in fourth ch from hook **(3 skipped chs count as one dc)** and in next 3 chs, ch 2, dc in next 5 chs, ★ skip next 2 chs, dc in next 5 chs, ch 2, dc in next 5 chs; repeat from ★ across.

To work Cluster (uses one ch-2 sp), ★ YO, insert hook in ch-2 sp indicated, YO and pull up a loop, YO and draw through 2 loops on hook; repeat from ★ 4 times **more**, YO and draw through all 6 loops on hook.

Row 2 (Right side)**:** Ch 3 **(counts as first dc, now and throughout)**, turn; skip first 3 dc, dc in next dc, ch 1, (dc, ch 1, work Cluster, ch 1, dc) in next ch-2 sp, ★ (ch 1, skip next dc, dc in next dc) twice, skip next 2 dc, (dc in next dc, ch 1, skip next dc) twice, (dc, ch 1, work Cluster, ch 1, dc) in next ch-2 sp; repeat from ★ across to last 5 dc, ch 1, skip next dc, dc in next dc, skip next 2 dc, dc in last dc.

Note: Loop a short piece of yarn around any stitch to mark Row 2 as **right** side.

Row 3: Ch 3, turn; (dc in next dc and in next ch-1 sp) twice, ch 2, skip next Cluster, dc in next ch-1 sp, ★ (dc in next dc and in next ch-1 sp) twice, skip next 2 dc, dc in next ch-1 sp, (dc in next dc and in next ch-1 sp) twice, ch 2, skip next Cluster, dc in next ch-1 sp; repeat from ★ across to last 3 dc, dc in next dc and in next ch-1 sp, dc in last 2 dc.

Row 4: Ch 3, turn; skip first 2 dc, dc in next 3 dc, (dc, ch 1, work Cluster, ch 1, dc) in next ch-2 sp, ★ dc in next 4 dc, skip next 2 dc, dc in next 4 dc, (dc, ch 1, work Cluster, ch 1, dc) in next ch-2 sp; repeat from ★ across to last 5 dc, dc in next 3 dc, skip next dc, dc in last dc.

Row 5: Ch 3, turn; skip first 2 dc, dc in next 3 dc and in next ch-1 sp, ch 2, skip next Cluster, dc in next ch-1 sp, ★ dc in next 4 dc, skip next 2 dc, dc in next 4 dc and in next ch-1 sp, ch 2, skip next Cluster, dc in next ch-1 sp; repeat from ★ across to last 5 dc, dc in next 3 dc, skip next dc, dc in last dc.

Repeat Rows 2-5 for pattern.

14 BUBBLES

Note: Uses Colors A, B, and C in the following sequence: ★ 2 Rows **each** Color A, Color B, Color C; repeat from ★ for stripe sequence.

With Color A, chain a multiple of 10 + 4 chs.

To treble crochet (abbreviated tr), YO twice, insert hook in st indicated, YO and pull up a loop (4 loops on hook), (YO and draw through 2 loops on hook) 3 times.

Row 1 (Right side)**:** Sc in second ch from hook and in next 2 chs, ★ hdc in next ch, dc in next ch, tr in next 3 chs, dc in next ch, hdc in next ch, sc in next 3 chs; repeat from ★ across.

Note: Loop a short piece of yarn around any stitch to mark Row 1 as **right** side.

Row 2: Ch 1, turn; sc in first 3 sc, ★ hdc in next hdc, dc in next dc, tr in next 3 tr, dc in next dc, hdc in next hdc, sc in next 3 sc; repeat from ★ across; finish off.

Row 3: With **right** side facing, join Color B with slip st in first sc; ch 4 **(counts as first tr, now and throughout)**, tr in next 2 sc, ★ dc in next hdc, hdc in next dc, sc in next 3 tr, hdc in next dc, dc in next hdc, tr in next 3 sc; repeat from ★ across.

Row 4: Ch 4, turn; tr in next 2 tr, ★ dc in next dc, hdc in next hdc, sc in next 3 sc, hdc in next hdc, dc in next dc, tr in next 3 tr; repeat from ★ across; finish off.

To work Puff St (uses one sc), ★ YO, insert hook from **front** to **back** around post of sc on row **below** next sc *(Fig. 4, page 159)*, YO and pull up a loop; repeat from ★ 2 times **more**, YO and draw through all 7 loops on hook. Skip sc behind Puff St.

Row 5: With **right** side facing, join Color C with sc in first tr *(see Joining With Sc, page 158)*; sc in next 5 sts, work Puff St, (sc in next 9 sts, work Puff St) across to last 6 sts, sc in last 6 sts.

Row 6: Ch 1, turn; sc in each sc and in each Puff St across; finish off.

Row 7: With **right** side facing, join Color A with sc in first sc; sc in next 2 sc, ★ hdc in next sc, dc in next sc, tr in next 3 sc, dc in next sc, hdc in next sc, sc in next 3 sc; repeat from ★ across.

Repeat Rows 2-7 for pattern.

15 RADIANCE

Note: Uses Colors A, B, C, and D in the following sequence: ★ 2 Rows **each** Color A, Color B, Color C, Color D; repeat from ★ for stripe sequence.

With Color A, chain a multiple of 24 + 2 chs.

To decrease (uses next 2 sts), ★ YO, insert hook in **next** st, YO and pull up a loop, YO and draw through 2 loops on hook; repeat from ★ once **more**, YO and draw through all 3 loops on hook **(counts as one dc)**.

To double decrease (uses next 3 sts), ★ YO, insert hook in **next** st, YO and pull up a loop, YO and draw through 2 loops on hook; repeat from ★ 2 times **more**, YO and draw through all 4 loops on hook **(counts as one dc)**.

To double crochet 5 together (abbreviated dc5tog), ★ YO, insert hook in **next** st, YO and pull up a loop, YO and draw through 2 loops on hook; repeat from ★ 4 times **more**, YO and draw through all 6 loops on hook **(counts as one dc)**.

Row 1 (Right side)**:** Decrease beginning in third ch from hook, dc in next 9 chs, 5 dc in next ch, dc in next 9 chs, ★ dc5tog, dc in next 9 chs, 5 dc in next ch, dc in next 9 chs; repeat from ★ across to last 3 chs, double decrease.

Note: Loop a short piece of yarn around any stitch to mark Row 1 as **right** side.

Row 2: Ch 2, turn; skip first st, decrease, dc in next 9 dc, 5 dc in next dc, dc in next 9 dc, ★ dc5tog, dc in next 9 dc, 5 dc in next dc, dc in next 9 dc; repeat from ★ across to last 3 dc, double decrease; finish off.

To work Long Front Post treble crochet (abbreviated LFPtr), working in **front** of previous row, YO twice, insert hook from **front** to **back** around post of dc on row **below** next dc *(Fig. 4, page 159)*, YO and pull up a loop even with loop on hook (4 loops on hook), (YO and draw through 2 loops on hook) 3 times. Skip dc behind LFPtr.

Row 3: With **right** side facing, join Color B with slip st in first st; ch 2, skip joining st, decrease, dc in next 5 dc, work LFPtr, dc in next 3 dc, 5 dc in next dc, dc in next 3 dc, work LFPtr, dc in next 5 dc, ★ dc5tog, dc in next 5 dc, work LFPtr, dc in next 3 dc, 5 dc in next dc, dc in next 3 dc, work LFPtr, dc in next 5 dc; repeat from ★ across to last 3 dc, double decrease.

Row 4: Ch 2, turn; skip first st, decrease, dc in next 9 sts, 5 dc in next dc, dc in next 9 sts, ★ dc5tog, dc in next 9 sts, 5 dc in next dc, dc in next 9 sts; repeat from ★ across to last 3 dc, double decrease; finish off.

Repeat Rows 3 and 4, working in stripe sequence.

16 PRECIOUS POPCORNS

Note: Uses MC and CC in the following sequence: ★ 5 Rows MC, 1 row CC; repeat from ★ for stripe sequence.

With MC, chain a multiple of 19 + 3 chs.

Row 1 (Right side)**:** Sc in second ch from hook, skip next ch, sc in next 8 chs, 3 sc in next ch, sc in next 8 chs, ★ skip next 2 chs, sc in next 8 chs, 3 sc in next ch, sc in next 8 chs; repeat from ★ across to last 2 chs, skip next ch, sc in last ch.

Note: Loop a short piece of yarn around any stitch to mark Row 1 as **right** side.

Row 2: Ch 1, turn; sc in first sc, skip next sc, sc in next 8 sc, 3 sc in next sc, sc in next 8 sc, ★ skip next 2 sc, sc in next 8 sc, 3 sc in next sc, sc in next 8 sc; repeat from ★ across to last 2 sc, skip next sc, sc in last sc.

To decrease (uses next 2 sc), ★ YO, insert hook in **next** sc, YO and pull up a loop, YO and draw through 2 loops on hook; repeat from ★ once **more**, YO and draw through all 3 loops on hook **(counts as one dc)**.

Row 3: Ch 3 **(counts as first dc, now and throughout)**, turn; skip first 2 sc, dc in next 8 sc, 3 dc in next sc, ★ dc in next 7 sc, decrease twice, dc in next 7 sc, 3 dc in next sc; repeat from ★ across to last 10 sc, dc in next 8 sc, skip next sc, dc in last sc.

Rows 4 and 5: Ch 1, turn; sc in first st, skip next st, sc in next 8 sts, 3 sc in next st, sc in next 8 sts, ★ skip next 2 sts, sc in next 8 sts, 3 sc in next sc, sc in next 8 sts; repeat from ★ across to last 2 sts, skip next st, sc in last st; at end of last row, finish off.

To work Popcorn (uses one sc), 3 dc in sc indicated, drop loop from hook, insert hook from **back** to **front** in first dc of 3-dc group, hook dropped loop and draw through st.

Row 6: With **wrong** side facing, join CC with slip st in first st; ch 3, skip joining st and next sc, (work Popcorn in next sc, ch 1, skip next sc) 4 times, (work Popcorn, ch 1) twice in next sc, skip next sc, work Popcorn in next sc, (ch 1, skip next sc, work Popcorn in next sc) 3 times, ★ skip next 2 sc, (work Popcorn in next sc, ch 1, skip next sc) 4 times, (work Popcorn, ch 1) twice in next sc, skip next sc, work Popcorn in next sc, (ch 1, skip next sc, work Popcorn in next sc) 3 times; repeat from ★ across to last 2 sc, skip next sc, dc in last sc; finish off.

Row 7: With **right** side facing, join MC with sc in first dc *(see Joining With Sc, page 158)*; skip next Popcorn, (sc in next ch-1 sp and in next Popcorn) 4 times, 3 sc in next ch-1 sp, (sc in next Popcorn and in next ch-1 sp) 4 times, ★ skip next 2 Popcorns, (sc in next ch-1 sp and in next Popcorn) 4 times, 3 sc in next ch-1 sp, (sc in next Popcorn and in next ch-1 sp) 4 times; repeat from ★ across to last 2 sts, skip next Popcorn, sc in last dc.

Repeat Rows 2-7 for pattern.

17 ON THE WAVES

Note: Uses Colors A, B, and C in the following sequence: ★ 2 Rows **each** Color A, Color B, Color C; repeat from ★ for stripe sequence.

With Color A, chain a multiple of 20 + 1 ch.

To decrease (uses next 2 sts), ★ YO, insert hook in **next** st, YO and pull up a loop, YO and draw through 2 loops on hook; repeat from ★ once **more**, YO and draw through all 3 loops on hook **(counts as one dc)**.

To double decrease (uses next 3 sts), ★ YO, insert hook in **next** st, YO and pull up a loop, YO and draw through 2 loops on hook; repeat from ★ 2 times **more**, YO and draw through all 4 loops on hook **(counts as one dc)**.

Row 1 (Right side)**:** Decrease beginning in third ch from hook, (dc in next 2 chs, 2 dc in next ch) twice, dc in next ch, place marker around last dc made for st placement, dc in next ch, (2 dc in next ch, dc in next 2 chs) twice, ★ double decrease twice, (dc in next 2 chs, 2 dc in next ch) twice, dc in next ch, place marker around last dc made for st placement, dc in next ch, (2 dc in next ch, dc in next 2 chs) twice; repeat from ★ across to last 3 chs, double decrease.

Note: Loop a short piece of yarn around any stitch to mark Row 1 as **right** side.

Row 2: Ch 2, turn; skip first dc, decrease, dc in next 2 dc, (2 dc in next st, dc in next 2 sts) 4 times, ★ double decrease twice, dc in next 2 sts, (2 dc in next st, dc in next 2 sts) 4 times; repeat from ★ across to last 3 sts, double decrease; finish off.

To work Front Post Cluster (abbreviated *FP Cluster*), working in **front** of previous row **(Fig. 6, page 159)**, ★ YO, insert hook from **front** to **back** around post of dc indicated 2 rows **below** **(Fig. 4, page 159)**, YO and pull up a loop even with loop on hook, YO and draw through 2 loops on hook; repeat from ★ 2 times **more**, YO and draw through all 4 loops on hook.

Row 3: With **right** side facing, join Color B with slip st in first dc; ch 2, skip joining st, decrease, dc in next 2 dc, 2 dc in next dc, dc in next 2 dc, work FP Cluster around first marked dc 2 rows **below**, remove marker, dc in next 2 dc, place marker around last dc made for st placement, dc in next 2 dc, work FP Cluster around next dc 2 rows **below**, dc in next 2 dc, 2 dc in next dc, dc in next 2 dc, ★ double decrease twice, dc in next 2 dc, 2 dc in next dc, dc in next 2 dc, work FP Cluster around next marked dc 2 rows **below**, remove marker, dc in next 2 dc, place marker around last dc made for st placement, dc in next 2 dc, work FP Cluster around next dc 2 rows **below**, dc in next 2 dc, 2 dc in next dc, dc in next 2 dc; repeat from ★ across to last 3 dc, double decrease.

Repeat Rows 2 and 3 for pattern, working in stripe sequence.

18 BOBBLES & EYELETS

Chain a multiple of 19 + 4 chs.

Row 1 (Right side)**:** Dc in fifth ch from hook **(4 skipped chs count as first dc and 1 skipped ch)**, ch 1, skip next ch, (dc in next ch, ch 1, skip next ch) 3 times, (dc, ch 3, dc) in next ch, ★ ch 1, (skip next ch, dc in next ch, ch 1) 3 times, YO, skip next ch, insert hook in next ch, YO and pull up a loop, YO and draw through 2 loops on hook, YO, skip next 2 chs, insert hook in next ch, YO and pull up a loop, YO and draw through 2 loops on hook, YO and draw through all 3 loops on hook, ch 1, skip next ch, (dc in next ch, ch 1, skip next ch) 3 times, (dc, ch 3, dc) in next ch; repeat from ★ across to last 10 chs, (ch 1, skip next ch, dc in next ch) 4 times, skip next ch, dc in last ch.

Note: Loop a short piece of yarn around any stitch to mark Row 1 as **right** side.

To double decrease (uses next 5 sts), YO insert hook in next st, YO and pull up a loop, YO and draw through 2 loops on hook, YO, skip next 3 sts, insert hook in next st, YO and pull up a loop, YO and draw through 2 loops on hook, YO and draw through all 3 loops on hook **(counts as one dc)**.

Row 2: Ch 3 **(counts as first dc, now and throughout)**, turn; skip first 2 dc, (dc in next ch-1 sp and in next dc) 4 times, (2 dc, ch 3, 2 dc) in next ch-3 sp, ★ (dc in next dc and in next ch-1 sp) 3 times, double decrease, (dc in next ch-1 sp and in next dc) 3 times, (2 dc, ch 3, 2 dc) in next ch-3 sp; repeat from ★ across to last 6 dc, (dc in next dc and in next ch-1 sp) 4 times, skip next dc, dc in last dc.

To decrease (uses next 3 sts), YO, insert hook in next st, YO and pull up a loop, YO and draw through 2 loops on hook, YO, skip next st, insert hook in next st, YO and pull up a loop, YO and draw through 2 loops on hook, YO and draw through all 3 loops on hook **(counts as one dc)**.

Row 3: Ch 3, turn; skip first 3 dc, (dc in next dc, ch 1, skip next dc) 4 times, (dc, ch 3, dc) in next ch-3 sp, ★ ch 1, skip next dc, (dc in next dc, ch 1, skip next dc) 3 times, decrease, ch 1, skip next dc, (dc in next dc, ch 1, skip next dc) 3 times, (dc, ch 3, dc) in next ch-3 sp; repeat from ★ across to last 11 dc, (ch 1, skip next dc, dc in next dc) 4 times, skip next 2 dc, dc in last dc.

Row 4: Ch 3, turn; skip first 2 dc, (dc in next ch-1 sp and in next dc) 4 times, (2 dc, ch 3, 2 dc) in next ch-3 sp, ★ (dc in next dc and in next ch-1 sp) 3 times, double decrease, (dc in next ch-1 sp and in next dc) 3 times, (2 dc, ch 3, 2 dc) in next ch-3 sp; repeat from ★ across to last 6 dc, (dc in next dc and in next ch-1 sp) 4 times, skip next dc, dc in last dc.

Row 5: Ch 3, turn; working in Front Loops Only **(Fig. 2, page 159)**, skip first 2 dc, dc in next 9 dc, (dc, ch 3, dc) in next ch-3 sp, ★ dc in next 7 dc, decrease, dc in next 7 dc, (dc, ch 3, dc) in next ch-3 sp; repeat from ★ across to last 11 dc, dc in next 9 dc, skip next dc, dc in last dc.

To work Cluster (uses one dc), ★ YO, insert hook in st indicated, YO and pull up a loop, YO and draw through 2 loops on hook; repeat from ★ 4 times **more**, YO and draw through all 6 loops on hook. Push Cluster to **right** side.

Row 6: Ch 3, turn; working in both loops, skip first 2 dc, dc in next 4 dc, work Cluster in next dc, dc in next 2 dc, work Cluster in next dc, (dc, ch 3, dc) in next ch-3 sp, dc in next dc, ★ (work Cluster in next dc, dc in next 2 dc) twice, decrease, (dc in next 2 dc, work Cluster in next dc) twice, dc in next dc, (dc, ch 3, dc) in next dc, dc in next dc; repeat from ★ across to last 10 dc, work Cluster in next dc, dc in next 2 dc, work Cluster in next dc, dc in next 4 dc, skip next dc, dc in last dc.

Row 7: Ch 3, turn; skip first 2 dc, dc in next 3 dc, (dc in next Cluster and in next 2 dc) twice, (dc, ch 3, dc) in next ch-3 sp, (dc in next 2 dc and in next Cluster) twice, ★ dc in next dc, decrease, dc in next dc, (dc in next Cluster and in next 2 dc) twice, (dc, ch 3, dc) in next ch-3 sp, (dc in next 2 dc and in next Cluster) twice; repeat from ★ across to last 5 dc, dc in next 3 dc, skip next dc, dc in last dc.

Row 8: Ch 3, turn; working in Back Loops Only **(Fig. 2, page 159)**, skip first 2 dc, dc in next 9 dc, (dc, ch 3, dc) in next ch-3 sp, ★ dc in next 7 dc, decrease, dc in next 7 dc, (dc, ch 3, dc) in next ch-3 sp; repeat from ★ across to last 11 dc, dc in next 9 dc, skip next dc, dc in last dc.

Row 9: Ch 3, turn; working in both loops, skip first 3 dc, (dc in next dc, ch 1, skip next dc) 4 times, (dc, ch 3, dc) in next ch-3 sp, ★ ch 1, skip next dc, (dc in next dc, ch 1, skip next dc) 3 times, decrease, ch 1, skip next dc, (dc in next dc, ch 1, skip next dc) 3 times, (dc, ch 3, dc) in next ch-3 sp; repeat from ★ across to last 11 dc, (ch 1, skip next dc, dc in next dc) 4 times, skip next 2 dc, dc in last dc.

Repeat Rows 2-9 for pattern.

19 COMFORT

Chain a multiple of 17 chs.

Row 1: Dc in fourth ch from hook **(3 skipped chs count as first dc)** and in next 5 chs, 3 dc in next ch, dc in next 7 chs, ★ skip next 2 chs, dc in next 7 chs, 3 dc in next ch, dc in next 7 chs; repeat from ★ across.

To work Front Post double crochet *(abbreviated FPdc)*, YO, insert hook from **front** to **back** around post of st indicated **(Fig. 4, page 159)**, YO and pull up a loop (3 loops on hook), (YO and draw through 2 loops on hook) twice. Skip st **behind** FPdc.

Row 2: Ch 3 **(counts as first dc, now and throughout)**, turn; working in Front Loops Only unless otherwise indicated **(Fig. 2, page 159)**, skip first 2 dc, dc in next 5 sts, work FPdc around next dc, 3 dc in **both** loops of next dc, work FPdc around next dc, ★ dc in next 6 sts, skip next 2 dc, dc in next 6 sts, work FPdc around next dc, 3 dc in **both** loops of next dc, work FPdc around next dc; repeat from ★ across to last 7 sts, dc in next 5 sts, skip next dc, dc in **both** loops of last dc.

Repeat Row 2 for pattern.

20 REVELRY

Note: Loop a short piece of yarn around **back** of any stitch on Row 1 to mark **right** side.

To treble crochet *(abbreviated tr)*, YO twice, insert hook in st indicated, YO and pull up a loop (4 loops on hook), (YO and draw through 2 loops on hook) 3 times.

To work Front Post treble crochet *(abbreviated FPtr)*, YO twice, insert hook from **front** to **back** around post of st indicated *(Fig. 4, page 159)*, YO and pull up a loop (4 loops on hook), YO and draw through 2 loops on hook) 3 times.

Row 2: With **right** side facing, join Color B with slip st in first dc; ch 2, dc in next dc, (work 2 FPtr around next dc, sc in next dc) 3 times, 3 tr in next ch-1 sp, (sc in next dc, work 2 FPtr around next dc) 3 times, ★ skip next 2 dc, (work 2 FPtr around next dc, sc in next dc) 3 times, 3 tr in next ch-1 sp, (sc in next dc, work 2 FPtr around next dc) 3 times; repeat from ★ across to last 2 dc, decrease.

Row 3: Ch 2, turn; working in Back Loops Only *(Fig. 2, page 159)*, skip first dc, dc in next st, skip next st, 2 dc in next sc, (skip next 2 sts, 2 dc in next sc) twice, skip next tr, (dc, ch 1, dc) in next tr, skip next tr, 2 dc in next sc, (skip next 2 sts, 2 dc in next sc) twice, ★ skip next 4 sts, 2 dc in next sc, (skip next 2 sts, 2 dc in next sc) twice, skip next tr, (dc, ch 1, dc) in next tr, skip next tr, 2 dc in next sc, (skip next 2 sts, 2 dc in next sc) twice; repeat from ★ across to last 3 sts, skip next st, decrease; finish off.

Note: Uses Colors A, B, and C in the following sequence: 1 Row Color A, ★ 2 rows Color B, 2 rows Color A, 1 row **each** Color C, Color A, Color B, Color A; repeat from ★ for stripe sequence.

With Color A, chain a multiple of 15 + 3 chs.

To decrease *(uses next 2 sts)*, ★ YO, insert hook in **next** st, YO and pull up a loop, YO and draw through 2 loops on hook; repeat from ★ once **more**, YO and draw through all 3 loops on hook **(counts as one dc)**.

Row 1 (Wrong side)**:** Dc in third ch from hook and in next 6 chs, (dc, ch 1, dc) in next ch, dc in next 6 chs, ★ skip next 2 chs, dc in next 6 chs, (dc, ch 1, dc) in next ch, dc in next 6 chs; repeat from ★ across to last 2 chs, decrease; finish off.

To work Back Post double crochet (abbreviated *BPdc*), YO, insert hook from **back** to **front** around post of dc indicated *(Fig. 4, page 159)*, YO and pull up a loop (3 loops on hook), (YO and draw through 2 loops on hook) twice.

Row 4: With **right** side facing and working in both loops, join Color A with slip st in first dc; ch 2, skip joining st, dc in next dc, work BPdc around each of next 6 dc, 3 tr in next ch-1 sp, work BPdc around each of next 6 dc, ★ skip next 2 dc, work BPdc around each of next 6 dc, 3 tr in next ch-1 sp, work BPdc around each of next 6 dc; repeat from ★ across to last 2 dc, decrease.

Row 5: Ch 2, turn; working in Back Loops Only, skip first dc, dc in next 2 sts, ch 1, skip next st, (dc in next st, ch 1, skip next st) twice, (dc, ch 1, dc) in next tr, (ch 1, skip next st, dc in next st) 3 times, ★ skip next 2 sts, (dc in next st, ch 1, skip next st) 3 times, (dc, ch 1, dc) in next tr, (ch 1, skip next st, dc in next st) 3 times; repeat from ★ across to last 2 dc, dc in last 2 dc; finish off.

To work Popcorn (uses one dc), 4 dc in dc indicated, drop loop from hook, insert hook from **front** to **back** in first dc of 4-dc group, hook dropped loop and draw through st.

Row 6: With **right** side facing and working in both loops, join Color C with slip st in first dc; ch 2, dc in next dc, (work Popcorn in next dc, ch 2) 3 times, 3 dc in next ch-1 sp, (ch 2, work Popcorn in next dc) 3 times, ★ skip next 2 dc, (work Popcorn in next dc, ch 2) 3 times, 3 dc in next ch-1 sp, (ch 2, work Popcorn in next dc) 3 times; repeat from ★ across to last 2 dc, decrease; finish off.

Row 7: With **wrong** side facing, join Color A with slip st in first dc; ch 2, skip joining st, dc in next Popcorn, 3 dc in each of next 2 Popcorns, skip next dc, (dc, ch 1, dc) in next dc, skip next dc, 3 dc in each of next 2 Popcorns, ★ skip next 2 Popcorns, 3 dc in each of next 2 Popcorns, skip next dc, (dc, ch 1, dc) in next dc, skip next dc, 3 dc in each of next 2 Popcorns; repeat from ★ across to last Popcorn and last dc, decrease; finish off.

Row 8: With **right** side facing and working in both loops, join Color B with slip st in first dc; ch 2, skip joining st, dc in next dc, work BPdc around each of next 6 dc, 3 tr in next ch-1 sp, work BPdc around each of next 6 dc, ★ skip next 2 dc, work BPdc around each of next 6 dc, 3 tr in next ch-1 sp, work BPdc around each of next 6 dc; repeat from ★ across to last 2 dc, decrease; finish off.

Row 9: With **wrong** side facing and working in both loops, join Color A with slip st in first dc; ch 2, skip joining st, dc in next 7 sts, (dc, ch 1, dc) in next tr, dc in next 6 sts, ★ skip next 2 sts, dc in next 6 sts, (dc, ch 1, dc) in next tr, dc in next 6 sts; repeat from ★ across to last 2 sts, decrease; finish off.

Repeat Rows 2-9 for pattern.

21 AUTUMN

Note: Uses Colors A, B, and C in the following sequence: ★ 1 Row **each** Color A, Color B, Color C, Color B; repeat from ★ for stripe sequence.

With Color A, chain a multiple of 39 + 1 ch.

Row 1 (Right side)**:** Dc in third ch from hook, skip next 2 chs, (3 dc in next ch, skip next 2 chs) 5 times, (3 dc, ch 1, 3 dc) in next ch, (skip next 2 chs, 3 dc in next ch) 5 times, ★ YO, skip next 2 chs, insert hook in next ch, YO and pull up a loop, YO and draw through 2 loops on hook, [YO, insert hook in **next** ch, YO and pull up a loop, YO and draw through 2 loops on hook] 3 times, YO and draw through all 5 loops on hook, skip next 2 chs, (3 dc in next ch, skip next 2 chs) 5 times, (3 dc, ch 1, 3 dc) in next ch, (skip next 2 chs, 3 dc in next ch) 5 times; repeat from ★ across to last 4 chs, YO, skip next 2 chs, insert hook in next ch, YO and pull up a loop, YO and draw through 2 loops on hook, YO, insert hook in next ch, YO and pull up a loop, YO and draw through 2 loops on hook, YO and draw through all 3 loops on hook; finish off.

Note: Loop a short piece of yarn around any stitch to mark Row 1 as **right** side.

To treble crochet (abbreviated tr), YO twice, insert hook in st or sp indicated, YO and pull up a loop (4 loops on hook), (YO and draw through 2 loops on hook) 3 times.

To work Cross St, skip next 3 dc, tr in sp **before** next dc *(Fig. 5, page 159)*, ch 2, working **behind** tr just made, tr in sp **before** first skipped dc.

Row 2: With **wrong** side facing, join Color B with slip st in first st; ch 2, work 6 Cross Sts, tr in same ch-1 sp, ch 2, working **behind** tr just made, tr in same sp (before last tr), ★ work 6 Cross Sts, skip next st, work 6 Cross Sts, tr in same ch-1 sp, ch 2, working **behind** tr just made, tr in same sp (before last tr); repeat from ★ across to last 6 3-dc groups, work 5 Cross Sts, skip next 3 dc, tr in sp **before** last dc, ch 2, working **behind** tr just made, tr in sp **before** first skipped dc to last step (2 loops on hook), YO, insert hook in last st, YO and pull up a loop (4 loops on hook), YO and draw through 2 loops on hook, YO and draw through last 3 loops on hook; finish off.

Row 3: With **right** side facing, join Color C with slip st in first st; ch 2, dc in next ch-2 sp, 3 dc in each of next 5 ch-2 sps, (3 dc, ch 1, 3 dc) in next ch-2 sp, 3 dc in each of next 5 ch-2 sps, ★ YO, insert hook in next ch-2 sp, YO and pull up a loop, YO and draw through 2 loops on hook, [YO insert hook in **next** tr, YO and pull up a loop, YO and draw through 2 loops on hook] twice, YO insert hook in next ch-2 sp, YO and pull up a loop, YO and draw through 2 loops on hook, YO and draw through all 5 loops on hook, 3 dc in each of next 5 ch-2 sps, (3 dc, ch 1, 3 dc) in next ch-2 sp, 3 dc in each of next 5 ch-2 sps; repeat from ★ across to last ch-2 sp, YO, insert hook in last ch-2 sp, YO and pull up a loop, YO and draw through 2 loops on hook, YO, insert hook in last tr, YO and pull up a loop, YO and draw through 2 loops on hook, YO and draw through all 3 loops on hook; finish off.

Repeat Rows 2 and 3 for pattern, working in stripe sequence.

22 LOOPY

Note: Uses MC and Colors A, B, C, and D in the following sequence: ★ 2 Rows **each** Color A, MC, Color B, MC, Color C, MC, Color D, MC; repeat from ★ for stripe sequence.

With Color A, chain a multiple of 18 + 2 chs.

Row 1 (Right side): Dc in third ch from hook and in next 7 chs, skip next 2 chs, dc in next 7 chs, ★ 2 dc in each of next 2 chs, dc in next 7 chs, skip next 2 chs, dc in next 7 chs; repeat from ★ across to last ch, 2 dc in last ch.

Note: Loop a short piece of yarn around any stitch to mark Row 1 as **right** side.

Row 2: Ch 3 **(counts as first dc, now and throughout)**, turn; dc in same st and in next 7 dc, skip next 2 dc, dc in next 7 dc, ★ 2 dc in each of next 2 dc, dc in next 7 dc, skip next 2 dc, dc in next 7 dc; repeat from ★ across to last dc, 2 dc in last dc; finish off.

Row 3: With **right** side facing, join MC with sc in first dc **(see Joining With Sc, page 158)**; sc in same st as joining, (ch 10, sc in next dc) 7 times, skip next 2 dc, (sc in next dc, ch 10) 7 times, ★ (sc, ch 10, sc) in each of next 2 dc, (ch 10, sc in next dc) 7 times, skip next 2 dc, (sc in next dc, ch 10) 7 times; repeat from ★ across to last dc, 2 sc in last dc.

Row 4: Ch 1, turn; keeping chs to **right** side, 2 sc in first sc, sc in next 7 sc, skip next 2 sc, sc in next 7 sc, ★ 2 sc in each of next 2 sc, sc in next 7 sc, skip next 2 sc, sc in next 7 sc; repeat from ★ across to last sc, 2 sc in last sc; finish off.

Row 5: With **right** side facing, join Color B with slip st in first sc; ch 3, dc in same st as joining and in next 7 sc, skip next 2 sc, dc in next 7 sc, ★ 2 dc in each of next 2 sc, dc in next 7 sc, skip next 2 sc, dc in next 7 sc; repeat from ★ across to last sc, 2 dc in last sc.

Row 6: Ch 3, turn; dc in same st and in next 7 dc, skip next 2 dc, dc in next 7 dc, ★ 2 dc in each of next 2 dc, dc in next 7 dc, skip next 2 dc, dc in next 7 dc; repeat from ★ across to last dc, 2 dc in last dc; finish off.

Repeat Rows 3-6 for pattern, working in stripe sequence.

Note: Uses Colors A, B, and C in the following sequence: 1 Row Color A, ★ 3 rows Color B, 2 rows Color A, 1 row Color B, 1 row Color C, 2 rows Color B, 1 row Color C, 1 row Color B, 1 row Color A; repeat from ★ for stripe sequence.

With Color A, chain a multiple of 15 + 3 chs.

To dc decrease (uses next 2 sts), ★ YO, insert hook in **next** st, YO and pull up a loop, YO and draw through 2 loops on hook; repeat from ★ once **more**, YO and draw through all 3 loops on hook **(counts as one dc)**.

Row 1 (Wrong side)**:** Dc in third ch from hook and in next 6 chs, 3 dc in next ch, dc in next 6 chs, ★ skip next 2 chs, dc in next 6 chs, 3 dc in next ch, dc in next 6 chs; repeat from ★ across to last 2 chs, dc decrease; finish off.

Note: Loop a short piece of yarn around **back** of any stitch on Row 1 to mark **right** side.

To work Back Post double crochet (abbreviated BPdc), YO, insert hook from **back** to **front** around post of st indicated **(Fig. 4, page 159)**, YO and pull up a loop (3 loops on hook), (YO and draw through 2 loops on hook) twice.

To work Front Post double crochet (abbreviated FPdc), YO, insert hook from **front** to **back** around post of st indicated **(Fig. 4, page 159)**, YO and pull up a loop (3 loops on hook), (YO and draw through 2 loops on hook) twice.

Row 2: With **right** side facing, join Color B with slip st in first dc; ch 2, skip joining st, dc in next dc, work BPdc around each of next 2 dc, work FPdc around each of next 2 dc, work BPdc around each of next 2 dc, 3 dc in next dc, work BPdc around each of next 2 dc, work FPdc around each of next 2 dc, work BPdc around each of next 2 dc, ★ skip next 2 dc, work BPdc around each of next 2 dc, work FPdc around each of next 2 dc, work BPdc around each of next 2 dc, 3 dc in next dc, work BPdc around each of next 2 dc, work FPdc around each of next 2 dc, work BPdc around each of next 2 dc; repeat from ★ across to last 2 sts, dc decrease.

Row 3: Ch 2, turn; working in Back Loops Only **(Fig. 2, page 159)**, skip first dc, dc in next 2 sts, ch 1, skip next st, (dc in next st, ch 1, skip next st) twice, 3 dc in next dc, (ch 1, skip next st, dc in next st) 3 times, ★ skip next 2 sts, (dc in next st, ch 1, skip next st) 3 times, 3 dc in next dc, (ch 1, skip next st, dc in next st) 3 times; repeat from ★ across to last 2 sts, dc decrease.

To work Popcorn, 4 dc in sp indicated, drop loop from hook, insert hook from **front** to **back** in first dc of 4-dc group, hook dropped loop and draw through st.

Row 4: Ch 2, turn; skip first dc, dc in both loops of next dc, skip next ch-1 sp, work (Popcorn, ch 6, Popcorn) in next ch-1 sp, skip next 2 dc, 3 dc in next dc, skip next ch-1 sp, work (Popcorn, ch 6, Popcorn) in next ch-1 sp, ★ skip next 2 ch-1 sps, work (Popcorn, ch 6, Popcorn) in next ch-1 sp, skip next 2 dc, 3 dc in next dc, skip next ch-1 sp, work (Popcorn, ch 6, Popcorn) in next ch-1 sp; repeat from ★ across to last ch-1 sp, skip last ch-1 sp, dc decrease; finish off.

Row 5: With **wrong** side facing, join Color A with slip st in first dc; ch 3, 6 hdc in next ch-6 sp, skip next Popcorn and next dc, 3 dc in next dc, 6 hdc in next ch-6 sp, ★ ch 1, 6 hdc in next ch-6 sp, skip next Popcorn and next dc, 3 dc in next dc, 6 hdc in next ch-6 sp; repeat from ★ across to last 2 sts, skip next Popcorn, dc in last dc.

To work Front Post treble crochet (abbreviated FPtr), YO twice, insert hook from **front** to **back** around post of st indicated, YO and pull up a loop (4 loops on hook), (YO and draw through 2 loops on hook) 3 times.

Row 6: Ch 2, turn; working in Back Loops Only, skip first dc, dc in next 7 sts, work 3 FPtr around next dc, skip dc just worked around, dc in next 6 sts, ★ skip next ch and next hdc, dc in next 6 sts, work 3 FPtr around next dc, skip dc just worked around, dc in next 6 sts; repeat from ★ across to last 2 sts, dc decrease; finish off.

To beginning sc decrease, pull up a loop in each of first 2 sts, YO and draw through all 3 loops on hook **(counts as one sc)**.

To sc decrease, pull up a loop in each of next 2 sts, YO and draw through all 3 loops on hook **(counts as one sc)**.

Row 7: With **wrong** side facing and working in both loops, join Color B with slip st in first dc; beginning sc decrease, sc in next 6 sts, 3 sc in next FPtr, sc in next 6 sts, ★ skip next 2 dc, sc in next 6 sts, 3 sc in next FPtr, sc in next 6 sts; repeat from ★ across to last 2 dc, sc decrease; finish off.

Row 8: With **right** side facing, join Color C with slip st in first sc; beginning sc decrease, sc in next 6 sc, 3 sc in next sc, sc in next 6 sc, ★ skip next 2 sc, sc in next 6 sc, 3 sc in next sc, sc in next 6 sc; repeat from ★ across to last 2 sc, sc decrease; finish off.

Row 9: With **wrong** side facing, join Color B with slip st in first sc; beginning sc decrease, sc in next 6 sc, 3 sc in next sc, sc in next 6 sc, ★ skip next 2 sc, sc in next 6 sc, 3 sc in next sc, sc in next 6 sc; repeat from ★ across to last 2 sc, sc decrease.

Row 10: Ch 1, turn; beginning sc decrease, sc in next 6 sc, 3 sc in next sc, sc in next 6 sc, ★ skip next 2 sc, sc in next 6 sc, 3 sc in next sc, sc in next 6 sc; repeat from ★ across to last 2 sc, sc decrease; finish off.

Row 11: With **wrong** side facing, join Color C with slip st in first sc; beginning sc decrease, sc in next 6 sc, 3 sc in next sc, sc in next 6 sc, ★ skip next 2 sc, sc in next 6 sc, 3 sc in next sc, sc in next 6 sc; repeat from ★ across to last 2 sc, sc decrease; finish off.

Row 12: With **right** side facing, join Color B with slip st in first sc; beginning sc decrease, sc in next 6 sc, 3 sc in next sc, sc in next 6 sc, ★ skip next 2 sc, sc in next 6 sc, 3 sc in next sc, sc in next 6 sc; repeat from ★ across to last 2 sc, sc decrease; finish off.

Row 13: With **wrong** side facing, join Color A with slip st in first sc; ch 2, skip joining st, dc in next 7 sc, 3 dc in next sc, dc in next 6 sc, ★ skip next 2 sc, dc in next 6 sc, 3 dc in next sc, dc in next 6 sc; repeat from ★ across to last 2 sc, dc decrease; finish off.

Repeat Rows 2-13 for pattern.

Note: Uses MC and Colors A and B in the following sequence: ★ 5 Rows MC, 1 row **each** Color A, Color B, Color A; repeat from ★ for stripe sequence.

With MC, chain a multiple of 15 + 14 chs.

Row 1: Hdc in second ch from hook and in next 5 chs, 3 hdc in next ch, hdc in next 6 chs, ★ skip next 2 chs, hdc in next 6 chs, 3 hdc in next ch, hdc in next 6 chs; repeat from ★ across.

To dc decrease (uses next 2 sts), ★ YO, insert hook in **next** st, YO and pull up a loop, YO and draw through 2 loops on hook; repeat from ★ once **more**, YO and draw through all 3 loops on hook **(counts as one dc)**.

Row 2 (Right side): Ch 2, turn; working in Back Loops Only *(Fig. 2, page 159)*, skip first hdc, dc in next 6 hdc, 3 dc in next hdc, ★ dc in next 6 hdc, skip next 2 hdc, dc in next 6 hdc, 3 dc in next hdc; repeat from ★ across to last 7 hdc, dc in next 5 hdc, dc decrease.

Note: Loop a short piece of yarn around any stitch to mark Row 2 as **right** side.

To work Back Post double crochet (abbreviated BPdc), YO, insert hook from **back** to **front** around post of st indicated *(Fig. 4, page 159)*, YO and pull up a loop (3 loops on hook), (YO and draw through 2 loops on hook) twice.

To work Front Post double crochet (abbreviated FPdc), YO, insert hook from **front** to **back** around post of st indicated *(Fig. 4, page 159)*, YO and pull up a loop (3 loops on hook), (YO and draw through 2 loops on hook) twice.

To work Back Post decrease (abbreviated BP decrease), YO, insert hook from **back** to **front** around post of st indicated, YO and pull up a loop (3 loops on hook), YO and draw through 2 loops on hook, pull up a loop in last st, YO and draw through all 3 loops on hook.

Row 3: Ch 1, turn; skip first dc, (work BPdc around next dc, work FPdc around next dc) 3 times, 3 dc in next dc, ★ (work FPdc around next dc, work BPdc around next dc) 3 times, skip next 2 dc, (work BPdc around next dc, work FPdc around next dc) 3 times, 3 dc in next dc; repeat from ★ across to last 7 dc, work FPdc around next dc, (work BPdc around next dc, work FPdc around next dc) twice, work BP decrease.

To double dc decrease (uses next 4 sts), YO, insert hook in next st, YO and pull up a loop, YO and draw through 2 loops on hook, YO, skip next 2 sts, insert hook in next st, YO and pull up a loop, YO and draw through 2 loops on hook, YO and draw through all 3 loops on hook **(counts as one dc)**.

Row 4: Ch 2, turn; working in Back Loops Only unless otherwise indicated, skip first st, (dc in next st, ch 1, skip next st) 3 times, 3 dc in **both** loops of next dc, ★ ch 1, skip next st, (dc in next st, ch 1, skip next st) twice, double dc decrease, ch 1, skip next st, (dc in next st, ch 1, skip next st) twice, 3 dc in **both** loops of next dc; repeat from ★ across to last 7 sts, ch 1, skip next st, (dc in next st, ch 1, skip next st) twice, dc decrease.

To hdc decrease (uses next 2 ch-1 sps), ★ YO, insert hook in **next** ch-1 sp, YO and pull up a loop; repeat from ★ once **more**, YO and draw through all 5 loops on hook **(counts as one hdc)**.

Row 5: Ch 1, turn; (hdc in next ch-1 sp and in next dc) 3 times, 3 hdc in next dc, hdc in next dc, (hdc in next ch-1 sp and in next dc) twice, ★ hdc decrease, hdc in next dc, (hdc in next ch-1 sp and in next dc) twice, 3 hdc in next dc, hdc in next dc, (hdc in next ch-1 sp and in next dc) twice; repeat from ★ across to last ch-1 sp, YO, insert hook in last ch-1 sp, YO and pull up a loop (3 loops on hook), pull up a loop in last dc, YO and draw through all 4 loops on hook; finish off.

To beginning sc decrease, pull up a loop in each of first 2 sts, YO and draw through all 3 loops on hook **(counts as one sc)**.

To sc decrease, pull up a loop in each of next 2 sts, YO and draw through all 3 loops on hook **(counts as one sc)**.

Row 6: With **right** side facing, join Color A with slip st in first st; beginning sc decrease, sc in next 5 hdc, working **around** previous row *(Fig. 6, page 159)*, 3 dc in same st as 3-hdc group on previous row, ★ sc in next 6 hdc, skip next hdc, sc in next 6 hdc, working **around** previous row, 3 dc in same st as 3-hdc group on previous row; repeat from ★ across to last 7 hdc, sc in next 5 hdc, sc decrease; finish off.

Row 7: With **wrong** side facing and working in Back Loops Only, join Color B with slip st in first sc; beginning sc decrease, sc in next 5 sts, 3 sc in next dc, ★ sc in next 6 sts, skip next 2 sc, sc in next 6 sts, 3 sc in next dc; repeat from ★ across to last 7 sts, sc in next 5 sts, sc decrease; finish off.

Row 8: With **right** side facing and working in Back Loops Only, join Color A with slip st in first st; beginning sc decrease, sc in next 5 sc, 3 sc in next sc, ★ sc in next 6 sc, skip next 2 sc, sc in next 6 sc, 3 sc in next sc; repeat from ★ across to last 7 sc, sc in next 5 sc, sc decrease; finish off.

Row 9: With **wrong** side facing and working in both loops, join MC with slip st in first sc; ch 1, skip joining st, hdc in next 6 sc, 3 hdc in next sc, ★ hdc in next 6 sc, skip next 2 sc, hdc in next 6 sc, 3 hdc in next sc; repeat from ★ across to last 7 sc, hdc in next 5 sc, YO, insert hook in next sc, YO and pull up a loop (3 loops on hook), pull up a loop in last sc, YO and draw through all 4 loops on hook.

Repeat Rows 2-9 for pattern.

25 FASCINATION

Chain a multiple of 23 + 6 chs.

Row 1: Dc in fourth ch from hook **(3 skipped chs count as first dc, now and throughout)** and in each ch across.

To decrease (uses next 2 sts), ★ YO, insert hook in **next** st, YO and pull up a loop, YO and draw through 2 loops on hook; repeat from ★ once **more**, YO and draw through all 3 loops on hook **(counts as one dc)**.

To work Front Post double crochet (abbreviated FPdc), YO, insert hook from **front** to **back** around post of st indicated **(Fig. 4, page 159)**, YO and pull up a loop (3 loops on hook), (YO and draw through 2 loops on hook) twice. Skip st **behind** FPdc.

Row 2: Ch 3 **(counts as first dc, now and throughout)**, turn; skip first dc, decrease, work FPdc around each of next 2 dc, (dc in next 2 dc, work FPdc around each of next 2 dc) twice, 3 dc in next dc, work FPdc around each of next 2 dc, (dc in next 2 dc, work FPdc around each of next 2 dc)

twice, ★ skip next 2 dc, work FPdc around each of next 2 dc, (dc in next 2 dc, work FPdc around each of next 2 dc) twice, 3 dc in next dc, work FPdc around each of next 2 dc, (dc in next 2 dc, work FPdc around each of next 2 dc) twice; repeat from ★ across to last 3 dc, decrease, dc in last dc.

Row 3: Ch 3, turn; skip first dc, decrease, dc in next st, (work FPdc around each of next 2 dc, dc in next 2 sts) twice, work FPdc around next dc, 3 dc in next dc, work FPdc around next dc, (dc in next 2 sts, work FPdc around each of next 2 dc) twice, dc in next st, ★ skip next 2 sts, dc in next st, (work FPdc around each of next 2 dc, dc in next 2 sts) twice, work FPdc around next dc, 3 dc in next dc, work FPdc around next dc, (dc in next 2 sts, work FPdc around each of next 2 dc) twice, dc in next st; repeat from ★ across to last 3 sts, decrease, dc in last dc.

Row 4: Ch 3, turn; working in Front Loops Only **(Fig. 2, page 159)**, skip first dc, decrease, dc in next 10 sts, 3 dc in next dc, dc in next 10 sts, ★ skip next 2 dc, dc in next 10 sts, 3 dc in next dc, dc in next 10 sts; repeat from ★ across to last 3 dc, decrease, dc in last dc.

Row 5: Ch 3, turn; working in Back Loops Only **(Fig. 2, page 159)**, skip first dc, decrease, dc in next 10 dc, 3 dc in next dc, dc in next 10 dc, ★ skip next 2 dc, dc in next 10 dc, 3 dc in next dc, dc in next 10 dc; repeat from ★ across to last 3 dc, decrease, dc in last dc.

Row 6: Ch 3, turn; working in both loops unless otherwise indicated, skip first dc, decrease, work FPdc around each of next 2 dc, (dc in next 2 dc, work FPdc around each of next 2 dc) twice, 3 dc in next dc, work FPdc around each of next 2 dc, (dc in next 2 dc, work FPdc around each of next 2 dc) twice, ★ skip next 2 dc, work FPdc around each of next 2 dc, (dc in next 2 dc, work FPdc around each of next 2 dc) twice, 3 dc in next dc, work FPdc around each of next 2 dc, (dc in next 2 dc, work FPdc around each of next 2 dc) twice; repeat from ★ across to last 3 dc, decrease, dc in last dc.

Repeat Rows 3-6 for pattern.

26 SPIKED CHEVRONS

Note: Uses MC and Colors A and B in the following sequence: ★ 4 Rows MC, 2 rows Color A, 4 rows MC, 2 rows Color B; repeat from ★ for stripe sequence.

With MC, chain a multiple of 33 + 32 chs.

Row 1 (Right side)**:** Sc in second ch from hook and in next 14 chs, 3 sc in next ch, sc in next 15 chs, ★ skip next 2 chs, sc in next 15 chs, 3 sc in next ch, sc in next 15 chs; repeat from ★ across.

Note: Loop a short piece of yarn around any stitch to mark Row 1 as **right** side.

Rows 2-4: Ch 1, turn; sc in first sc, skip next sc, sc in next 14 sc, 3 sc in next sc, ★ sc in next 15 sc, skip next 2 sc, sc in next 15 sc, 3 sc in next sc; repeat from ★ across to last 16 sc, sc in next 14 sc, skip next sc, sc in last sc; at end of last row, finish off.

To work Long Double Crochet (abbreviated LDC)*,* working **around** previous rows *(Fig. 6, page 159)*, dc in sc indicated.

Row 5: With **right** side facing, join Color A with sc in first sc *(see Joining With Sc, page 158)*; skip next sc, LDC in sc 2 rows **below** next sc, sc in next sc, [LDC in sc 3 rows **below** next sc, sc in next sc, LDC in sc 2 rows **below** next sc, sc in next sc] 3 times, 3 sc in next sc, sc in next sc, LDC in sc 2 rows **below** next sc, ★ sc in next sc, [LDC in sc 3 rows **below** next sc, sc in next sc, LDC in sc 2 rows **below** next sc, sc in next sc] 3 times, skip next 2 sc, sc in next sc, LDC in sc 2 rows **below** next sc, sc in next sc, [LDC in sc 3 rows **below** next sc, sc in next sc, LDC in sc 2 rows **below** next sc, sc in next sc] 3 times, 3 sc in next sc, sc in next sc, LDC in sc 2 rows **below** next sc; repeat from ★ across to last 14 sc, [sc in next sc, LDC in sc 3 rows **below** next sc, sc in next sc, LDC in sc 2 rows **below** next sc] 3 times, skip next sc, sc in last sc.

Row 6: Ch 1, turn; sc in first sc, skip next st, sc in next 14 sts, 3 sc in next sc, ★ sc in next 15 sts, skip next 2 sc, sc in next 15 sts, 3 sc in next sc; repeat from ★ across to last 16 sts, sc in next 14 sts, skip next st, sc in last sc; finish off.

Row 7: With **right** side facing, join MC with sc in first sc; skip next sc, sc in next 14 sc, 3 sc in next sc, ★ sc in next 15 sc, skip next 2 sc, sc in next 15 sc, 3 sc in next sc; repeat from ★ across to last 16 sc, sc in next 14 sc, skip next sc, sc in last sc.

Rows 8-10: Ch 1, turn; sc in first sc, skip next sc, sc in next 14 sc, 3 sc in next sc, ★ sc in next 15 sc, skip next 2 sc, sc in next 15 sc, 3 sc in next sc; repeat from ★ across to last 16 sc, sc in next 14 sc, skip next sc, sc in last sc; at end of last row, finish off.

Rows 11 and 12: With Color B, repeat Rows 5 and 6.

Row 13: With **right** side facing, join MC with sc in first sc; skip next sc, sc in next 14 sc, 3 sc in next sc, ★ sc in next 15 sc, skip next 2 sc, sc in next 15 sc, 3 sc in next sc; repeat from ★ across to last 16 sc, sc in next 14 sc, skip next sc, sc in last sc.

Repeat Rows 2-13 for pattern.

27 WAFFLE RIPPLE

Note: Uses MC and Colors A and B in the following sequence: ★ 4 Rows MC, 2 rows Color A, 2 rows MC, 2 rows Color B; repeat from ★ for stripe sequence.

With MC, chain a multiple of 23 + 6 chs.

Row 1 (Right side)**:** Dc in fourth ch from hook **(3 skipped chs count as first dc)** and in each ch across.

Note: Loop a short piece of yarn around any stitch to mark Row 1 as **right** side.

To decrease (uses next 2 sts), ★ YO, insert hook in **next** st, YO and pull up a loop, YO and draw through 2 loops on hook; repeat from ★ once **more**, YO and draw through all 3 loops on hook **(counts as one dc)**.

To work Front Post double crochet *(abbreviated FPdc)*, YO, insert hook from **front** to **back** around post of st indicated *(Fig. 4, page 159)*, YO and pull up a loop (3 loops on hook), (YO and draw through 2 loops on hook) twice. Skip st behind FPdc.

Row 2: Ch 3 **(counts as first dc, now and throughout)**, turn; skip first dc, decrease, work FPdc around each of next 2 dc, (dc in next 2 dc, work FPdc around each of next 2 dc) twice, 3 dc in next dc, work FPdc around each of next 2 dc, (dc in next 2 dc, work FPdc around each of next 2 dc) twice, ★ skip next 2 dc, work FPdc around each of next 2 dc, (dc in next 2 dc, work FPdc around each of next 2 dc) twice, 3 dc in next dc, work FPdc around each of next 2 dc, (dc in next 2 dc, work FPdc around each of next 2 dc) twice; repeat from ★ across to last 3 dc, decrease, dc in last dc.

Row 3: Ch 3, turn; skip first dc, decrease, dc in next st, (work FPdc around each of next 2 dc, dc in next 2 sts) twice, work FPdc around next dc, 3 dc in next dc, work FPdc around next dc, (dc in next 2 sts, work FPdc around each of next 2 dc) twice, dc in next st, ★ skip next 2 sts, dc in next st, (work FPdc around each of next 2 dc, dc in next 2 sts) twice, work FPdc around next dc, 3 dc in next dc, work FPdc around next dc, (dc in next 2 sts, work FPdc around each of next 2 dc) twice, dc in next st; repeat from ★ across to last 3 sts, decrease, dc in last dc.

Row 4: Ch 3, turn; skip first dc, decrease, dc in next 2 sts, (work FPdc around each of next 2 dc, dc in next 2 sts) twice, 3 dc in next dc, dc in next 2 sts, (work FPdc around each of next 2 dc, dc in next 2 sts) twice, ★ skip next 2 dc, dc in next 2 sts, (work FPdc around each of next 2 dc, dc in next 2 sts) twice, 3 dc in next dc, dc in next 2 sts, (work FPdc around each of next 2 dc, dc in next 2 sts) twice; repeat from ★ across to last 3 dc, decrease, dc in last dc; finish off.

Row 5: With **right** side facing, join Color A with slip st in first dc; ch 3, skip joining st, decrease, work FPdc around next dc, (dc in next 2 sts, work FPdc around each of next 2 dc) twice, dc in next dc, 3 dc in next dc, dc in next dc, (work FPdc around each of next 2 dc, dc in next 2 sts) twice, work FPdc around next dc, ★ skip next 2 dc, work FPdc around next dc, (dc in next 2 sts, work FPdc around each of next 2 dc) twice, dc in next dc, 3 dc in next dc, dc in next dc, (work FPdc around each of next 2 dc, dc in next 2 sts) twice, work FPdc around next dc; repeat from ★ across to last 3 dc, decrease, dc in last dc.

Row 6: Ch 3, turn; skip first dc, decrease, work FPdc around each of next 2 dc, (dc in next 2 sts, work FPdc around each of next 2 dc) twice, 3 dc in next dc, work FPdc around each of next 2 dc, (dc in next 2 sts, work FPdc around each of next 2 dc) twice, ★ skip next 2 sts, work FPdc around each of next 2 dc, (dc in next 2 sts, work FPdc around each of next 2 dc) twice, 3 dc in next dc, work FPdc around each of next 2 dc, (dc in next 2 sts, work FPdc around each of next 2 dc) twice; repeat from ★ across to last 3 sts, decrease, dc in last dc; finish off.

Row 7: With **right** side facing, join MC with slip st in first dc; ch 3, skip joining st, decrease, dc in next st, (work FPdc around each of next 2 dc, dc in next 2 sts) twice, work FPdc around next dc, 3 dc in next dc, work FPdc around next dc, (dc in next 2 sts, work FPdc around each of next 2 dc) twice, dc in next st, ★ skip next 2 sts, dc in next st, (work FPdc around each of next 2 dc, dc in next 2 sts) twice, work FPdc around next dc, 3 dc in next dc, work FPdc around next dc, (dc in next 2 sts, work FPdc around each of next 2 dc) twice, dc in next st; repeat from ★ across to last 3 sts, decrease, dc in last dc.

Repeat Rows 4-7 for pattern, working in stripe sequence.

28 TUMBLEWEED

Note: Uses MC and CC in the following sequence: ★ 2 Rows **each** MC, CC; repeat from ★ for stripe sequence.

With MC, chain a multiple of 6 + 4 chs.

Row 1 (Right side)**:** 3 Dc in fourth ch from hook **(3 skipped chs count as first dc)**, skip next 2 chs, sc in next ch, ★ skip next 2 chs, 3 dc in next ch, (sc, hdc, dc) around post of last dc made **(Fig. 4, page 159)**, skip next 2 chs, sc in next ch; repeat from ★ across to last 3 chs, skip next 2 chs, 4 dc in last ch.

Note: Loop a short piece of yarn around any stitch to mark Row 1 as **right** side.

Row 2: Ch 1, turn; sc in first dc, skip next 3 dc, 3 dc in next sc, (sc, hdc, dc) around post of last dc made, skip next 3 sts, sc in next dc, ★ skip next 2 dc, 3 dc in next sc, (sc, hdc, dc) around post of last dc made, skip next 3 sts, sc in next dc; repeat from ★ across; finish off.

Row 3: With **right** side facing, join CC with slip st in first sc; ch 3 **(counts as one dc)**, 3 dc in same st as joining, skip next 3 sts, sc in next dc, ★ skip next 2 dc, 3 dc in next sc, (sc, hdc, dc) around post of last dc made, skip next 3 sts, sc in next dc; repeat from ★ across to last 3 sts, skip next 2 dc, 4 dc in last sc.

Repeat Rows 2 and 3 for pattern, working in stripe sequence.

29 RUFFLED DELIGHT

Note: Loop a short piece of yarn around any stitch to mark Row 1 as **right** side.

To decrease (uses next ch-1 sp and last 2 dc), YO, insert hook in next ch-1 sp, YO and pull up a loop, YO and draw through 2 loops on hook, YO, skip next dc, insert hook in last dc, YO and pull up a loop, YO and draw through 2 loops on hook, YO and draw through all 3 loops on hook **(counts as one dc)**.

To double decrease (uses next 2 ch-1 sps), ★ YO, insert hook in **next** ch-1 sp, YO and pull up a loop, YO and draw through 2 loops on hook; repeat from ★ once **more**, YO and draw through all 3 loops on hook **(counts as one dc)**.

Row 2: With **wrong** side facing, join Color B with slip st in first st; ch 2, dc in next ch-1 sp, (dc, ch 1, dc) in next 3 ch-1 sps, (dc, ch 1, dc, ch 3, dc, ch 1, dc) in next ch-3 sp, ★ (dc, ch 1, dc) in next 2 ch-1 sps, double decrease, (dc, ch 1, dc) in next 2 ch-1 sps, (dc, ch 1, dc, ch 3, dc, ch 1, dc) in next ch-3 sp; repeat from ★ across to last 4 ch-1 sps, (dc, ch 1, dc) in next 3 ch-1 sps, decrease; finish off.

Row 3: With **right** side facing, join Color C with slip st in first st; ch 2, dc in next ch-1 sp, (dc, ch 1, dc) in next 3 ch-1 sps, (dc, ch 1, dc, ch 3, dc, ch 1, dc) in next ch-3 sp, ★ (dc, ch 1, dc) in next 2 ch-1 sps, double decrease, (dc, ch 1, dc) in next 2 ch-1 sps, (dc, ch 1, dc, ch 3, dc, ch 1, dc) in next ch-3 sp; repeat from ★ across to last 4 ch-1 sps, (dc, ch 1, dc) in next 3 ch-1 sps, decrease; finish off.

Row 4: With **wrong** side facing, join Color B with slip st in first st; ch 2, dc in next ch-1 sp, (dc, ch 1, dc) in next 3 ch-1 sps, (dc, ch 1, dc, ch 3, dc, ch 1, dc) in next ch-3 sp, ★ (dc, ch 1, dc) in next 2 ch-1 sps, double decrease, (dc, ch 1, dc) in next 2 ch-1 sps, (dc, ch 1, dc, ch 3, dc, ch 1, dc) in next ch-3 sp; repeat from ★ across to last 4 ch-1 sps, (dc, ch 1, dc) in next 3 ch-1 sps, decrease; finish off.

Note: Uses Colors A, B, and C in the following sequence: 1 Row Color A, ★ 1 row Color B, 1 row Color C, 1 row Color B, 3 rows Color A, 1 row Color C, 1 row Color B, 1 row Color C, 3 rows Color A; repeat from ★ for stripe sequence.

With Color A, chain a multiple of 23 + 9 chs.

Row 1 (Right side)**:** Dc in fifth ch from hook, [skip next 2 chs, (dc, ch 1, dc) in next ch] 4 times, ch 3, (dc, ch 1, dc) in next ch, ★ [skip next 2 chs, (dc, ch 1, dc) in next ch] twice, YO, skip next 2 chs, insert hook in next ch, YO and pull up a loop, YO and draw through 2 loops on hook, YO, skip next 3 chs, insert hook in next ch, YO and pull up a loop, YO and draw through 2 loops on hook, YO and draw through all 3 loops on hook, [skip next 2 chs, (dc, ch 1, dc) in next ch] 3 times, ch 3, (dc, ch 1, dc) in next ch; repeat from ★ across to last 14 chs, [skip next 2 chs, (dc, ch 1, dc) in next ch] 3 times, YO, skip next 2 chs, insert hook in next ch, YO and pull up a loop, YO and draw through 2 loops on hook, YO, skip next ch, insert hook in next ch, YO and pull up a loop, YO and draw through 2 loops on hook, YO and draw through all 3 loops on hook; finish off.

Row 5: With **right** side facing, join Color A with slip st in first st; ch 2, dc in next ch-1 sp, (dc, ch 1, dc) in next 3 ch-1 sps, (dc, ch 1, dc, ch 3, dc, ch 1, dc) in next ch-3 sp, ★ (dc, ch 1, dc) in next 2 ch-1 sps, double decrease, (dc, ch 1, dc) in next 2 ch-1 sps, (dc, ch 1, dc, ch 3, dc, ch 1, dc) in next ch-3 sp; repeat from ★ across to last 4 ch-1 sps, (dc, ch 1, dc) in next 3 ch-1 sps, decrease.

Rows 6 and 7: Ch 2, turn; dc in next ch-1 sp, (dc, ch 1, dc) in next 3 ch-1 sps, (dc, ch 1, dc, ch 3, dc, ch 1, dc) in next ch-3 sp, ★ (dc, ch 1, dc) in next 2 ch-1 sps, double decrease, (dc, ch 1, dc) in next 2 ch-1 sps, (dc, ch 1, dc, ch 3, dc, ch 1, dc) in next ch-3 sp; repeat from ★ across to last 4 ch-1 sps, (dc, ch 1, dc) in next 3 ch-1 sps, decrease; at end of last row, finish off.

Repeat Rows 2-7 for pattern, working in stripe sequence.

The Ruffle is worked around the post of sts **(Fig. 4, page 159)**, every third row as follows: With **right** side and bottom of piece facing, join corresponding color yarn with sc around first st **(see Joining With Sc, page 158)**; (ch 5, sc around next st) across; finish off.

30 LITTLE RUFFLES WAVES

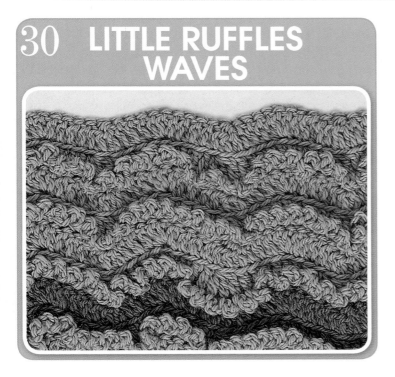

Note: Uses MC and Colors A and B in the following sequence: ★ 2 Rows **each** MC, Color A, MC, Color B; repeat from ★ for stripe sequence.

With MC, chain a multiple of 10 + 3 chs.

To decrease (uses next 3 sts), ★ YO, insert hook in **next** st, YO and pull up a loop, YO and draw through 2 loops on hook; repeat from ★ 2 times **more**, YO and draw through all 4 loops on hook **(counts as one dc)**.

Row 1 (Right side)**:** Dc in third ch from hook and in next 3 chs, decrease, dc in next 3 chs, ★ 3 dc in next ch, dc in next 3 chs, decrease, dc in next 3 chs; repeat from ★ across to last ch, 2 dc in last ch.

Note: Loop a short piece of yarn around any stitch to mark Row 1 as **right** side.

Row 2: Ch 3 **(counts as first dc, now and throughout)**, turn; working in Front Loops Only **(Fig. 2, page 159)**, dc in same st and in next 3 dc, decrease, dc in next 3 dc, ★ 3 dc in next dc, dc in next 3 dc, decrease, dc in next 3 dc; repeat from ★ across to last dc, 2 dc in last dc; finish off.

Row 3: With **right** side facing and working in Back Loops Only **(Fig. 2, page 159)**, join Color A with slip st in first dc; ch 3, dc in same st as joining and in next 3 dc, decrease, dc in next 3 dc, ★ 3 dc in next dc, dc in next 3 dc, decrease, dc in next 3 dc; repeat from ★ across to last dc, 2 dc in last dc.

Repeat Rows 2 and 3 for pattern, working in stripe sequence.

The Ruffle is worked in the free loops of sts **(Fig. 3, page 159)**, every second row as follows: With **right** side and bottom of piece facing, join MC with slip st in first dc; (ch 3, slip st in next st) across; finish off.

Note: Uses Colors A, B, and C.

With Color A, chain a multiple of 22 + 10 chs.

To decrease (uses next 3 sts), ★ YO, insert hook in **next** st, YO and pull up a loop, YO and draw through 2 loops on hook; repeat from ★ 2 times **more**, YO and draw through all 4 loops on hook **(counts as one dc)**.

Row 1 (Right side)**:** Dc in fourth ch from hook **(3 skipped chs count as first dc)** and in next 5 chs, decrease, dc in next 5 chs, 3 dc in next ch, ★ dc in next 9 chs, decrease, dc in next 9 chs, 3 dc in next ch; repeat from ★ across to last 14 chs, dc in next 5 chs, decrease, dc in next 5 chs, 2 dc in last ch.

Note: Loop a short piece of yarn around any stitch to mark Row 1 as **right** side.

Row 2: Ch 3 **(counts as first dc, now and throughout)**, turn; dc in same st and in next 5 dc, decrease, dc in next 5 dc, 3 dc in next dc, ★ dc in next 9 dc, decrease, dc in next 9 dc, 3 dc in next dc; repeat from ★ across to last 14 dc, dc in next 5 dc, decrease, dc in next 5 dc, 2 dc in last dc; finish off.

To FP decrease (uses next 3 sts), † YO, insert hook from **front** to **back** around post of next dc

38

(Fig. 4, page 159), YO and pull up a loop, YO and draw through 2 loops on hook †, YO, insert hook from **front** to **back** around post of center leg of next decrease, YO and pull up a loop, YO and draw through 2 loops on hook, repeat from † to † once, YO and draw through all 4 loops on hook. Skip 3 sts **behind** FP decrease.

Row 3: With **right** side facing, join Color B with slip st in first dc; ch 3, dc in same st as joining and in next 5 dc, FP decrease, dc in next 5 dc, 3 dc in next dc, ★ dc in next 9 dc, FP decrease, dc in next 9 dc, 3 dc in next dc; repeat from ★ across to last 14 dc, dc in next 5 dc, FP decrease, dc in next 5 dc, 2 dc in last dc; finish off.

Row 4: With **wrong** side facing and working in Back Loops Only *(Fig. 2, page 159)*, join Color C with sc in first dc *(see Joining With Sc, page 158)*; ch 1, sc in same st, ★ (sc, ch 1, sc) in each dc across to next FP decrease, skip FP decrease; repeat from ★ across to last 7 dc, (sc, ch 1, sc) in last 7 dc; finish off.

Row 5: With **right** side facing, working **behind** sts on Row 4 *(Fig. 6, page 159)*, and in free loops of sts on Row 3 *(Fig. 3, page 159)*, join Color B with slip st in first dc; ch 3, dc in same st as joining and in next 5 dc, decrease, dc in next 5 dc, 3 dc in next dc, ★ dc in next 9 dc, decrease, dc in next 9 dc, 3 dc in next dc; repeat from ★ across to last 14 sts, dc in next 5 dc, decrease, dc in next 5 dc, 2 dc in last dc; finish off.

Row 6: With **wrong** side facing and working in both loops of sts, join Color A with slip st in first dc; ch 3, dc in same st as joining and in next 5 dc, decrease, dc in next 5 dc, 3 dc in next dc, ★ dc in next 9 dc, decrease, dc in next 9 dc, 3 dc in next dc; repeat from ★ across to last 14 dc, dc in next 5 dc, decrease, dc in next 5 dc, 2 dc in last dc.

Rows 7 and 8: Ch 3, turn; dc in same st and in next 5 dc, decrease, dc in next 5 dc, 3 dc in next dc, ★ dc in next 9 dc, decrease, dc in next 9 dc, 3 dc in next dc; repeat from ★ across to last 14 dc, dc in next 5 dc, decrease, dc in next 5 dc, 2 dc in last dc; at end of last row, finish off.

Repeat Rows 3-8 for pattern.

32 PRETTY POSIES

Note: Uses MC and CC in the following sequence: ★ 4 Rows MC, 2 rows CC; repeat from ★ for stripe sequence.

With MC, chain a multiple of 16 + 4 chs.

To dc decrease (uses next 3 sts), ★ YO, insert hook in **next** st, YO and pull up a loop, YO and draw through 2 loops on hook; repeat from ★ 2 times **more**, YO and draw through all 4 loops on hook **(counts as one dc)**.

Row 1 (Right side)**:** Dc in fourth ch from hook **(3 skipped chs count as first dc)** and in next 6 chs, dc decrease, dc in next 6 chs, ★ 3 dc in next ch, dc in next 6 chs, dc decrease, dc in next 6 chs; repeat from ★ across to last ch, 2 dc in last ch.

Note: Loop a short piece of yarn around any stitch to mark Row 1 as **right** side.

Rows 2-4: Ch 3 **(counts as first dc, now and throughout)**, turn; dc in same st and in next 6 dc, dc decrease, dc in next 6 dc, ★ 3 dc in next dc, dc in next 6 dc, dc decrease, dc in next 6 dc; repeat from ★ across to last dc, 2 dc in last dc; at end of last row, finish off.

To sc decrease, pull up a loop in each of next 3 dc, YO and draw through all 4 loops on hook **(counts as one sc)**.

Row 5: With **right** side facing, join CC in with sc in first dc **(see Joining With Sc, page 158)**; sc in same st as joining and in next 4 dc, [working from **top** to **bottom** around post of dc **(Fig. 4, page 159)**, (slip st, ch 3) 4 times around next dc, turn work (clockwise), slip st around post of previous dc, working from **bottom** to **top**, (ch 3, slip st around post of same dc) 3 times **(flower made)**], skip dc of flower, sc in next dc, sc decrease, sc in next dc, [working from **top** to **bottom** around post of dc, (slip st, ch 3) 4 times around next dc, turn work, slip st around post of previous dc, working from **bottom** to **top**, (ch 3, slip st around post of same dc) 3 times **(flower made)**], skip dc of flower, sc in next 4 dc, ★ 3 sc in next dc, sc in next 4 dc, [working from **top** to **bottom** around post of dc, (slip st, ch 3) 4 times around next dc, turn work, slip st around post of previous dc, working from **bottom** to **top**, (ch 3, slip st around post of same dc) 3 times **(flower made)**], skip dc of flower, sc in next dc, sc decrease, sc in next dc, [working from **top** to **bottom** around post of dc, (slip st, ch 3) 4 times around next dc, turn work, slip st around post of previous dc, working from **bottom** to **top**, (ch 3, slip st around post of same dc) 3 times **(flower made)**], skip dc of flower, sc in next 4 dc; repeat from ★ across to last dc, 2 sc in last dc.

Row 6: Ch 1, turn; 2 sc in first sc, sc in next 5 sc and in next flower, sc decrease, sc in next flower and in next 5 sc, ★ 3 sc in next sc, sc in next 5 sc and in next flower, sc decrease, sc in next flower and in next 5 sc; repeat from ★ across to last sc, 2 sc in last sc; finish off.

Row 7: With **right** side facing, join MC with slip st in first sc; ch 3, dc in same st as joining and in next 6 sc, dc decrease, dc in next 6 sc, ★ 3 dc in next sc, dc in next 6 sc, dc decrease, dc in next 6 sc; repeat from ★ across to last sc, 2 dc in last sc.

Repeat Rows 2-7 for pattern.

33 POPCORN ARCHES

Note: Uses MC and CC in the following sequence: 5 Rows MC, ★ 2 rows CC, 6 rows MC; repeat from ★ for stripe sequence.

With MC, chain a multiple of 16 + 2 chs.

Row 1 (Right side): 2 Sc in second ch from hook, sc in next 7 chs, skip next ch, sc in next 7 chs, ★ 3 sc in next ch, sc in next 7 chs, skip next ch, sc in next 7 chs; repeat from ★ across to last ch, 2 sc in last sc.

Note: Loop a short piece of yarn around any stitch to mark Row 1 as **right** side.

Row 2: Ch 1, turn; 2 sc in first sc, sc in next 7 sc, skip next 2 sc, sc in next 7 sc, ★ 3 sc in next sc, sc in next 7 sc, skip next 2 sc, sc in next 7 sc; repeat from ★ across to last sc, 2 sc in last sc.

To work Front Popcorn (uses one sc), 5 dc in sc indicated, drop loop from hook, insert hook from **front** to **back** in first dc of 5-dc group, hook dropped loop and draw through st.

Row 3: Ch 1, turn; 2 sc in first sc, sc in next 3 sc, work Front Popcorn in next sc, sc in next 3 sc, skip next 2 sc, sc in next 3 sc, work Front

Popcorn in next sc, sc in next 3 sc, ★ 3 sc in next sc, sc in next 3 sc, work Front Popcorn in next sc, sc in next 3 sc, skip next 2 sc, sc in next 3 sc, work Front Popcorn in next sc, sc in next 3 sc; repeat from ★ across to last sc, 2 sc in last sc.

Rows 4 and 5: Ch 1, turn; 2 sc in next 7 sts, skip next 2 sc, sc in next ... next sc, sc in next 7 sts, skip next 2 sc ... 7 sts; repeat from ★ across to last sc, 2 ... at end of last row, finish off.

To work Back Popcorn (uses one sc), 5 dc in sc indicated, drop loop from hook, insert hook from **back** to **front** in first dc of 5-dc group, hook dropped loop and draw through st.

Row 6: With **wrong** side facing, join CC with sc in first sc *(see Joining With Sc, page 158)*; sc in same st as joining and in next 3 sc, work Back Popcorn in next sc, sc in next 3 sc, skip next 2 sc, sc in next 3 sc, work Back Popcorn in next sc, sc in next 3 sc, ★ 3 sc in next sc, sc in next 3 sc, work Back Popcorn in next sc, sc in next 3 sc, skip next 2 sc, sc in next 3 sc, work Back Popcorn in next sc, sc in next 3 sc; repeat from ★ across to last sc, 2 sc in last sc.

Row 7: Ch 1, turn; 2 sc in first sc, sc in next 7 sts, skip next 2 sc, sc in next 7 sts, ★ 3 sc in next sc, sc in next 7 sts, skip next 2 sc, sc in next 7 sts; repeat from ★ across to last sc, 2 sc in last sc; finish off.

Row 8: With **wrong** side facing, join MC with sc in first sc; sc in same st as joining and in next 7 sc, skip next 2 sc, sc in next 7 sc, ★ 3 sc in next sc, sc in next 7 sc, skip next 2 sc, sc in next 7 sc; repeat from ★ across to last sc, 2 sc in last sc.

Rows 9 and 10: Ch 1, turn; 2 sc in first sc, sc in next 7 sc, skip next 2 sc, sc in next 7 sc, ★ 3 sc in next sc, sc in next 7 sc, skip next 2 sc, sc in next 7 sc; repeat from ★ across to last sc, 2 sc in last sc.

Repeat Rows 3-10 for pattern.

34 ILLUSION

Note: Uses Colors A, B, C, and D in the following sequence: ★ 1 Row **each** Color A, Color B, Color C, Color D; repeat from ★ for stripe sequence.

With Color A, chain a multiple of 28 + 17 chs.

To decrease (uses next 3 sts), ★ YO, insert hook in **next** st, YO and pull up a loop, YO and draw through 2 loops on hook; repeat from ★ 2 times **more**, YO and draw through all 4 loops on hook **(counts as one dc)**.

Row 1 (Right side)**:** Dc in fourth ch from hook **(3 skipped chs count as first dc)** and in next 5 chs, ch 3, ★ dc in next 6 chs, skip next 2 chs, sc in next 6 chs, ch 3, sc in next 6 chs, skip next 2 chs, dc in next 6 chs, ch 3; repeat from ★ across to last 8 chs, dc in next 5 chs, decrease; finish off.

Note: Loop a short piece of yarn around any stitch to mark Row 1 as **right** side.

To work Cluster, ch 3, YO, insert hook in third ch from hook, YO and pull up a loop, YO and draw through 2 loops on hook, ★ YO, insert hook in **same** ch, YO and pull up a loop, YO and draw through 2 loops on hook; repeat from ★ once **more**, YO and draw through all 4 loops on hook.

Row 2: With **wrong** side facing, join Color B with sc in first dc *(see Joining With Sc, page 158)*; sc in next 5 dc, work Cluster, skip next ch-3, sc in next 5 dc, ★ skip next 2 sts, dc in next 5 sc, (dc, ch 3, dc) in next ch-3 sp, dc in next 5 sc, skip next 2 sts, sc in next 5 dc, work Cluster, skip next ch-3, sc in next 5 dc; repeat from ★ across to last 2 dc, skip next dc, sc in last dc; finish off.

To treble crochet (abbreviated tr), YO twice, insert hook in sp indicated, YO and pull up a loop (4 loops on hook), (YO and draw through 2 loops on hook) 3 times.

Row 3: With **right** side facing, join Color C with slip st in first sc; ch 3 **(counts as first dc, now and throughout)**, skip first 2 sc, dc in next 4 sc, working **behind** Cluster, (2 tr, ch 3, 2 tr) in skipped ch-3 sp one row **below** next Cluster, ★ dc in next 4 sc, skip next 2 sts, sc in next 5 dc, (sc, ch 3, sc) in next ch-3 sp, sc in next 5 dc, skip next 2 sts, dc in next 4 dc, working **behind** Cluster, (2 tr, ch 3, 2 tr) in skipped ch-3 sp one row **below** next Cluster; repeat from ★ across to last 6 sc, dc in next 3 sc, decrease; finish off.

Row 4: With **wrong** side facing, join Color D with sc in first dc; sc in next 5 sts, work Cluster, skip next ch-3, sc in next 5 sts, ★ skip next 2 sts, dc in next 5 sc, (dc, ch 3, dc) in next ch-3 sp, dc in next 5 sc, skip next 2 sts, sc in next 5 sts, work Cluster, skip next ch-3, sc in next 5 sts; repeat from ★ across to last 2 dc, skip next dc, sc in last dc; finish off.

Repeat Rows 3 and 4 for pattern, working in stripe sequence.

35 SHADES OF FALL

Note: Uses Colors A, B, C, D, and E in the following sequence: ★ 2 Rows **each** Color A, Color B, Color C, Color D, Color E; repeat from ★ for stripe sequence.

With Color A, chain a multiple of 14 + 2 chs.

To dc decrease (uses next 2 sts), ★ YO, insert hook in **next** st, YO and pull up a loop, YO and draw through 2 loops on hook; repeat from ★ once **more**, YO and draw through all 3 loops on hook **(counts as one dc)**.

To double dc decrease (uses next 3 sts), ★ YO, insert hook in **next** st, YO and pull up a loop, YO and draw through 2 loops on hook; repeat from ★ 2 times **more**, YO and draw through all 4 loops on hook **(counts as one dc)**.

Row 1 (Right side)**:** Dc in third ch from hook and in next 5 chs, 3 dc in next ch, dc in next 5 chs, ★ double dc decrease, dc in next 5 chs, 3 dc in next ch, dc in next 5 chs; repeat from ★ across to last 2 chs, dc decrease.

Note: Loop a short piece of yarn around any stitch to mark Row 1 as **right** side.

To treble crochet (abbreviated tr), YO twice, insert hook in st or sp indicated, YO and pull up a loop (4 loops on hook), (YO and draw through 2 loops on hook) 3 times.

To tr decrease (uses next 2 dc), ★ YO twice, insert hook in **next** dc, YO and pull up a loop, (YO and draw through 2 loops on hook) twice; repeat from ★ once **more**, YO and draw through all 3 loops on hook **(counts as one tr)**.

To double tr decrease (uses next 3 dc), ★ YO twice, insert hook in **next** dc, YO and pull up a loop, (YO and draw through 2 loops on hook) twice; repeat from ★ 2 times **more**, YO and draw through all 4 loops on hook **(counts as one tr)**.

Row 2: Ch 3, turn; tr in next 6 dc, (tr, ch 1, tr) in next dc, tr in next 5 dc, ★ double tr decrease, tr in next 5 dc, (tr, ch 1, tr) in next dc, tr in next 5 dc; repeat from ★ across to last 2 dc, tr decrease; finish off.

To work Front Post double treble crochet (abbreviated FPdtr), working in **front** of previous row **(Fig. 6, page 159)**, YO 3 times, insert hook from **front** to **back** around post of st indicated **(Fig. 4, page 159)**, YO and pull up a loop (5 loops on hook), (YO and draw through 2 loops on hook) 4 times.

Row 3: With **right** side facing, join Color B with slip st in first tr; ch 2, dc in next 6 tr, work FPdtr around first dc of 3-dc group 2 rows **below**, dc in next ch-1 sp, work FPdtr around third dc of same 3-dc group 2 rows **below**, dc in next 5 tr, ★ double dc decrease, dc in next 5 tr, work FPdtr around first dc of 3-dc group 2 rows **below**, dc in next ch-1 sp, work FPdtr around third dc of same 3-dc group 2 rows **below**, dc in next 5 tr; repeat from ★ across to last 2 tr, dc decrease.

Row 4: Ch 3, turn; tr in next 6 sts, (tr, ch 1, tr) in next dc, tr in next 5 dc, ★ double tr decrease, tr in next 5 dc, (tr, ch 1, tr) in next dc, tr in next 5 dc; repeat from ★ across to last 2 dc, tr decrease; finish off.

Row 5: With **right** side facing, join Color C with slip st in first tr; ch 2, dc in next 6 tr, work FPdtr around next FPdtr 2 rows **below**, dc in next ch-1 sp, work FPdtr around next FPdtr 2 rows **below**, dc in next 5 tr, ★ double dc decrease, dc in next 5 tr, work FPdtr around next FPdtr 2 rows **below**, dc in next ch-1 sp, work FPdtr around next FPdtr 2 rows **below**, dc in next 5 tr; repeat from ★ across to last 2 tr, dc decrease.

Row 6: Ch 3, turn; tr in next 6 sts, (tr, ch 1, tr) in next dc, tr in next 5 sts, ★ double tr decrease, tr in next 5 sts, (tr, ch 1, tr) in next dc, tr in next 5 sts; repeat from ★ across to last 2 dc, tr decrease; finish off.

Repeat Rows 5 and 6 for pattern, working in stripe sequence.

36 POPCORN LACE

Chain a multiple of 12 chs.

Row 1: Dc in fourth ch from hook **(3 skipped chs count as one dc)** and in next 3 chs, ch 2, dc in next 5 chs, ★ skip next 2 chs, dc in next 5 chs, ch 2, dc in next 5 chs; repeat from ★ across.

To work Popcorn (uses one ch-2 sp), 5 dc in ch-2 sp indicated, drop loop from hook, insert hook from **front** to **back** in first dc of 5-dc group, hook dropped loop and draw through st.

Row 2 (Right side)**:** Ch 4 **(counts as first dc plus ch 1)**, turn; skip first 3 dc, dc in next dc, ch 1, (dc, ch 1, work Popcorn, ch 1, dc) in next ch-2 sp, ★ (ch 1, skip next dc, dc in next dc) twice, skip next 2 dc, (dc in next dc, ch 1, skip next dc) twice, (dc, ch 1, work Popcorn, ch 1, dc) in next ch-2 sp; repeat from ★ across to last 5 dc, ch 1, skip next dc, dc in next dc, ch 1, skip next 2 dc, dc in last dc.

Note: Loop a short piece of yarn around any stitch to mark Row 2 as **right** side.

Row 3: Ch 3 **(counts as first dc)**, turn; skip next ch-1 sp, (dc in next dc and in next ch-1 sp) twice, ch 2, dc in next ch-1 sp, ★ (dc in next dc and in next ch-1 sp) twice, skip next 2 dc, dc in next ch-1 sp, (dc in next dc and in next ch-1 sp) twice, ch 2, dc in next ch-1 sp; repeat from ★ across to last 2 ch-1 sps, dc in next dc and in next ch-1 sp, dc in next dc, skip last ch-1 sp, dc in last dc.

Repeat Rows 2 and 3 for pattern.

37 GUMBALLS

Chain a multiple of 15 + 5 chs.

Row 1 (Right side)**:** Dc in fifth ch from hook, ch 1, skip next ch, (dc in next ch, ch 1, skip next ch) twice, 3 dc in next ch, ch 3, 3 dc in next ch, ch 1, (skip next ch, dc in next ch, ch 1) twice, ★ YO, skip next ch, insert hook in next ch, YO and pull up a loop, YO and draw through 2 loops on hook, [YO, insert hook in **next** ch, YO and pull up a loop, YO and draw through 2 loops on hook] twice, YO and draw through all 4 loops on hook, ch 1, skip next ch, (dc in next ch, ch 1, skip next ch) twice, 3 dc in next ch, ch 3, 3 dc in next ch, ch 1, (skip next ch, dc in next ch, ch 1) twice; repeat from ★ across to last 4 chs, [YO, skip next ch, insert hook in **next** ch, YO and pull up a loop, YO and draw through 2 loops on hook] twice, YO and draw through all 3 loops on hook.

Note: Loop a short piece of yarn around any stitch to mark Row 1 as **right** side.

To work Cluster (uses next 5 sts), YO, insert hook in next dc, YO and pull up a loop, YO and draw through 2 loops on hook, YO twice, skip next ch, insert hook in next st, YO and pull up a loop, (YO and draw through 2 loops on hook) twice, [YO twice, insert hook in **same** st, YO and pull up a loop, (YO and draw through 2 loops on hook) twice] 3 times, YO, skip next ch, insert hook in next dc, YO and pull up a loop, YO and draw through 2 loops on hook, YO and draw through all 7 loops on hook.

Row 2: Ch 2, turn; (skip next ch, dc in next dc, ch 1) 3 times, (3 dc, ch 3, 3 dc) in next ch-3 sp, ch 1, skip next 2 dc, (dc in next dc, ch 1, skip next ch) twice, ★ work Cluster, ch 1, (skip next ch, dc in next dc, ch 1) twice, (3 dc, ch 3, 3 dc) in next ch-3 sp, ch 1, skip next 2 dc, (dc in next dc, ch 1, skip next ch) twice; repeat from ★ across to last 2 dc, [YO, insert hook in **next** dc, YO and pull up a loop, YO and draw through 2 loops on hook] twice, YO and draw through all 3 loops on hook.

To decrease (uses next 5 sts), YO, insert hook in next dc, YO and pull up a loop, YO and draw through 2 loops on hook, ★ YO, skip **next** ch, insert hook in **next** st, YO and pull up a loop, YO and draw through 2 loops on hook; repeat from ★ once **more**, YO and draw through all 4 loops on hook.

Row 3: Ch 2, turn; (skip next ch, dc in next dc, ch 1) 3 times, (3 dc, ch 3, 3 dc) in next ch-3 sp, ch 1, skip next 2 dc, (dc in next dc, ch 1, skip next ch) twice, ★ decrease, ch 1, (skip next ch, dc in next dc, ch 1) twice, (3 dc, ch 3, 3 dc) in next ch-3 sp, ch 1, skip next 2 dc, (dc in next dc, ch 1, skip next ch) twice; repeat from ★ across to last 2 dc, [YO, insert hook in **next** dc, YO and pull up a loop, YO and draw through 2 loops on hook] twice, YO and draw through all 3 loops on hook.

Repeat Rows 2 and 3 for pattern.

38 TRES CHIC

Chain a multiple of 16 + 3 chs.

To decrease (uses next 2 sts), ★ YO, insert hook in **next** st, YO and pull up a loop, YO and draw through 2 loops on hook; repeat from ★ once **more**, YO and draw through all 3 loops on hook **(counts as one dc)**.

Row 1 (Right side)**:** Dc in third ch from hook and in next 6 chs, 2 dc in next ch, ch 2, 2 dc in next ch, ★ dc in next 5 chs, decrease twice, dc in next 5 chs, 2 dc in next ch, ch 2, 2 dc in next ch; repeat from ★ across to last 8 chs, dc in next 6 chs, decrease.

Note: Loop a short piece of yarn around any stitch to mark Row 1 as **right** side.

To work Popcorn (uses one ch-2 sp), 5 dc in ch-2 sp indicated, drop loop from hook, insert hook from **back** to **front** in first dc of 5-dc group, hook dropped loop and draw through st.

Row 2: Ch 3 **(counts as first dc, now and throughout)**, turn; skip first 2 dc, dc in next 6 sts, 2 dc in next dc, work Popcorn in next ch-2 sp, 2 dc in next dc, ★ dc in next 5 sts, decrease twice, dc in next 5 sts, 2 dc in next dc, work Popcorn in next ch-2 sp, 2 dc in next dc; repeat from ★ across to last 8 sts, dc in next 6 sts, skip next dc, dc in last dc.

To work Front Post treble crochet (abbreviated FPtr), YO twice, working in **front** of previous row **(Fig. 6, page 159)**, insert hook from **front** to **back** around post of st indicated **(Fig. 4, page 159)**, YO and pull up a loop (4 loops on hook), (YO and draw through 2 loops on hook) 3 times. Skip dc behind FPtr.

Row 3: Ch 3, turn; skip first 2 dc, dc in next 5 dc, work FPtr around dc one row **below** next dc, 2 dc in next dc, ch 2, skip next Popcorn, 2 dc in next dc, work FPtr around next dc one row **below**, ★ dc in next 4 dc, decrease twice, dc in next 4 dc, work FPtr around dc one row **below** next dc, 2 dc in next dc, ch 2, skip next Popcorn, 2 dc in next dc, work FPtr around next dc one row **below**; repeat from ★ across to last 7 dc, dc in next 5 dc, skip next dc, dc in last dc.

Repeat Rows 2 and 3 for pattern.

39 ASCENDING CLUSTERS

Note: Uses MC and Colors A and B in the following sequence: ★ 4 Rows MC, 2 rows Color A, 2 rows Color B; repeat from ★ for stripe sequence.

With MC, chain a multiple of 17 + 16 chs.

Row 1 (Right side)**:** Sc in second ch from hook and in next 6 chs, 3 sc in next ch, sc in next 7 chs, ★ skip next 2 chs, sc in next 7 chs, 3 sc in next ch, sc in next 7 chs; repeat from ★ across.

Note: Loop a short piece of yarn around any stitch to mark Row 1 as **right** side.

Rows 2-4: Ch 1, turn; sc in first sc, skip next sc, sc in next 6 sts, 3 sc in next sc, ★ sc in next 7 sts, skip next 2 sc, sc in next 7 sts, 3 sc in next sc; repeat from ★ across to last 8 sts, sc in next 6 sts, skip next sc, sc in last sc; at end of last row, finish off.

To work Front Post Cluster *(abbreviated FP Cluster)*, working in **front** of previous 3 rows *(Fig. 6, page 159)*, ★ YO twice, insert hook from **front** to **back** around post of sc indicated *(Fig. 4, page 159)*, YO and pull up a loop, (YO and draw through 2 loops on hook) twice; repeat from ★ 2 times **more**, YO and draw through all 4 loops on hook. Skip sc **behind** FP Cluster.

Row 5: With **right** side facing, join Color A with sc in first sc *(see Joining With Sc, page 158)*; skip next sc, sc in next 2 sc, work FP Cluster around sc 3 rows **below** next sc (sc **before** 3-sc group), sc in next 3 sc, 3 sc in next sc, sc in next 3 sc, work FP Cluster around sc 3 rows **below** next sc (sc **after** 3-sc group), ★ sc in next 3 sc, skip next 2 sc, sc in next 3 sc, work FP Cluster around sc 3 rows **below** next sc (sc **before** 3-sc group), sc in next 3 sc, 3 sc in next sc, sc in next 3 sc, work FP Cluster around sc 3 rows **below** next sc (sc **after** 3-sc group); repeat from ★ across to last 4 sc, sc in next 2 sc, skip next sc, sc in last sc.

Row 6: Ch 1, turn; sc in first sc, skip next sc, sc in next 6 sts, 3 sc in next sc, ★ sc in next 7 sts, skip next 2 sc, sc in next 7 sts, 3 sc in next sc; repeat from ★ across to last 8 sts, sc in next 6 sts, skip next sc, sc in last sc; finish off.

Row 7: With **right** side facing, join Color B with sc in first sc; skip next sc, sc in next 6 sc, 3 sc in next sc, ★ sc in next 7 sc, skip next 2 sc, sc in next 7 sc, 3 sc in next sc; repeat from ★ across to last 8 sc, sc in next 6 sc, skip next sc, sc in last sc.

Row 8: Ch 1, turn; sc in first sc, skip next sc, sc in next 6 sc, 3 sc in next sc, ★ sc in next 7 sc, skip next 2 sc, sc in next 7 sc, 3 sc in next sc; repeat from ★ across to last 8 sc, sc in next 6 sc, skip next sc, sc in last sc; finish off.

Row 9: With **right** side facing, join MC with sc in first sc; skip next sc, sc in next 2 sc, work FP Cluster around sc 3 rows **below** next sc (sc **before** 3-sc group), sc in next 3 sc, 3 sc in next sc, sc in next 3 sc, work FP Cluster around sc 3 rows **below** next sc (sc **after** 3-sc group), ★ sc in next 3 sc, skip next 2 sc, sc in next 3 sc, work FP Cluster around sc 3 rows **below** next sc (sc **before** 3-sc group), sc in next 3 sc, 3 sc in next sc, sc in next 3 sc, work FP Cluster around sc 3 rows **below** next sc (sc **after** 3-sc group); repeat from ★ across to last 4 sc, sc in next 2 sc, skip next sc, sc in last sc.

Repeat Rows 2-9 for pattern.

40 COUNTRY CABLE

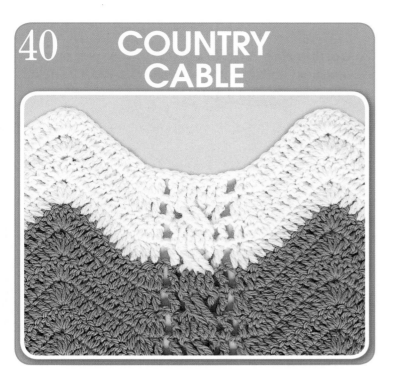

Note: Uses Colors A, B, and C in the following sequence: ★ 4 Rows **each** Color A, Color B, Color C; repeat from ★ for stripe sequence.

With Color A, chain a multiple of 29 + 25 chs.

To decrease (uses next 3 sts), ★ YO, insert hook in **next** st, YO and pull up a loop, YO and draw through 2 loops on hook; repeat from ★ 2 times **more**, YO and draw through all 4 loops on hook **(counts as one dc)**.

To treble crochet (abbreviated tr), YO twice, insert hook in st indicated, YO and pull up a loop (4 loops on hook), (YO and draw through 2 loops on hook) 3 times.

Row 1 (Right side)**:** Decrease beginning in fourth ch from hook **(3 skipped chs count as first dc)**, dc in next 7 chs, 5 dc in next ch, dc in next 7 chs, decrease, dc in next ch, ★ ch 1, skip next ch, tr in next ch, skip next ch, 2 tr in next ch, working in **front** of last 2 tr, 2 tr in skipped ch, tr in next ch, ch 1, skip next ch, dc in next ch, decrease, dc in next 7 chs, 5 dc in next ch, dc in next 7 chs, decrease, dc in next ch; repeat from ★ across.

Note: Loop a short piece of yarn around any stitch to mark Row 1 as **right** side.

To work Back Post treble crochet (abbreviated BPtr), YO twice, insert hook from **back** to **front** around post of st indicated **(Fig. 4, page 159)**, YO and pull up a loop (4 loops on hook), (YO and draw through 2 loops on hook) 3 times.

Row 2: Ch 3 **(counts as first dc, now and throughout)**, turn; decrease, dc in next 7 dc, 5 dc in next dc, dc in next 7 dc, decrease, dc in next dc, ★ ch 1, tr in next tr, work BPtr around each of next 4 sts, tr in next tr, ch 1, dc in next dc, decrease, dc in next 7 dc, 5 dc in next dc, dc in next 7 dc, decrease, dc in next dc; repeat from ★ across.

To work Front Post treble crochet (abbreviated FPtr), YO twice, insert hook from **front** to **back** around post of st indicated **(Fig. 4, page 159)**, YO and pull up a loop (4 loops on hook), (YO and draw through 2 loops on hook) 3 times.

Row 3: Ch 3, turn; decrease, dc in next 7 dc, 5 dc in next dc, dc in next 7 dc, decrease, dc in next dc, ★ ch 1, tr in next tr, skip next 2 BPtr, work FPtr around each of next 2 BPtr, working in **front** of last 2 FPtr, work FPtr around each skipped BPtr, tr in next tr, ch 1, dc in next dc, decrease, dc in next 7 dc, 5 dc in next dc, dc in next 7 dc, decrease, dc in next dc; repeat from ★ across.

Row 4: Ch 3, turn; decrease, dc in next 7 dc, 5 dc in next dc, dc in next 7 dc, decrease, dc in next dc, ★ ch 1, tr in next tr, work BPtr around each of next 4 sts, tr in next tr, ch 1, dc in next dc, decrease, dc in next 7 dc, 5 dc in next dc, dc in next 7 dc, decrease, dc in next dc; repeat from ★ across; finish off.

Row 5: With **right** side facing, join Color B with slip st in first dc; ch 3, decrease, dc in next 7 dc, 5 dc in next dc, dc in next 7 dc, decrease, dc in next dc, ★ ch 1, tr in next tr, skip next 2 BPtr, work FPtr around each of next 2 BPtr, working in **front** of last 2 FPtr, work FPtr around each skipped BPtr, tr in next tr, ch 1, dc in next dc, decrease, dc in next 7 dc, 5 dc in next dc, dc in next 7 dc, decrease, dc in next dc; repeat from ★ across.

Repeat Rows 2-5 for pattern, working in stripe sequence.

41 BOBBITY

Note: Uses MC and CC in the following sequence: ★ 4 Rows **each** MC, CC; repeat from ★ for stripe sequence.

With MC, chain a multiple of 23 + 3 chs.

To decrease, pull up a loop in each of next 2 sts, YO and draw through all 3 loops on hook **(counts as one sc)**.

Row 1 (Right side)**:** Decrease beginning in second ch from hook, ★ sc in next 10 chs, 3 sc in next ch, sc in next 10 chs, decrease; repeat from ★ across.

Note: Loop a short piece of yarn around any stitch to mark Row 1 as **right** side.

To beginning decrease, pull up a loop in each of first 2 sts, YO and draw through all 3 loops on hook **(counts as one sc)**.

To treble crochet (abbreviated tr), YO twice, insert hook in st indicated, YO and pull up a loop (4 loops on hook), (YO and draw through 2 loops on hook) 3 times.

To double decrease (uses next 3 sts), pull up a loop in next st, skip next st, pull up a loop in next st, YO and draw through all 3 loops on hook.

Row 2: Ch 1, turn; beginning decrease, pushing all tr to **right** side, (sc, tr, sc) in next st, skip next sc, (sc, tr, sc) in next st, sc in next sc, (ch 1, skip next sc, sc in next sc) twice, (sc, tr, sc) in each of next 5 sc, sc in next sc, (ch 1, skip next sc, sc in next sc) twice, (sc, tr, sc) in next st, skip next sc, (sc, tr, sc) in next st, ★ double decrease, (sc, tr, sc) in next st, skip next sc, (sc, tr, sc) in next st, sc in next sc, (ch 1, skip next sc, sc in next sc) twice, (sc, tr, sc) in each of next 5 sc, sc in next sc, (ch 1, skip next sc, sc in next sc) twice, (sc, tr, sc) in next st, skip next sc, (sc, tr, sc) in next st; repeat from ★ across to last 2 sc, decrease.

Row 3: Ch 1, turn; beginning decrease, skip next tr, decrease, skip next tr, sc in next 2 sc and in next ch-1 sp, sc in next sc and in next ch-1 sp, (decrease, skip next tr) twice, sc in next 2 sc, 3 sc in next tr, sc in next 2 sc, (skip next tr, decrease) twice, sc in next ch-1 sp and in next sc, sc in next ch-1 sp and in next 2 sc, skip next tr, decrease, ★ skip next tr, double decrease, skip next tr, decrease, skip next tr, sc in next 2 sc and in next ch-1 sp, sc in next sc and in next ch-1 sp, (decrease, skip next tr) twice, sc in next 2 sc, 3 sc in next tr, sc in next 2 sc, (skip next tr, decrease) twice, sc in next ch-1 sp and in next sc, sc in next ch-1 sp and in next 2 sc, skip next tr, decrease; repeat from ★ across to last 3 sts, skip next tr, decrease.

Row 4: Ch 1, turn; beginning decrease, sc in next 10 sc, 3 sc in next sc, sc in next 10 sc, ★ double decrease, sc in next 10 sc, 3 sc in next sc, sc in next 10 sc; repeat from ★ across to last 2 sc, decrease; finish off.

To work Long Double Crochet (abbreviated LDC), working **around** previous 2 rows **(Fig. 6, page 159)**, YO, insert hook in ch-1 sp 2 rows **below** next sc, YO and pull up a loop even with loop on hook (3 loops on hook), (YO and draw through 2 loops on hook) twice.

Row 5: With **right** side facing and using CC, pull up a loop in first 2 sc, YO and draw through all 3 loops on hook **(counts as one sc)**; (sc in next sc, work LDC) twice, sc in next 6 sc, 3 sc in next sc, sc in next 6 sc, (work LDC, sc in next sc) twice, ★ double decrease, (sc in next sc, work LDC) twice, sc in next 6 sc, 3 sc in next sc, sc in next 6 sc, (work LDC, sc in next sc) twice; repeat from ★ across to last 2 sc, decrease.

Repeat Rows 2-5 for pattern, working in stripe sequence.

42 HIGHS & LOWS

Note: Uses MC and Colors A and B in the following sequence: ★ 1 Row **each** MC, Color A, MC, Color B; repeat from ★ for stripe sequence.

With MC, chain a multiple of 19 + 17 chs.

Row 1 (Right side)**:** Dc in fourth ch from hook **(3 skipped chs count as first dc)** and in next 5 chs, 5 dc in next ch, dc in next 7 chs, ★ skip next 4 chs, dc in next 7 chs, 5 dc in next ch, dc in next 7 chs; repeat from ★ across; finish off.

Note: Loop a short piece of yarn around any stitch to mark Row 1 as **right** side.

Row 2: With **right** side facing and working in Front Loops Only **(Fig. 2, page 159)**, join Color A with sc in third dc **(see Joining With Sc, page 158)**; (ch 1, skip next dc, sc in next dc) 3 times, (sc, ch 1, sc, ch 1, sc) in next st, sc in next dc, (ch 1, skip next dc, sc in next dc) 3 times, ★ ch 1, skip next 4 dc, sc in next dc, (ch 1, skip next dc, sc in next dc) 3 times, (sc, ch 1, sc, ch 1, sc) in next st, sc in next dc, (ch 1, skip next dc, sc in next dc) 3 times; repeat from ★ across to last 2 dc, leave last 2 dc unworked; finish off.

Row 3: With **right** side facing, working **behind** sts on previous row **(Fig. 6, page 159)**, and in free loops of sts one row **below (Fig. 3, page 159)**, join MC with slip st in same st as first sc on previous row (third dc); ch 3, dc in next 6 dc, 2 dc in next dc, hdc in center sc on previous row, 2 dc in same st as last 2 dc, dc in next 7 dc, ★ skip next 4 dc, dc in next 7 dc, 2 dc in next dc, hdc in center sc on previous row, 2 dc in same st as last 2 dc, dc in next 7 dc; repeat from ★ across to last 2 dc, leave last 2 dc unworked; finish off.

Repeat Rows 2 and 3 for pattern, working in stripe sequence.

43 BUDS IN BLOOM

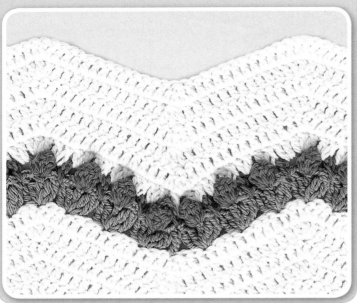

Note: Uses MC and Colors A and B in the following sequence: ★ 6 Rows MC, 1 row Color A, 1 row Color B; repeat from ★ for stripe sequence.

With MC, chain a multiple of 28 + 1 ch.

To decrease (uses next 3 sts), ★ YO, insert hook in **next** st, YO and pull up a loop, YO and draw through 2 loops on hook; repeat from ★ 2 times **more**, YO and draw through all 4 loops on hook **(counts as one dc).**

Row 1 (Right side)**:** Dc in fourth ch from hook **(3 skipped chs count as first dc)** and in next 11 chs, 3 dc in next ch, ★ dc in next 12 chs, decrease, dc in next 12 chs, 3 dc in next ch; repeat from ★ across to last 13 chs, dc in last 13 chs.

Note: Loop a short piece of yarn around any stitch to mark Row 1 as **right** side.

Rows 2-6: Ch 3 **(counts as first dc, now and throughout)**, turn; skip first 2 dc, dc in next 12 dc, 3 dc in next dc, dc in next 12 dc, ★ decrease, dc in next 12 dc, 3 dc in next dc, dc in next 12 dc; repeat from ★ across to last 2 dc, skip next dc, dc in last dc; at end of last row, finish off.

To treble crochet (abbreviated tr), YO twice, insert hook in st indicated, YO and pull up a loop (4 loops on hook), (YO and draw through 2 loops on hook) 3 times.

To work Cluster (uses one st), ★ YO twice, insert hook in st indicated, YO and pull up a loop, (YO and draw through 2 loops on hook) twice; repeat from ★ once **more**, YO and draw through all 3 loops on hook.

Row 7: With **right** side facing, join Color A with slip st in first dc; ch 3, skip next 2 dc, work (Cluster, ch 2, tr, ch 2, Cluster) in next dc, [skip next 3 dc, work (Cluster, ch 2, tr, ch 2, Cluster) in next dc] twice, [skip next 2 dc, work (Cluster, ch 2, tr, ch 2, Cluster) in next dc] twice, [skip next 3 dc, work (Cluster, ch 2, tr, ch 2, Cluster) in next dc] twice, ★ skip next 2 dc, tr in next dc, skip next 2 dc, work (Cluster, ch 2, tr, ch 2, Cluster) in next dc, [skip next 3 dc, work (Cluster, ch 2, tr, ch 2, Cluster) in next dc] twice, [skip next 2 dc, work (Cluster, ch 2, tr, ch 2, Cluster) in next dc] twice, [skip next 3 dc, work (Cluster, ch 2, tr, ch 2, Cluster) in next dc] twice; repeat from ★ across to last 3 dc, skip next 2 dc, dc in last dc; finish off.

To work Popcorn (uses one tr), 5 dc in tr indicated, drop loop from hook, insert hook from **back** to **front** in first dc of 5-dc group, hook dropped loop and draw through st.

Row 8: With **wrong** side facing, join Color B with sc in first dc **(see Joining With Sc, page 158)**; ★ ch 3, skip next ch-2 sp, work Popcorn in next tr, ch 3, [skip next ch-2 sp and next Cluster, sc in sp **before** next Cluster **(Fig. 5, page 159)**, ch 3, skip next ch-2 sp, work Popcorn in next tr, ch 3] 6 times, skip next ch-2 sp and next Cluster, sc in next st; repeat from ★ across; finish off.

Row 9: With **right** side facing, join MC with slip st in first sc; ch 3, ★ skip next ch-3 sp, 2 dc in each of next 6 ch-3 sps, 3 dc in next Popcorn, 2 dc in each of next 6 ch-3 sps, skip next ch-3 sp, dc in next sc; repeat from ★ across.

Repeat Rows 2-9 for pattern.

44 ROSEBUDS

Note: Uses Colors A, B, C, and D in the following sequence: ★ 2 Rows Color A, 2 rows Color B, 1 row Color C, 1 row Color D, 2 rows Color B; repeat from ★ for stripe sequence.

With Color A, chain a multiple of 30 + 12 chs.

To decrease (uses next 2 sts), ★ YO, insert hook in **next** st, YO and pull up a loop, YO and draw through 2 loops on hook; repeat from ★ once **more**, YO and draw through all 3 loops on hook.

Row 1 (Right side): Dc in fourth ch from hook **(3 skipped chs counts as first dc)** and in next 6 chs, decrease twice, ★ dc in next 7 chs, 2 dc in each of next 2 chs, dc in next 7 chs, decrease twice; repeat from ★ across to last 8 chs, dc in last 8 chs.

Note: Loop a short piece of yarn around any stitch to mark Row 1 as **right** side.

Row 2: Ch 3 **(counts as first dc, now and throughout)**, turn; dc in first 7 dc, decrease twice, ★ dc in next 7 dc, 2 dc in each of next 2 dc, dc in next 7 dc, decrease twice; repeat from ★ across to last 7 dc, dc in next 6 dc, 2 dc in last dc; finish off.

Row 3: With **right** side facing, join Color B with slip st in first dc; ch 3, dc in same st as joining and in next 6 dc, decrease twice, ★ dc in next 7 dc, 2 dc in each of next 2 dc, dc in next 7 dc, decrease twice; repeat from ★ across to last 7 dc, dc in next 6 dc, 2 dc in last dc.

Row 4: Ch 3, turn; dc in first 7 dc, decrease twice, ★ dc in next 7 dc, 2 dc in each of next 2 dc, dc in next 7 dc, decrease twice; repeat from ★ across to last 7 dc, dc in next 6 dc, 2 dc in last dc; finish off.

Row 5: With **right** side facing, join Color C with sc in first sc *(see Joining With Sc, page 158)*; sc in next dc, (ch 9, sc in next 3 dc) across; finish off.

To work Popcorn (uses one sc), 5 dc in sc indicated, drop loop from hook, insert hook from **back** to **front** in first dc of 5-dc group, hook dropped loop and draw through st.

Row 6: With **wrong** side facing, join Color D with sc in first sc; work Popcorn in next sc, ★ keeping ch-9 sp to **right** side of work, sc in next 2 sc, work Popcorn in next sc; repeat from ★ across to last 3 sc, keeping ch-9 sp to **right** side of work, sc in last 3 sc; finish off.

Row 7: With **right** side facing, join Color B with slip st in first sc; ch 3, dc in same st as joining and in next 6 sts, decrease twice, ★ dc in next 7 sts, 2 dc in each of next 2 sts, dc in next 7 sts, decrease twice; repeat from ★ across to last 7 sts, dc in next 6 sts, 2 dc in last sc.

Row 8: Ch 3, turn; dc in first 7 dc, decrease twice, ★ dc in next 7 dc, 2 dc in each of next 2 dc, dc in next 7 dc, decrease twice; repeat from ★ across to last 7 dc, dc in next 6 dc, 2 dc in last dc; finish off.

Row 9: With **right** side facing, join Color A with slip st in first dc; ch 3, dc in same st as joining and in next 6 dc, decrease twice, ★ dc in next 7 dc, 2 dc in each of next 2 dc, dc in next 7 dc, decrease twice; repeat from ★ across to last 7 dc, dc in next 6 dc, 2 dc in last dc.

Repeat Rows 2-9 for pattern.

45 BOUNTIFUL

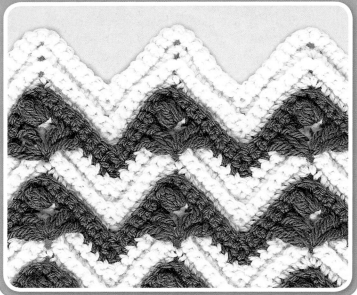

Note: Uses MC and CC in the following sequence: ★ 4 Rows MC, 2 rows CC; repeat from ★ for stripe sequence.

With MC, chain a multiple of 17 + 16 chs.

Row 1 (Right side)**:** Sc in second ch from hook and in next 6 chs, 3 sc in next ch, sc in next 7 chs, ★ skip next 2 chs, sc in next 7 chs, 3 sc in next ch, sc in next 7 chs; repeat from ★ across.

Note: Loop a short piece of yarn around any stitch to mark Row 1 as **right** side.

Rows 2-4: Ch 1, turn; working in Back Loops Only *(Fig. 2, page 159)*, sc in first sc, skip next sc, sc in next 6 sc, 3 sc in next sc, ★ sc in next 7 sc, skip next 2 sc, sc in next 7 sc, 3 sc in next sc; repeat from ★ across to last 8 sc, sc in next 6 sc, skip next sc, sc in last sc; at end of last row, finish off.

To work Long Double Crochet (abbreviated LDC), YO, working in **front** of previous rows *(Fig. 6, page 159)*, insert hook in same st as 3-sc group 4 rows **below**, YO and pull up a loop even with loops on hook (3 loops on hook), (YO and draw through 2 loops on hook) twice. Skip st **behind** LDC.

To work Popcorn (uses one sc), 4 hdc in sc indicated, drop loop from hook, insert hook from **front** to **back** in first hdc of 4-hdc group, hook dropped loop and draw through st.

Row 5: With **right** side facing and working in both loops, join CC with sc in first sc; skip next sc, sc in next 2 sc, (work LDC, sc in next sc) twice, (sc, work Popcorn, sc) in next sc, (sc in next sc, work LDC) twice, ★ sc in next 3 sc, skip next 2 sc, sc in next 3 sc, (work LDC, sc in next sc) twice, (sc, work Popcorn, sc) in next sc, (sc in next sc, work LDC) twice; repeat from ★ across to last 4 sc, sc in next 2 sc, skip next sc, sc in last sc.

Row 6: Ch 1, turn; sc in first sc, skip next sc, sc in next 6 sts, 3 sc in next Popcorn, ★ sc in next 7 sts, skip next 2 sc, sc in next 7 sts, 3 sc in next Popcorn; repeat from ★ across to last 8 sts, sc in next 6 sts, skip next sc, sc in last sc; finish off.

Row 7: With **right** side facing and working in Back Loops Only, join MC with sc in first sc; skip next sc, sc in next 6 sc, 3 sc in next sc, ★ sc in next 7 sc, skip next 2 sc, sc in next 7 sc, 3 sc in next sc; repeat from ★ across to last 8 sc, sc in next 6 sc, skip next sc, sc in last sc.

Repeat Rows 2-7 for pattern.

46 SNOW ON THE MEADOW

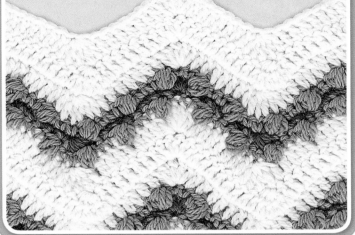

Note: Uses MC and Colors A and B in the following sequence: ★ 3 Rows MC, 1 row **each** Color A, Color B, Color A; repeat from ★ for stripe sequence.

With MC, chain a multiple of 20 + 4 chs.

To double crochet 5 together (abbreviated *dc5tog*), ★ YO, insert hook in **next** st, YO and pull up a loop, YO and draw through 2 loops on hook; repeat from ★ 4 times **more**, YO and draw through all 6 loops on hook **(counts as one dc)**.

Row 1 (Right side)**:** 2 Dc in fourth ch from hook **(3 skipped chs count as first dc)**, dc in next 7 chs, dc5tog, dc in next 7 chs, ★ 5 dc in next ch, dc in next 7 chs, dc5tog, dc in next 7 chs; repeat from ★ across to last ch, 3 dc in last ch.

Note: Loop a short piece of yarn around any stitch to mark Row 1 as **right** side.

Rows 2 and 3: Ch 3 **(counts as first dc, now and throughout)**, turn; 2 dc in same st, dc in next 7 dc, dc5tog, dc in next 7 dc, ★ 5 dc in next dc, dc in next 7 dc, dc5tog, dc in next 7 dc; repeat from ★ across to last dc, 3 dc in last dc; at end of last row, finish off.

To work Puff St (uses one st), ★ YO insert hook in st indicated, YO and pull up a loop; repeat from ★ 2 times **more**, YO and draw through all 7 loops on hook. Push Puff St to **right** side.

Row 4: With **wrong** side facing, join Color A with sc in first dc *(see Joining With Sc, page 158)*; sc in next dc, work Puff St in next dc, (sc in next 3 dc, work Puff St in next dc) across to last 2 dc, sc in last 2 dc; finish off.

To single crochet 5 together (abbreviated *sc5tog*), pull up a loop in each of next 5 sts, YO and draw through all 6 loops on hook **(counts as one sc)**.

Row 5: With **right** side facing, join Color B with sc in first sc; 2 sc in same st as joining, sc in next 7 sts, sc5tog, sc in next 7 sts, ★ 5 sc in next sc, sc in next 7 sts, sc5tog, sc in next 7 sts; repeat from ★ across to last sc, 3 sc in last sc; finish off.

Row 6: With **wrong** side facing, join Color A with sc in first sc; sc in next sc, work Puff St in next sc, (sc in next 3 sc, work Puff St in next sc) across to last 2 sc, sc in last 2 sc; finish off.

Row 7: With **right** side facing, join MC with slip st in first sc; ch 3, 2 dc in same st as joining, dc in next 7 sts, dc5tog, dc in next 7 sts, ★ 5 dc in next sc, dc in next 7 sts, dc5tog, dc in next 7 sts; repeat from ★ across to last sc, 3 dc in last sc.

Repeat Rows 2-7 for pattern.

47 BERRIES

Chain a multiple of 26 + 1 ch.

To decrease (uses next 2 sts), ★ YO, insert hook in **next** st, YO and pull up a loop, YO and draw through 2 loops on hook; repeat from ★ once **more**, YO and draw through all 3 loops on hook **(counts as one dc)**.

Row 1 (Right side)**:** Dc in third ch from hook and in next 9 chs, ch 1, skip next ch, dc in next ch, ch 3, dc in next ch, ch 1, ★ skip next ch, dc in next 8 chs, decrease, skip next 2 chs, decrease, dc in next 8 chs, ch 1, skip next ch, dc in next ch, ch 3, dc in next ch, ch 1; repeat from ★ across to last 12 chs, skip next ch, dc in next 9 chs, decrease.

Note: Loop a short piece of yarn around any stitch to mark Row 1 as **right** side.

To work Cluster, ch 3, YO, insert hook in third ch from hook, YO and pull up a loop, YO and draw through 2 loops on hook, ★ YO, insert hook in **same** ch, YO and pull up a loop, YO and draw through 2 loops on hook; repeat from ★ 2 times **more**, YO and draw through all 5 loops on hook.

Row 2: Ch 2, turn; skip first dc, dc in next dc, decrease, dc in next 4 dc, work Cluster, dc in next ch-1 sp, work Cluster, (dc, ch 3, dc) in next ch-3 sp, work Cluster, dc in next ch-1 sp, work Cluster, skip next 2 dc, dc in next 4 dc, ★ decrease, skip next 2 dc, decrease, dc in next 4 dc, work Cluster, dc in next ch-1 sp, work Cluster, (dc, ch 3, dc) in next ch-3 sp, work Cluster, dc in next ch-1 sp, work Cluster, skip next 2 dc, dc in next 4 dc; repeat from ★ across to last 4 dc, decrease twice.

Row 3: Ch 2, turn; skip first dc, dc in next dc, decrease, dc in next 2 dc, (ch 2, skip next Cluster, dc in next dc) twice, ch 1, (dc, ch 3, dc) in next ch-3 sp, ch 1, (dc in next dc, ch 2, skip next Cluster) twice, dc in next 2 dc, ★ decrease, skip next 2 dc, decrease, dc in next 2 dc, (ch 2, skip next Cluster, dc in next dc) twice, ch 1, (dc, ch 3, dc) in next ch-3 sp, ch 1, (dc, in next dc, ch 2, skip next Cluster) twice, dc in next 2 dc; repeat from ★ across to last 4 dc, decrease twice.

Row 4: Ch 2, turn; skip first dc, dc in next dc, decrease, 2 dc in next ch-2 sp, dc in next dc and in next ch-2 sp, work Cluster, dc in next ch-1 sp, work Cluster, (dc, ch 3, dc) in next ch-3 sp, work Cluster, dc in next ch-1 sp, work Cluster, dc in next ch-2 sp and in next dc, 2 dc in next ch-2 sp, ★ decrease, skip next 2 dc, decrease, 2 dc in next ch-2 sp, dc in next dc and in next ch-2 sp, work Cluster, dc in next ch-1 sp, work Cluster, (dc, ch 3, dc) in next ch-3 sp, work Cluster, dc in next ch-1 sp, work Cluster, dc in next ch-2 sp and in next dc, 2 dc in next ch-2 sp; repeat from ★ across to last 4 dc, decrease twice.

Repeat Rows 3 and 4 for pattern.

48 DIMENSIONS

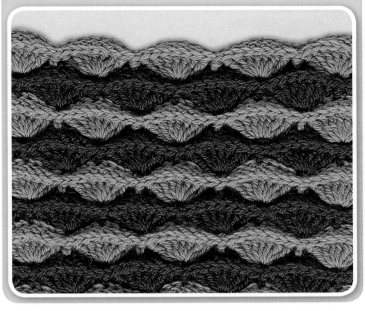

Note: Uses MC and CC in the following sequence:
★ 2 Rows **each** MC, CC; repeat from ★ for
stripe sequence.

With MC, chain a multiple of 8 + 2 chs.

To treble crochet *(abbreviated tr)*, YO twice,
insert hook in st indicated, YO and pull up
a loop (4 loops on hook), (YO and draw through
2 loops on hook) 3 times.

Row 1 (Right side)**:** Sc in second ch from hook,
★ skip next 3 chs, 7 tr in next ch, skip next 3 chs,
sc in next ch; repeat from ★ across.

Note: Loop a short piece of yarn around any stitch
to mark Row 1 as **right** side.

To work Front Post single crochet *(abbreviated
FPsc)*, insert hook from **front** to **back** around post
of next st *(Fig. 4, page 159)*, YO and pull up a
loop, YO and draw through both loops on hook.

Row 2: Ch 1, turn; sc in first sc, work FPsc
around each st across to last sc, sc in last sc;
finish off.

Row 3: With **right** side facing, join CC with
slip st in first sc; ch 4 **(counts as first tr)**, 3 tr in
same st as joining, skip next 3 sts, sc in next st,
★ skip next 3 sts, 7 tr in next st, skip next 3 sts,
sc in next st; repeat from ★ across to last 4 sts, skip
next 3 sts, 4 tr in last sc.

Row 4: Ch 1, turn; sc in first tr, work FPsc around
each st across to last tr, sc in last tr; finish off.

Row 5: With **right** side facing, join MC with sc in
first sc *(see Joining With Sc, page 158)*; ★ skip
next 3 sts, 7 tr in next st, skip next 3 sts, sc in next
st; repeat from ★ across.

Repeat Rows 2-5 for pattern.

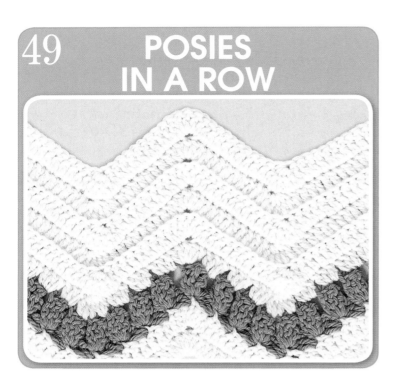

Note: Uses MC and Colors A and B in the following sequence: 2 Rows MC, ★ 1 row Color A, 1 row Color B, 6 rows MC; repeat from ★ for stripe sequence.

With MC, chain a multiple of 24 + 4 chs.

To double crochet 5 together *(abbreviated dc5tog)*, ★ YO, insert hook in **next** st, YO and pull up a loop, YO and draw through 2 loops on hook; repeat from ★ 4 times **more**, YO and draw through all 6 loops on hook **(counts as one dc)**.

Row 1 (Right side)**:** 2 Dc in fourth ch from hook **(3 skipped chs count as first dc)**, dc in next 9 chs, dc5tog, dc in next 9 chs, ★ 5 dc in next ch, dc in next 9 chs, dc5tog, dc in next 9 chs; repeat from ★ across to last ch, 3 dc in last ch.

Note: Loop a short piece of yarn around any stitch to mark Row 1 as **right** side.

Row 2: Ch 3 **(counts as first dc, now and throughout)**, turn; working in Back Loops Only **(Fig. 2, page 159)**, 2 dc in same st, dc in next 9 dc, dc5tog, dc in next 9 dc, ★ 5 dc in next dc, dc in next 9 dc, dc5tog, dc in next 9 dc; repeat from ★ across to last dc, 3 dc in last dc; finish off.

To work Cluster *(uses one st)*, ★ YO, insert hook in st indicated, YO and pull up a loop, YO and draw through 2 loops on hook; repeat from ★ once **more**, YO and draw through all 3 loops on hook.

Row 3: With **right** side facing and working in both loops, join Color A with slip st in first dc; ch 3, work Cluster in same st as joining, ★ skip next 2 dc, (slip st, ch 3, work Cluster) in next dc; repeat from ★ across to last 3 dc, skip next 2 dc, slip st in last dc; finish off.

To treble crochet *(abbreviated tr)*, YO twice, insert hook in st indicated, YO and pull up a loop (4 loops on hook), (YO and draw through 2 loops on hook) 3 times.

To work Popcorn *(uses one slip st)*, 4 tr in slip st indicated, drop loop from hook, insert hook from **back** to **front** in first tr of 4-tr group, hook dropped loop and draw through st.

Row 4: With **wrong** side facing, join Color B with slip st in first slip st; [ch 4 **(counts as first tr)**, 3 tr in same st as joining, drop loop from hook, insert hook from **back** to **front** in first tr of 4-tr group, hook dropped loop and draw through st **(beginning Popcorn made)**], [ch 3, skip next Cluster and ch-3, work Popcorn in next slip st] 3 times, [ch 2, skip next Cluster and ch-3, work Popcorn in next slip st] twice, ★ [ch 3, skip next Cluster and ch-3, work Popcorn in next slip st] 6 times, [ch 2, skip next Cluster and ch-3, work Popcorn in next slip st] twice; repeat from ★ across to last 3 Clusters, [ch 3, skip next Cluster and ch-3, work Popcorn in next slip st] 3 times; finish off.

To work sp decrease *(uses 2 sps and one Popcorn)*, † YO, insert hook in **next** sp, YO and pull up a loop, YO and draw through 2 loops on hook, YO, insert hook in **same** sp, YO and pull up a loop, YO and draw through 2 loops on hook †, YO, insert hook in **next** Popcorn, YO and pull up a loop, YO and draw through 2 loops on hook, repeat from † to † once, YO and draw through all 6 loops on hook **(counts as one dc)**.

Row 5: With **right** side facing, join MC with slip st in first Popcorn; ch 3, 2 dc in same st as joining, 3 dc in each of next 3 ch-3 sps, work sp decrease, 3 dc in each of next 3 ch-3 sps, ★ 5 dc in next Popcorn, 3 dc in each of next 3 ch-3 sps, work sp decrease, 3 dc in each of next 3 ch-3 sps; repeat from ★ across to last Popcorn, 3 dc in last Popcorn.

Rows 6-10: Ch 3, turn; working in Back Loops Only, 2 dc in same st, dc in next 9 dc, dc5tog, dcin next 9 dc, ★ 5 dc in next dc, dc in next 9 dc, dc5tog, dc in next 9 dc; repeat from ★ across to last dc, 3 dc in last dc; at end of last row, finish off.

Repeat Rows 3-10 for pattern.

50 PUFF STITCH CHEVRONS

Chain a multiple of 21 + 2 chs.

Row 1 (Right side)**:** 3 Sc in second ch from hook, sc in next 9 chs, skip next 2 chs, sc in next 9 chs, ★ 5 sc in next ch, sc in next 9 chs, skip next 2 chs, sc in next 9 chs; repeat from ★ across to last ch, 3 sc in last ch.

Note: Loop a short piece of yarn around any stitch to mark Row 1 as **right** side.

Rows 2 and 3: Ch 1, turn; 2 sc in first sc, sc in next 10 sc, skip next 2 sc, sc in next 10 sc, ★ 3 sc in next sc, sc in next 10 sc, skip next 2 sc, sc in next 10 sc; repeat from ★ across to last sc, 2 sc in last sc.

To work Puff St (uses one sc), ★ YO, insert hook in sc indicated, YO and pull up a loop; repeat from ★ 2 times **more**, YO and draw through all 7 loops on hook.

Row 4: Ch 4 **(counts as first dc plus ch 1, now and throughout)**, turn; skip first 2 sc, work Puff St in next sc, (ch 1, skip next sc, work Puff St in next sc) 4 times, skip next 2 sc, work Puff St in next sc, ★ (ch 1, skip next sc, work Puff St in next sc) 10 times, skip next 2 sc, work Puff St in next sc; repeat from ★ across to last 10 sc, ch 1, skip next sc, (work Puff St in next sc, ch 1, skip next sc) 4 times, dc in last sc.

Row 5: Ch 1, turn; 3 sc in first dc, sc in next ch, (sc in next Puff St and in next ch) 4 times, skip next 2 Puff Sts, sc in next ch, (sc in next Puff St and in next ch) 4 times, ★ 5 sc in next Puff St, sc in next ch, (sc in next Puff St and in next ch) 4 times, skip next 2 Puff Sts, sc in next ch, (sc in next Puff St and in next ch) 4 times; repeat from ★ across to last dc, 3 sc in last dc.

Repeat Rows 2-5 for pattern.

51 JOYFUL

Chain a multiple of 17 + 2 chs.

To decrease (uses next 2 sts), ★ YO, insert hook in **next** st, YO and pull up a loop, YO and draw through 2 loops on hook; repeat from ★ once **more**, YO and draw through all 3 loops on hook **(counts as one dc)**.

To double decrease (uses next 3 sts), ★ YO, insert hook in **next** st, YO and pull up a loop, YO and draw through 2 loops on hook; repeat from ★ 2 times **more**, YO and draw through all 4 loops on hook **(counts as one dc)**.

Row 1: Dc in third ch from hook and in next 7 chs, ch 2, dc in next 7 chs, ★ double decrease, dc in next 7 chs, ch 2, dc in next 7 chs; repeat from ★ across to last 2 chs, decrease.

To work Cluster (uses next 3 sts), † YO, insert hook in **next** st, YO and pull up a loop, YO and draw through 2 loops on hook †, YO twice, insert hook in **next** st, YO and pull up a loop, (YO and draw through 2 loops on hook) twice, ★ YO twice, insert hook in **same** st, YO and pull up a loop, (YO and draw through 2 loops on hook) twice; repeat from ★ 2 times **more**, repeat from † to † once, YO and draw through all 7 loops on hook.

Row 2 (Right side): Ch 2, turn; skip first dc, dc in next 6 dc, ch 1, (dc, ch 2, dc) in next ch-2 sp, ch 1, skip next dc, dc in next 5 dc, ★ work Cluster, dc in next 5 dc, ch 1, (dc, ch 2, dc) in next ch-2 sp, ch 1, skip next dc, dc in next 5 dc; repeat from ★ across to last 2 dc, decrease.

Note: Loop a short piece of yarn around any stitch to mark Row 2 as **right** side.

Row 3: Ch 2, turn; skip first dc, dc in next 4 dc, ch 1, dc in next ch-1 sp, ch 1, (dc, ch 2, dc) in next ch-2 sp, ch 1, dc in next ch-1 sp, ch 1, skip next dc, dc in next 3 dc, ★ double decrease, dc in next 3 dc, ch 1, dc in next ch-1 sp, ch 1, (dc, ch 2, dc) in next ch-2 sp, ch 1, dc in next ch-1 sp, ch 1, skip next dc, dc in next 3 dc; repeat from ★ across to last 2 dc, decrease.

Row 4: Ch 2, turn; skip first dc, dc in next 2 dc, ch 1, (dc in next ch-1 sp, ch 1) twice, (dc, ch 2, dc) in next ch-2 sp, ch 1, (dc in next ch-1 sp, ch 1) twice, skip next dc, dc in next dc, ★ work Cluster, dc in next dc, ch 1, (dc in next ch-1 sp, ch 1) twice, (dc, ch 2, dc) in next ch-2 sp, ch 1, (dc in next ch-1 sp, ch 1) twice, skip next dc, dc in next dc; repeat from ★ across to last 2 dc, decrease.

Row 5: Ch 2, turn; skip first dc, dc in next dc, (dc in next ch-1 sp and in next dc) 3 times, (dc, ch 2, dc) in next ch-2 sp, (dc in next dc and in next ch-1 sp) 3 times, ★ double decrease, (dc in next ch-1 sp and in next dc) 3 times, (dc, ch 2, dc) in next ch-2 sp, (dc in next dc and in next ch-1 sp) 3 times; repeat from ★ across to last 2 dc, decrease.

Repeat Rows 2-5 for pattern.

52 HOPSCOTCH

Chain a multiple of 16 + 1 ch.

Row 1: Sc in second ch from hook and in next 7 chs, ch 2, ★ sc in next 7 chs, skip next 2 chs, sc in next 7 chs, ch 2; repeat from ★ across to last 8 chs, sc in last 8 chs.

To decrease (uses next 2 sts), ★ YO, insert hook in **next** st, YO and pull up a loop, YO and draw through 2 loops on hook; repeat from ★ once **more**, YO and draw through all 3 loops on hook **(counts as one dc)**.

To double decrease (uses next 3 sts), ★ YO, insert hook in **next** st, YO and pull up a loop, YO and draw through 2 loops on hook; repeat from ★ 2 times **more**, YO and draw through all 4 loops on hook **(counts as one dc)**.

To double crochet 4 together (abbreviated *dc4tog*), ★ YO, insert hook in **next** st, YO and pull up a loop, YO and draw through 2 loops on hook; repeat from ★ 3 times **more**, YO and draw through all 5 loops on hook **(counts as one dc)**.

Row 2 (Right side)**:** Ch 2, turn; skip first sc, decrease, dc in next 5 sc, (dc, ch 2, dc) in next ch-2 sp, ★ ch 1, skip next sc, (dc in next sc, ch 1, skip next sc) twice, dc4tog, dc in next 5 sc, (dc, ch 2, dc) in next ch-2 sp; repeat from ★ across to last 8 sc, ch 1, skip next sc, (dc in next sc, ch 1, skip next sc) twice, double decrease.

Note: Loop a short piece of yarn around any stitch to mark Row 2 as **right** side.

To work Cluster, ch 3, YO, insert hook in third ch from hook, YO and pull up a loop, YO and draw through 2 loops on hook, YO, insert hook in same ch, YO and pull up a loop, YO and draw through 2 loops on hook, YO and draw through all 3 loops on hook.

Row 3: Ch 1, turn; sc in first dc, (sc in next ch-1 sp and in next dc) 3 times, (sc, ch 2, sc) in next ch-2 sp, sc in next dc, work Cluster, ★ skip next dc, sc in next 4 sts, skip next dc, (sc in next ch-1 sp and in next dc) 3 times, (sc, ch 2, sc) in next ch-2 sp, sc in next dc, work Cluster; repeat from ★ across to last 6 sts, skip next dc, sc in last 5 sts.

To treble crochet (abbreviated *tr*), YO twice, insert hook in st indicated, YO and pull up a loop (4 loops on hook), (YO and draw through 2 loops on hook) 3 times.

Row 4: Ch 2, turn; skip first sc, decrease, dc in next 2 sc, working **behind** next Cluster *(Fig. 6, page 159)*, tr in skipped dc one row **below** Cluster, dc in next 2 sc, (dc, ch 2, dc) in next ch-2 sp, ★ ch 1, skip next sc, (dc in next sc, ch 1, skip next sc) twice, dc4tog, dc in next 2 sc, working **behind** next Cluster, tr in skipped dc one row **below** Cluster, dc in next 2 sc, (dc, ch 2, dc) in next ch-2 sp; repeat from ★ across to last 8 sc, ch 1, skip next sc, (dc in next sc, ch 1, skip next sc) twice, double decrease.

Repeat Rows 3 and 4 for pattern.

53 WOVEN RIBBONS

Note: Uses MC and Colors A and B in the following sequence: ★ 4 Rows MC, 1 row Color A, 4 rows MC, 1 row Color B; repeat from ★ for stripe sequence.

With MC, chain a multiple of 32 + 3 chs.

To decrease (uses next 2 sts), ★ YO, insert hook in **next** st, YO and pull up a loop, YO and draw through 2 loops on hook; repeat from ★ once **more**, YO and draw through all 3 loops on hook **(counts as one dc)**.

Row 1 (Right side)**:** Working in back ridges of beginning ch *(Fig. 1, page 159)*, 2 dc in fourth ch from hook **(3 skipped chs count as one dc)**, dc in next 12 chs, decrease, dc in next ch, decrease, dc in next 12 chs, ★ 2 dc in next ch, dc in next ch, 2 dc in next ch, dc in next 12 chs, decrease, dc in next ch, decrease, dc in next 12 chs; repeat from ★ across to last 2 chs, 2 dc in next ch, dc in last ch.

Note: Loop a short piece of yarn around any stitch to mark Row 1 as **right** side.

Row 2: Ch 4 **(counts as first dc plus ch 1, now and throughout)**, turn; dc in first dc, [skip next 2 dc, (dc, ch 1, dc) in next dc] 4 times, [skip next 3 dc, (dc, ch 1, dc) in next dc] twice, ★ [skip next 2 dc, (dc, ch 1, dc) in next dc] 3 times, skip next 2 dc, dc in next dc, (ch 1, dc in same st) twice, [skip next 2 dc, (dc, ch 1, dc) in next dc] 4 times, [skip next 3 dc, (dc, ch 1, dc) in next dc] twice; repeat from ★ across to last 12 dc, [skip next 2 dc, (dc, ch 1, dc) in next dc] 4 times.

Row 3: Ch 3 **(counts as first dc, now and throughout)**, turn; ★ 2 dc in next ch-1 sp, (dc in next 2 dc and in next ch-1 sp) 4 times, decrease, dc in next ch-1 sp, decrease, (dc in next ch-1 sp and in next 2 dc) 4 times, 2 dc in next ch-1 sp, dc in next dc; repeat from ★ across.

Row 4: Ch 4, turn; dc in first dc, [skip next 2 dc, (dc, ch 1, dc) in next dc] 4 times, [skip next 3 dc, (dc, ch 1, dc) in next dc] twice, ★ [skip next 2 dc, (dc, ch 1, dc) in next dc] 3 times, skip next 2 dc, dc in next dc, (ch 1, dc in same st) twice, [skip next 2 dc, (dc, ch 1, dc) in next dc] 4 times, [skip next 3 dc, (dc, ch 1, dc) in next dc] twice; repeat from ★ across to last 12 dc, [skip next 2 dc, (dc, ch 1, dc) in next dc] 4 times; finish off.

Row 5: With **right** side facing, join Color A with slip st in first dc; ch 3, dc in same st as joining, (ch 1, skip next ch, dc in next 2 dc) 4 times, ch 1, skip next ch, decrease, dc in next ch-1 sp, decrease, (ch 1, skip next ch, dc in next 2 dc) 4 times, ★ ch 1, skip next ch-1 sp, 3 dc in next dc, (ch 1, skip next ch, dc in next 2 dc) 4 times, ch 1, skip next ch, decrease, dc in next ch-1 sp, decrease, (ch 1, skip next ch, dc in next 2 dc) 4 times; repeat from ★ across to last ch-1 sp, ch 1, skip last ch-1 sp, 2 dc in last dc; finish off.

To treble crochet (abbreviated *tr*), YO twice, insert hook in sp indicated, YO and pull up a loop (4 loops on hook), (YO and draw through 2 loops on hook) 3 times.

Row 6: With **right** side facing and working in Back Loops Only *(Fig. 2, page 159)*, join MC with slip st in first dc; slip st in next dc, working in **front** of previous row *(Fig. 6, page 159)*, tr in ch-1 sp one row **below** next ch, (slip st in next 2 dc, working in **front** of previous row, tr in ch-1 sp one row **below** next ch) 4 times, slip st in next dc, working in **front** of previous row, tr in ch-1 sp one row **below** (before dc), slip st in next dc, working in **front** of previous row, tr in same ch-1 sp one row **below** (after dc), slip st in next dc, working in **front** of previous row, tr in ch-1 sp one row **below** next ch, (slip st in next 2 dc, working in **front** of previous row, tr in ch-1 sp one row **below** next ch) 4 times, ★ slip st in next 3 dc, working in **front** of previous row, tr in ch-1 sp one row **below** next ch, (slip st in next 2 dc, working in **front** of previous row, tr in ch-1 sp one row **below** next ch) 4 times, slip st in next dc, working in **front** of previous row, tr in ch-1 sp one row **below** (before dc), slip st in next dc, working in **front** of previous row, tr in same ch-1 sp one row **below** (after dc), slip st in next dc, working in **front** of previous row, tr in ch-1 sp one row **below** next ch, (slip st in next 2 dc, working in **front** of previous row, tr in ch-1 sp one row **below** next ch) 4 times; repeat from ★ across to last 2 dc, slip st in last 2 dc.

Row 7: Ch 4, turn; working in both loops, dc in first st, [skip next 2 sts, (dc, ch 1, dc) in next st] 4 times, [skip next 4 sts, (dc, ch 1, dc) in next st] twice, ★ [skip next 2 sts, (dc, ch 1, dc) in next st] 3 times, skip next 2 sts, dc in next st, (ch 1, dc in same st) twice, [skip next 2 sts, (dc, ch 1, dc) in next st] 4 times, [skip next 4 sts, (dc, ch 1, dc) in next st] twice; repeat from ★ across to last 12 sts, [skip next 2 sts, (dc, ch 1, dc) in next st] 4 times.

Repeat Rows 3-7 for pattern, working in stripe sequence.

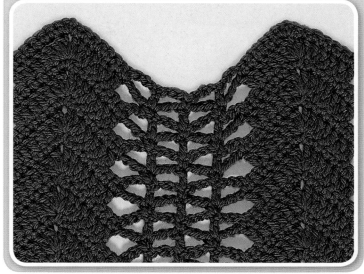

Chain a multiple of 26 + 22 chs.

Row 1 (Right side)**:** Sc in second ch from hook, ch 3, skip next 4 chs, dc in next 5 chs, (2 dc, ch 1, 2 dc) in next ch, dc in next 5 chs, ch 3, skip next 4 chs, sc in next ch, ★ ch 3, skip next 2 chs, dc in next ch, ch 3, skip next 2 chs, sc in next ch, ch 3, skip next 4 chs, dc in next 5 chs, (2 dc, ch 1, 2 dc) in next ch, dc in next 5 chs, ch 3, skip next 4 chs, sc in next ch; repeat from ★ across.

Note: Loop a short piece of yarn around any stitch to mark Row 1 as **right** side.

Row 2: Ch 6 **(counts as first dc plus ch 3)**, turn; sc in next 7 dc, (sc, ch 1, sc) in next ch-1 sp, sc in next 7 dc, ch 3, dc in next sc, ★ ch 3, sc in next dc, ch 3, dc in next sc, ch 3, sc in next 7 dc, (sc, ch 1, sc) in next ch-1 sp, sc in next 7 dc, ch 3, dc in next sc; repeat from ★ across.

Row 3: Ch 1, turn; sc in first dc, ch 3, skip next 3 sc, dc in next 5 sc, (2 dc, ch 1, 2 dc) in next ch-1 sp, dc in next 5 sc, ch 3, skip next 3 sc, sc in next dc, ★ ch 3, dc in next sc, ch 3, sc in next dc, ch 3, skip next 3 sc, dc in next 5 sc, (2 dc, ch 1, 2 dc) in next ch-1 sp, dc in next 5 sc, ch 3, skip next 3 sc, sc in next dc; repeat from ★ across.

Repeat Rows 2 and 3 for pattern.

55 GLOWING

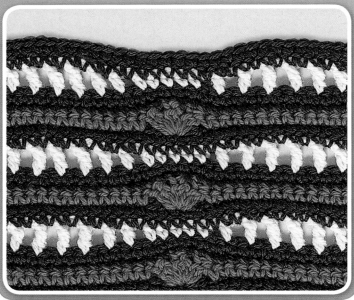

Note: Uses MC and Colors A and B in the following sequence: ★ 2 Rows MC, 1 row Color A, 2 rows MC, 1 row Color B; repeat from ★ for stripe sequence.

With MC, chain a multiple of 20 + 2 chs.

Row 1 (Right side)**:** Sc in second ch from hook and in each ch across.

Note: Loop a short piece of yarn around any stitch to mark Row 1 as **right** side.

Row 2: Ch 1, turn; sc in each sc across; finish off.

To treble crochet (abbreviated tr), YO twice, insert hook in sc indicated, YO and pull up a loop (4 loops on hook), (YO and draw through 2 loops on hook) 3 times.

Row 3: With **right** side facing, join Color A with sc in first sc **(see Joining With Sc, page 158)**; sc in next 2 sc, ch 1, skip next sc, hdc in next sc, ch 1, skip next sc, dc in next sc, (ch 1, skip next sc, tr in next sc) 3 times, ch 1, skip next sc, dc in next sc, ch 1, skip next sc, hdc in next sc, ★ ch 1, skip next sc, sc in next 5 sc, ch 1, skip next sc, hdc in next sc, ch 1, skip next sc, dc in next sc, (ch 1, skip next sc, tr in next sc) 3 times, ch 1, skip next sc, dc in next sc, ch 1, skip next sc, hdc in next sc; repeat from ★ across to last 4 sc, ch 1, skip next sc, sc in last 3 sc; finish off.

Row 4: With **wrong** side facing, join MC with sc in first sc; sc in each st and in each ch-1 sp across.

Row 5: Ch 1, turn; sc in each sc across; finish off.

To work Cluster (uses one st), ★ YO, insert hook in st indicated, YO and pull up a loop, YO and draw through 2 loops on hook; repeat from ★ once **more**, YO and draw through all 3 loops on hook.

Row 6: With **wrong** side facing, join Color B with slip st in first sc; ch 3 **(counts as first dc)**, work (Cluster, ch 1, Cluster) in same st as joining, skip next 2 sc, sc in next 15 sc, ★ skip next 2 sc, work Cluster in next sc, (ch 1, work Cluster in same st) twice, skip next 2 sc, sc in next 15 sc; repeat from ★ across to last 3 sc, skip next 2 sc, work (Cluster, ch 1, Cluster, dc) in last sc; finish off.

Row 7: With **right** side facing, join MC with sc in first dc; sc in next Cluster, skip next ch, sc in next Cluster and in next 15 sc, ★ (sc in next Cluster and in next ch) twice, sc in next Cluster and in next 15 sc; repeat from ★ across to last 4 sts, sc in next Cluster, skip next ch, sc in next Cluster and in last dc.

Repeat Rows 2-7 for pattern.

56 STATELY

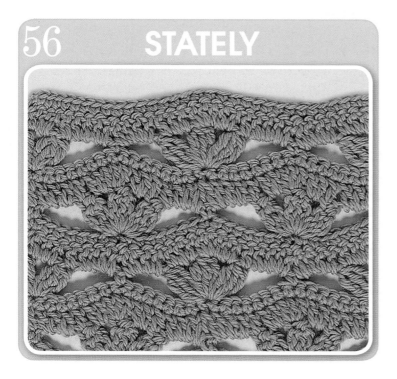

Chain a multiple of 17 + 1 ch.

Row 1 (Right side): Dc in fourth ch from hook **(3 skipped chs count as first dc)** and in next 5 chs, 3 dc in next ch, dc in next 6 chs, ★ [YO, insert hook in next ch, YO and pull up a loop, YO and draw through 2 loops on hook, YO, skip next 2 chs, insert hook in next ch, YO and pull up a loop, YO and draw through 2 loops on hook, YO and draw through all 3 loops on hook **(counts as one dc)**], dc in next 6 chs, 3 dc in next ch, dc in next 6 chs; repeat from ★ across to last 2 chs, [(YO, insert hook in **next** ch, YO and pull up a loop, YO and draw through 2 loops on hook) twice, YO and draw through all 3 loops on hook **(counts as one dc)**].

Note: Loop a short piece of yarn around any stitch to mark Row 1 as **right** side.

Row 2: Ch 1, turn; sc in each dc across.

To treble crochet (abbreviated tr), YO twice, insert hook in st indicated, YO and pull up a loop (4 loops on hook), (YO and draw through 2 loops on hook) 3 times.

To work Cluster (uses one st), ★ YO twice, insert hook in st indicated, YO and pull up a loop, (YO and draw through 2 loops on hook) twice; repeat from ★ once **more**, YO and draw through all 3 loops on hook.

To work double Cluster (uses one st), ★ YO twice, insert hook in st indicated, YO and pull up a loop, (YO and draw through 2 loops on hook) twice; repeat from ★ 2 times **more**, YO and draw through all 4 loops on hook.

Row 3: Ch 3, turn; (tr, ch 2, work double Cluster) in first sc, ch 3, skip next 7 sc, sc in next sc, ch 3, ★ skip next 7 sc, work double Cluster in next sc, (ch 2, work double Cluster in same st) twice, ch 3, skip next 7 sc, sc in next sc, ch 3; repeat from ★ across to last 8 sc, skip next 7 sc, work (double Cluster, ch 2, Cluster) in last sc.

To decrease (uses 2 sps), YO, insert hook in **same** sp, YO and pull up a loop, YO and draw through 2 loops on hook, YO, insert hook in **next** sp, YO and pull up a loop, YO and draw through 2 loops on hook, YO and draw through all 3 loops on hook **(counts as one dc)**.

Row 4: Ch 3 **(counts as first dc)**, turn; dc in first Cluster, 2 dc in next ch-2 sp, dc in next Cluster, 3 dc in next ch-3 sp, decrease, 3 dc in same ch-3 sp, dc in next Cluster, 2 dc in next ch-2 sp, ★ 3 dc in next Cluster, 2 dc in next ch-2 sp, dc in next Cluster, 3 dc in next ch-3 sp, decrease, 3 dc in same ch-3 sp, dc in next Cluster, 2 dc in next ch-2 sp; repeat from ★ across to last tr, 2 dc in last tr.

Row 5: Ch 1, turn; sc in each dc across.

Row 6: Ch 1, turn; sc in first sc, ★ ch 3, skip next 7 sc, work double Cluster in next sc, (ch 2, work double Cluster in same st) twice, ch 3, skip next 7 sc, sc in next sc; repeat from ★ across.

Row 7: Ch 3 **(counts as first dc)**, turn; 3 dc in next ch-3 sp, dc in next Cluster, 2 dc in next ch-2 sp, 3 dc in next Cluster, 2 dc in next ch-2 sp, dc in next Cluster, 3 dc in next ch-3 sp, ★ decrease, 3 dc in same ch-3 sp, dc in next Cluster, 2 dc in next ch-2 sp, 3 dc in next Cluster, 2 dc in next ch-2 sp, dc in next Cluster, 3 dc in next ch-3 sp; repeat from ★ across to last sc, dc in last sc.

Repeat Rows 2-7 for pattern.

57 SUMMERTIME

Note: Uses MC and CC in the following sequence: ★ 2 Rows **each** MC, CC; repeat from ★ for stripe sequence.

With MC, chain a multiple of 16 + 2 chs.

Row 1 (Right side)**:** Sc in second ch from hook and in each ch across.

Note: Loop a short piece of yarn around any stitch to mark Row 1 as **right** side.

Row 2: Ch 1, turn; sc in each sc across; finish off.

To treble crochet (abbreviated tr), YO twice, insert hook in st indicated, YO and pull up a loop (4 loops on hook), (YO and draw through 2 loops on hook) 3 times.

Row 3: With **right** side facing, join CC with slip st in first sc; ch 4 **(counts as first tr, now and throughout)**, tr in next sc, ch 1, skip next sc, dc in next sc, ch 1, skip next sc, hdc in next sc, ch 1, skip next sc, (sc in next sc, ch 1, skip next sc) twice, hdc in next sc, ch 1, skip next sc, dc in next sc, ch 1, ★ skip next sc, (tr in next sc, ch 1, skip next sc) twice, dc in next sc, ch 1, skip next sc, hdc in next sc, ch 1, skip next sc, (sc in next sc, ch 1, skip next sc) twice, hdc in next sc, ch 1, skip next sc, dc in next sc, ch 1; repeat from ★ across to last 3 sc, skip next sc, tr in last 2 sc.

Row 4: Ch 4, turn; tr in next tr, ch 1, dc in next dc, ch 1, hdc in next hdc, ch 1, (sc in next sc, ch 1) twice, hdc in next hdc, ch 1, dc in next dc, ch 1, ★ (tr in next tr, ch 1) twice, dc in next dc, ch 1, hdc in next hdc, ch 1, (sc in next sc, ch 1) twice, hdc in next hdc, ch 1, dc in next dc, ch 1; repeat from ★ to last 2 tr, tr in last 2 tr; finish off.

Row 5: With **right** side facing, join MC with sc in first tr *(see Joining With Sc, page 158)*; sc in each st and in each ch-1 sp across.

Row 6: Ch 1, turn; sc in each st across; finish off.

Row 7: With **right** side facing, join CC with sc in first sc; sc in next sc, ch 1, skip next sc, hdc in next sc, ch 1, skip next sc, dc in next sc, ch 1, skip next sc, (tr in next sc, ch 1, skip next sc) twice, dc in next sc, ch 1, skip next sc, hdc in next sc, ch 1, ★ skip next sc, (sc in next sc, ch 1, skip next sc) twice, hdc in next sc, ch 1, skip next sc, dc in next sc, ch 1, skip next sc, (tr in next sc, ch 1, skip next sc) twice, dc in next sc, ch 1, skip next sc, hdc in next sc, ch 1; repeat from ★ across to last 3 sc, skip next sc, sc in last 2 sc.

Row 8: Ch 1, turn; sc in first 2 sc, ch 1, hdc in next hdc, ch 1, dc in next dc, ch 1, (tr in next tr, ch 1) twice, dc in next dc, ch 1, hdc in next hdc, ch 1, ★ (sc in next sc, ch 1) twice, hdc in next hdc, ch 1, dc in next dc, ch 1, (tr in next tr, ch 1) twice, dc in next dc, ch 1, hdc in next hdc, ch 1; repeat from ★ across to last 2 sc, sc in last 2 sc; finish off.

Row 9: With **right** side facing, join MC with sc in first sc; sc in each st and in each ch-1 sp across.

Repeat Rows 2-9 for pattern.

58 DEFINED WAVES

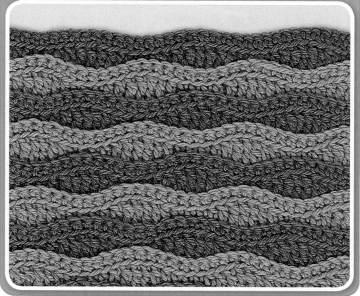

Note: Uses MC and CC in the following sequence: ★ 2 Rows **each** MC, CC; repeat from ★ for stripe sequence.

With MC, chain a multiple of 10 + 4 chs.

Row 1 (Right side)**:** Sc in second ch from hook and in next 2 chs, ★ hdc in next ch, dc in next 5 chs, hdc in next ch, sc in next 3 chs; repeat from ★ across.

Note: Loop a short piece of yarn around any stitch to mark Row 1 as **right** side.

Row 2: Ch 1, turn; sc in Front Loop Only *(Fig. 2, page 159)* of each st across; finish off.

To treble crochet (abbreviated *tr*), YO twice, insert hook in sc indicated, YO and pull up a loop (4 loops on hook), (YO and draw through 2 loops on hook) 3 times.

Row 3: With **right** side facing and working in Back Loops Only *(Fig. 2, page 159)*, join CC with slip st of first sc; ch 4 **(counts as first tr, now and throughout)**, tr in next 2 sc, ★ dc in next sc, hdc in next sc, sc in next 3 sc, hdc in next sc, dc in next sc, tr in next 3 sc; repeat from ★ across.

Row 4: Ch 1, turn; sc in Front Loop Only of each st across; finish off.

Row 5: With **right** side facing and working in Back Loops Only, join MC with sc in first sc *(see Joining With Sc, page 158)*; sc in next 2 sc, ★ hdc in next sc, dc in next sc, tr in next 3 sc, dc in next sc, hdc in next sc, sc in next 3 sc; repeat from ★ across.

Repeat Rows 2-5 for pattern.

Note: Uses MC and CC in the following sequence: 1 Row MC, ★ 2 rows **each** CC, MC; repeat from ★ for stripe sequence.

With MC, chain a multiple of 12 + 2 chs.

To treble crochet (abbreviated tr), YO twice, insert hook in st indicated, YO and pull up a loop (4 loops on hook), (YO and draw through 2 loops on hook) 3 times.

To double treble crochet (abbreviated dtr), YO 3 times, insert hook in st indicated, YO and pull up a loop (5 loops on hook), (YO and draw through 2 loops on hook) 4 times.

Row 1 (Right side)**:** Sc in second ch from hook and in next ch, hdc in next ch, dc in next ch, tr in next ch, dtr in next 3 chs, tr in next ch, dc in next ch, hdc in next ch, ★ sc in next 3 chs, hdc in next ch, dc in next ch, tr in next ch, dtr in next 3 chs, tr in next ch, dc in next ch, hdc in next ch; repeat from ★ across to last 2 chs, sc in last 2 chs; finish off.

Note: Loop a short piece of yarn around any stitch to mark Row 1 as **right** side.

To work Front Post single crochet (abbreviated FPsc), insert hook from **front** to **back** around post of st indicated *(Fig. 4, page 159)*, YO and pull up a loop, YO and draw through both loops on hook.

To work Front Post half double crochet (abbreviated FPhdc), YO, insert hook from **front** to **back** around post of st indicated, YO and pull up a loop, YO and draw through all 3 loops on hook.

To work Front Post double crochet (abbreviated FPdc), YO, insert hook from **front** to **back** around post of st indicated, YO and pull up a loop (3 loops on hook), (YO and draw through 2 loops on hook) twice.

To work Front Post treble crochet (abbreviated FPtr), YO twice, insert hook from **front** to **back** around post of st indicated, YO and pull up a loop (4 loops on hook), (YO and draw through 2 loops on hook) 3 times.

To work Front Post double treble crochet (abbreviated FPdtr), YO 3 times, insert hook from **front** to **back** around post of st indicated, YO and pull up a loop (5 loops on hook), (YO and draw through 2 loops on hook) 4 times.

Row 2: With **wrong** side facing and inserting hook from **front** to **back**, join CC with slip st around post of first sc *(Fig. 4, page 159)*; ch 5 **(counts as first FPdtr)**, FPdtr around next st, FPtr around next st, FPdc around next st, FPhdc around next st, FPsc around each of next 3 sts, FPhdc around next st, FPdc around next st, FPtr around next st, ★ FPdtr around each of next 3 sts, FPtr around next st, FPdc around next st, FPhdc around next st, FPsc around each of next 3 sts, FPhdc around next st, FPdc around next st, FPtr around next st; repeat from ★ across to last 2 sts, FPdtr around each of last 2 sts.

Row 3: Ch 5 **(counts as first dtr)**, turn; dtr in next st, tr in next st, dc in next st, hdc in next st, sc in next 3 sts, hdc in next st, dc in next st, tr in next st, ★ dtr in each of next 3 sts, tr in next st, dc in next st, hdc in next st, sc in next 3 sts, hdc in next st, dc in next st, tr in next st; repeat from ★ across to last 2 sts, dtr in last 2 sts; finish off.

Row 4: With **wrong** side facing, join MC with slip st around post of first dtr; ch 1, FPsc around same st and around next st, FPhdc around next st, FPdc around next st, FPtr around next st, FPdtr around each of next 3 sts, FPtr around next st, FPdc around next st, FPhdc around next st, ★ FPsc around each of next 3 sts, FPhdc around next st, FPdc around next st, FPtr around next st, FPdtr around each of next 3 sts, FPtr around next st, FPdc around next st, FPhdc around next st; repeat from ★ across to last 2 sts, FPsc around each of last 2 sts.

Row 5: Ch 1, turn; sc in first 2 sts, hdc in next st, dc in next st, tr in next st, dtr in next 3 sts, tr in next st, dc in next st, hdc in next st, ★ sc in next 3 sts, hdc in next st, dc in next st, tr in next st, dtr in next 3 sts, tr in next st, dc in next st, hdc in next st; repeat from ★ across to last 2 sts, sc in last 2 sts; finish off.

Repeat Rows 2-5 for pattern.

60 CROSS STITCH WAVES

Note: Uses Colors A, B, and C in the following sequence: ★ 2 Rows **each** Color A, Color B, Color C, Color B; repeat from ★ for stripe sequence.

With Color A, chain a multiple of 20 + 14 chs.

To work Cross St (uses next 2 sts), skip next st, dc in next st, working **around** dc just made, dc in skipped st.

Row 1 (Right side): Work Cross St beginning in fifth ch from hook **(3 skipped chs count as first dc)**, work 4 Cross Sts, (sc in next 10 chs, work 5 Cross Sts) across to last ch, dc in last ch.

Note: Loop a short piece of yarn around any stitch to mark Row 1 as **right** side.

Row 2: Ch 3 **(counts as first dc, now and throughout)**, turn; work 5 Cross Sts, (sc in next 10 sc, work 5 Cross Sts) across to last dc, dc in last dc; finish off.

Row 3: With **right** side facing, join Color B with sc in first dc *(see Joining With Sc, page 158)*; sc in each st across.

Row 4: Ch 1, turn; sc in each sc across; finish off.

Row 5: With **right** side facing, join Color C with sc in first sc; (sc in next 10 sc, work 5 Cross Sts) across to last 11 sc, sc in last 11 sc.

Row 6: Ch 1, turn; sc in first 11 sc, work 5 Cross Sts, (sc in next 10 sc, work 5 Cross Sts) across to last 11 sc, sc in last 11 sc; finish off.

Row 7: With **right** side facing, join Color B with sc in first sc; sc in each st across.

Row 8: Ch 1, turn; sc in each sc across; finish off.

Row 9: With **right** side facing, join Color A with slip st in first sc; ch 3, work 5 Cross Sts, (sc in next 10 sc, work 5 Cross Sts) across to last sc, dc in last sc.

Repeat Rows 2-9 for pattern.

61 3 D SHELLS

Note: Uses MC and Colors A and B in the following sequence: 2 Rows MC, ★ 4 rows **each** Color A, MC, Color B, MC; repeat from ★ for stripe sequence.

With MC, chain a multiple of 15 + 14 chs.

Row 1: Sc in second ch from hook, ch 3, skip next 2 chs, sc in next ch, ch 1, skip next 2 chs, (dc, ch 3, dc) in next ch, ch 1, skip next 2 chs, sc in next ch, ★ (ch 3, skip next 2 chs, sc in next ch) 3 times, ch 1, skip next 2 chs, (dc, ch 3, dc) in next ch, ch 1, skip next 2 chs, sc in next ch; repeat from ★ across to last 3 chs, ch 3, skip next 2 chs, sc in last ch.

Row 2 (Right side)**:** Ch 3 **(counts as first hdc plus ch 1, now and throughout)**, turn; sc in next ch-3 sp, ch 1, skip next ch-1 sp, 7 dc in next ch-3 sp, ch 1, skip next ch-1 sp, sc in next ch-3 sp, ★ (ch 3, sc in next ch-3 sp) twice, ch 1, skip next ch-1 sp, 7 dc in next ch-3 sp, ch 1, skip next ch-1 sp, sc in next ch-3 sp; repeat from ★ across to last sc, ch 1, hdc in last sc; finish off.

Note: Loop a short piece of yarn around any stitch to mark Row 2 as **right** side.

To treble crochet (abbreviated tr), YO twice, insert hook in st indicated, YO and pull up a loop (4 loops on hook), (YO and draw through 2 loops on hook) 3 times.

Row 3: With **wrong** side facing, join Color A with sc in first hdc *(see Joining With Sc, page 158)*; ch 3, skip next ch-1 sp, working in **front** of next ch-1 sp *(Fig. 6, page 159)*, dc in skipped sc one row **below**, ch 3, working in **front** of next 7-dc group, tr in ch two rows **below** (between dc), ch 3, working in **front** of next ch-1 sp, dc in skipped sc one row **below**, ch 3, ★ (sc in next ch-3 sp, ch 3) twice, working in **front** of next ch-1 sp, dc in skipped sc one row **below**, ch 3, working in **front** of next 7-dc group, tr in ch two rows **below** (between dc), ch 3, working in **front** of next ch-1 sp, dc in skipped sc one row **below**, ch 3; repeat from ★ across to last ch-1 sp, skip last ch-1 sp, sc in last hdc.

Row 4: Ch 3, turn; sc in next ch-3 sp, (ch 3, sc in next ch-3 sp) across to last sc, ch 1, hdc in last sc.

Row 5: Ch 1, turn; sc in first hdc, ch 3, skip next ch-1 sp, sc in next ch-3 sp, ch 1, working **behind** previous 2 rows, (dc, ch 3, dc) in center dc of 7-dc group 2 rows **below**, ch 1, sc in next ch-3 sp, ★ (ch 3, sc in next ch-3 sp) 3 times, ch 1, working **behind** previous 2 rows, (dc, ch 3, dc) in center dc of 7-dc group 2 rows **below**, ch 1, sc in next ch-3 sp; repeat from ★ across to last ch-1 sp, ch 3, skip last ch-1 sp, sc in last hdc.

Row 6: Ch 3, turn; sc in next ch-3 sp, ch 1, skip next ch-1 sp, 7 dc in next ch-3 sp, ch 1, skip next ch-1 sp, sc in next ch-3 sp, ★ (ch 3, sc in next ch-3 sp) twice, ch 1, skip next ch-1 sp, 7 dc in next ch-3 sp, ch 1, skip next ch-1 sp, sc in next ch-3 sp; repeat from ★ across to last sc, ch 1, hdc in last sc; finish off.

Row 7: With **wrong** side facing, join MC with sc in first hdc; ch 3, skip next ch-1 sp, working in **front** of next ch-1 sp, dc in skipped sc one row **below**, ch 3, working in **front** of next 7-dc group, tr in center dc of 7-dc group five rows **below**

68

(between dc), ch 3, working in **front** of next ch-1 sp, dc in skipped sc one row **below**, ch 3, ★ (sc in next ch-3 sp, ch 3) twice, working in **front** of next ch-1 sp, dc in skipped sc one row **below**, ch 3, working in **front** of next 7-dc group, tr in center dc of 7-dc group five rows **below** (between

dc), ch 3, working in **front** of next ch-1 sp, dc in skipped sc one row **below**, ch 3; repeat from ★ across to last ch-1 sp, skip last ch-1 sp, sc in last hdc.

Repeat Rows 4-7 for pattern, working in stripe sequence.

62 SHARP RELIEF CHEVRONS

Chain a multiple of 16 + 2 chs.

To decrease (uses next 2 sts), ★ YO, insert hook in **next** st, YO and pull up a loop, YO and draw through 2 loops on hook; repeat from ★ once **more**, YO and draw through all 3 loops on hook **(counts as one dc).**

To double decrease (uses next 3 sts), ★ YO, insert hook in **next** st, YO and pull up a loop, YO and draw through 2 loops on hook; repeat from ★ 2 times **more**, YO and draw through all 4 loops on hook **(counts as one dc).**

To double crochet 5 together (abbreviated dc5tog), ★ YO, insert hook in **next** st, YO and pull up a loop, YO and draw through 2 loops on hook; repeat from ★ 4 times **more**, YO and draw through all 6 loops on hook **(counts as one dc).**

Row 1 (Right side)**:** Decrease beginning in third ch from hook, dc in next 5 chs, (2 dc, ch 1, 2 dc) in next ch, dc in next 5 chs, ★ dc5tog, dc in next 5 chs, (2 dc, ch 1, 2 dc) in next ch, dc in next 5 chs; repeat from ★ across to last 3 chs, double decrease.

Note: Loop a short piece of yarn around any stitch to mark Row 1 as **right** side.

To work Front Post double crochet (abbreviated FPdc), YO, insert hook from **front** to **back** around post of st indicated **(Fig. 4, page 159)**, YO and pull up a loop (3 loops on hook), (YO and draw through 2 loops on hook) twice.

Row 2: Ch 2, turn; skip first dc, decrease, work FPdc around each of next 5 sts, (2 dc, ch 1, 2 dc) in next ch-1 sp, work FPdc around each of next 5 sts, ★ dc5tog, work FPdc around each of next 5 sts, (2 dc, ch 1, 2 dc) in next ch-1 sp, work FPdc around each of next 5 sts; repeat from ★ across to last 3 sts, double decrease.

To work Back Post double crochet (abbreviated BPdc), YO, insert hook from **back** to **front** around post of st indicated **(Fig. 4, page 159)**, YO and pull up a loop (3 loops on hook), (YO and draw through 2 loops on hook) twice.

Row 3: Ch 2, turn; skip first dc, decrease, work BPdc around each of next 5 sts, (2 dc, ch 1, 2 dc) in next ch-1 sp, work BPdc around each of next 5 sts, ★ dc5tog, work BPdc around each of next 5 sts, (2 dc, ch 1, 2 dc) in next ch-1 sp, work BPdc around each of next 5 sts; repeat from ★ across to last 3 sts, double decrease.

Repeat Rows 2 and 3 for pattern.

63 COZY

Chain a multiple of 20 + 4 chs.

Row 1 (Right side)**:** 2 Dc in fourth ch from hook **(3 skipped chs count as first dc)** and in next ch, (ch 1, skip next ch, dc in next ch) 3 times, skip next ch, dc in next 2 chs, ★ skip next ch, (dc in next ch, ch 1, skip next ch) 3 times, 2 dc in each of next 4 chs, (ch 1, skip next ch, dc in next ch) 3 times, skip next ch, dc in next 2 chs; repeat from ★ across to last 10 chs, skip next ch, (dc in next ch, ch 1, skip next ch) 3 times, 2 dc in each of next 2 chs, dc in last ch.

Note: Loop a short piece of yarn around any stitch to mark Row 1 as **right** side.

To work Back Post double crochet (abbreviated BPdc), YO, insert hook from **back** to **front** around post of st indicated **(Fig. 4, page 159)**, YO and pull up a loop (3 loops on hook), (YO and draw through 2 loops on hook) twice.

To work Back Post decrease (abbreviated BP decrease) (uses next 2 sts), ★ YO, insert hook from **back** to **front** around post of **next** st, YO and pull up a loop, YO and draw through 2 loops on hook; repeat from ★ once **more**, YO and draw through all 3 loops on hook.

Row 2: Ch 3 **(counts as first dc, now and throughout)**, turn; 2 dc in each of next 2 dc, ch 1, skip next dc, (work BPdc around next dc, ch 1) 3 times, work BP decrease twice, ch 1, (work BPdc around next dc, ch 1) 3 times, ★ skip next dc, 2 dc in each of next 4 dc, ch 1, skip next dc, (work BPdc around next dc, ch 1) 3 times, work BP decrease twice, ch 1, (work BPdc around next dc, ch 1) 3 times; repeat from ★ across to last 4 dc, skip next dc, 2 dc in each of next 2 dc, dc in last dc.

To work Front Post double crochet (abbreviated FPdc), YO, insert hook from **front** to **back** around post of st indicated **(Fig. 4, page 159)**, YO and pull up a loop (3 loops on hook), (YO and draw through 2 loops on hook) twice.

To work Front Post decrease (abbreviated FP decrease) (uses next 2 sts), ★ YO, insert hook from **front** to **back** around post of **next** st, YO and pull up a loop, YO and draw through 2 loops on hook; repeat from ★ once **more**, YO and draw through all 3 loops on hook.

Row 3: Ch 3, turn; 2 dc in each of next 2 dc, ch 1, skip next dc, (work FPdc around next st, ch 1) 3 times, work FP decrease twice, ch 1, (work FPdc around next st, ch 1) 3 times, ★ skip next dc, 2 dc in each of next 4 dc, ch 1, skip next dc, (work FPdc around next st, ch 1) 3 times, work FP decrease twice, ch 1, (work FPdc around next st, ch 1) 3 times; repeat from ★ across to last 4 dc, skip next dc, 2 dc in each of next 2 dc, dc in last dc.

Repeat Rows 2 and 3 for pattern.

64 CALYPSO

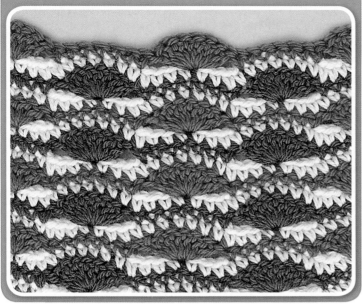

Note: Uses Colors A, B, and C in the following sequence: ★ 1 Row **each** Color A, Color B, Color C, Color B; repeat from ★ for stripe sequence.

With Color A, chain a multiple of 14 + 4 chs.

Row 1 (Wrong side): 3 Dc in fourth ch from hook **(3 skipped chs count as first dc)**, skip next 3 chs, sc in next 7 chs, ★ skip next 3 chs, 7 dc in next ch, skip next 3 chs, sc in next 7 chs; repeat from ★ across to last 4 chs, skip next 3 chs, 4 dc in last ch; finish off.

Note: Loop a short piece of yarn around **back** of any stitch on Row 1 to mark **right** side.

Row 2: With **right** side facing, join Color B with sc in first dc *(see Joining With Sc, page 158)*; sc in each st across; finish off.

Row 3: With **wrong** side facing, join Color C with sc in first sc; sc in next 3 sc, skip next 3 sc, 7 dc in next sc, ★ skip next 3 sc, sc in next 7 sc, skip next 3 sc, 7 dc in next sc; repeat from ★ across to last 7 sc, skip next 3 sc, sc in last 4 sc; finish off.

Row 4: With **right** side facing, join Color B with sc in first sc; sc in each st across; finish off.

Row 5: With **wrong** side facing, join Color A with slip st in first sc; ch 3 **(counts as first dc)**, 3 dc in same st as joining, skip next 3 sc, sc in next 7 sc, ★ skip next 3 sc, 7 dc in next sc, skip next 3 sc, sc in next 7 sc; repeat from ★ across to last 4 sc, skip next 3 sc, 4 dc in last sc; finish off.

Repeat Rows 2-5 for pattern.

65 SPARTAN

Chain a multiple of 20 + 1 ch.

Row 1 (Right side)**:** Sc in second ch from hook and in next 9 chs, ch 2, ★ sc in next 9 chs, skip next 2 chs, sc in next 9 chs, ch 2; repeat from ★ across to last 10 chs, sc in last 10 chs.

Note: Loop a short piece of yarn around any stitch to mark Row 1 as **right** side.

To double crochet 4 together (abbreviated dc4tog), ★ YO, insert hook in **next** st, YO and pull up a loop, YO and draw through 2 loops on hook; repeat from ★ 3 times **more**, YO and draw through all 5 loops on hook **(counts as one dc)**.

To double decrease (uses next 3 sts), ★ YO, insert hook in **next** st, YO and pull up a loop, YO and draw through 2 loops on hook; repeat from ★ 2 times **more**, YO and draw through all 4 loops on hook **(counts as one dc)**.

Row 2: Ch 3 **(counts as first dc, now and throughout)**, turn; skip first 2 sc, (dc in next sc, ch 1, skip next sc) 4 times, (dc, ch 3, dc) in next ch-2 sp, dc in next 7 sc, ★ dc4tog, ch 1, skip next sc, (dc in next sc, ch 1, skip next sc) 3 times, (dc, ch 3, dc) in next ch-2 sp, dc in next 7 sc; repeat from ★ across to last 3 sc, double decrease.

Row 3: Ch 1, turn; sc in first 9 dc, (sc, ch 2, sc) in next ch-3 sp, (sc in next dc and in next ch-1 sp) 4 times, ★ skip next dc, sc in next 8 dc, (sc, ch 2, sc) in next ch-3 sp, (sc in next dc and in next ch-1 sp) 4 times; repeat from ★ across to last 2 dc, skip next dc, sc in last dc.

Rows 4-7: Repeat Rows 2 and 3 twice.

Row 8: Ch 3, turn; skip first 2 sc, dc in next 8 sc, (dc, ch 3, dc) in next ch-2 sp, ch 1, (skip next sc, dc in next sc, ch 1) 3 times, ★ skip next sc, dc4tog, dc in next 7 sc, (dc, ch 3, dc) in next ch-2 sp, ch 1, (skip next sc, dc in next sc, ch 1) 3 times; repeat from ★ across to last 4 sc, skip next sc, double decrease.

Row 9: Ch 1, turn; sc in first dc, (sc in next ch-1 sp and in next dc) 4 times, (sc, ch 2, sc) in next ch-3 sp, sc in next 8 dc, ★ skip next dc, (sc in next ch-1 sp and in next dc) 4 times, (sc, ch 2, sc) in next ch-3 sp, sc in next 8 dc; repeat from ★ across to last 2 dc, skip next dc, sc in last dc.

Rows 10-13: Repeat Rows 8 and 9 twice.

Repeat Rows 2-13 for pattern.

66 DAINTY CHEVRON

Note: Uses MC and CC in the following sequence: 1 Row MC, ★ 2 rows **each** CC, MC; repeat from ★ for stripe sequence.

With MC, chain a multiple of 8 + 4 chs.

Row 1 (Right side)**:** 2 Dc in fourth ch from hook **(3 skipped chs count as first dc)**, skip next 3 chs, sc in next ch, ★ skip next 3 chs, 5 dc in next ch, skip next 3 chs, sc in next ch; repeat from ★ across to last 4 chs, skip next 3 chs, 3 dc in last ch; finish off.

Note: Loop a short piece of yarn around any stitch to mark Row 1 as **right** side.

To double crochet 5 together (abbreviated *dc5tog*), ★ YO, insert hook in **next** st, YO and pull up a loop, YO and draw through 2 loops on hook; repeat from ★ 4 times **more**, YO and draw through all 6 loops on hook **(counts as one dc)**.

Row 2: With **wrong** side facing, join CC with sc in first dc *(see Joining With Sc, page 158)*; ★ ch 3, dc5tog, ch 3, sc in next dc; repeat from ★ across.

Row 3: Ch 3 **(counts as first dc, now and throughout)**, turn; 2 dc in first sc, skip next ch-3, sc in next st, ★ skip next ch-3, 5 dc in next sc, skip next ch-3, sc in next st; repeat from ★ across to last ch-3, skip last ch-3, 3 dc in last sc; finish off.

Row 4: With **wrong** side facing, join MC with sc in first dc; ★ ch 3, dc5tog, ch 3, sc in next dc; repeat from ★ across.

Row 5: Ch 3, turn; 2 dc in first sc, skip next ch-3, sc in next st, ★ skip next ch-3, 5 dc in next sc, skip next ch-3, sc in next st; repeat from ★ across to last ch-3, skip last ch-3, 3 dc in last sc; finish off.

Repeat Rows 2-5 for pattern.

67 RICKRACK

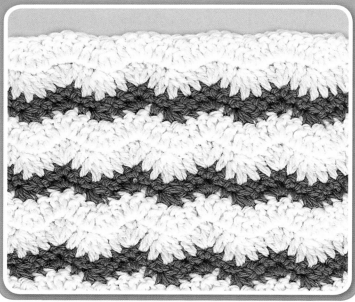

Note: Uses MC and CC in the following sequence: ★ 2 Rows **each** MC, CC; repeat from ★ for stripe sequence.

With MC, chain a multiple of 6 + 4 chs.

To dc decrease (uses next 3 sts), ★ YO, insert hook in **next** st, YO and pull up a loop, YO and draw through 2 loops on hook; repeat from ★ 2 times **more**, YO and draw through all 4 loops on hook **(counts as one dc)**.

Row 1 (Right side)**:** Dc in fourth ch from hook **(3 skipped chs count as first dc)** and in next ch, dc decrease, dc in next ch, ★ 3 dc in next ch, dc in next ch, dc decrease, dc in next ch; repeat from ★ across to last ch, 2 dc in last ch.

Note: Loop a short piece of yarn around any stitch to mark Row 1 as **right** side.

Row 2: Ch 3 **(counts as first dc, now and throughout)**, turn; dc in first 2 dc, dc decrease, dc in next dc, ★ 3 dc in next dc, dc in next dc, dc decrease, dc in next dc; repeat from ★ across to last dc, 2 dc in last dc; finish off.

To sc decrease, pull up a loop in each of next 3 sts, YO and draw through all 4 loops on hook **(counts as one sc)**.

Row 3: With **right** side facing, join CC with sc in first dc **(see Joining With Sc, page 158)**; sc in same st as joining and in next dc, sc decrease, sc in next dc, ★ 3 sc in next dc, sc in next dc, sc decrease, sc in next dc; repeat from ★ across to last dc, 2 sc in last dc.

Row 4: Ch 1, turn; 2 sc in first sc, sc in next sc, sc decrease, sc in next sc, ★ 3 sc in next sc, sc in next sc, sc decrease, sc in next sc; repeat from ★ across to last sc, 2 sc in last sc; finish off.

Row 5: With **right** side facing, join MC with slip st in first sc; ch 3, dc in same st as joining and in next sc, dc decrease, dc in next sc, ★ 3 dc in next sc, dc in next sc, dc decrease, dc in next sc; repeat from ★ across to last sc, 2 dc in last sc.

Repeat Rows 2-5 for pattern.

68 POLKA DOTS

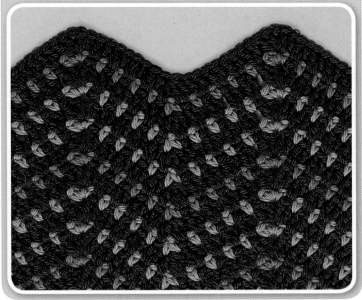

Note: Uses MC and Colors A, B, and C in the following sequence: ★ 1 Row **each** MC, Color A, MC, Color B, MC, Color C; repeat from ★ for stripe sequence.

With MC, chain a multiple of 22 + 3 chs.

Row 1 (Right side)**:** Dc in fourth ch from hook, (skip next ch, 2 dc in next ch) 4 times, skip next ch, (2 dc, ch 1, 2 dc) in next ch, (skip next ch, 2 dc in next ch) 4 times, ★ skip next ch, [YO, insert hook in **next** ch, YO and pull up a loop, YO and draw through 2 loops on hook] 3 times, YO and draw through all 4 loops on hook, (skip next ch, 2 dc in next ch) 4 times, skip next ch, (2 dc, ch 1, 2 dc) in next ch, (skip next ch, 2 dc in next ch) 4 times; repeat from ★ across to last 3 chs, skip next ch, [YO, insert hook in **next** ch, YO and pull up a loop, YO and draw through 2 loops on hook] twice, YO and draw through all 3 loops on hook; finish off.

Note: Loop a short piece of yarn around any stitch to mark Row 1 as **right** side.

Row 2: With **right** side facing, skip first dc and join Color A with sc *(see Joining With Sc, page 158)* in sp **before** next dc *(Fig. 5, page 159)*; ch 1, skip next 2 dc, (sc in sp **before** next dc, ch 1, skip next 2 dc) 4 times, 3 sc in next ch-1 sp, ★ ch 1, skip next 2 dc, (sc in sp **before** next dc, ch 1, skip next 2 dc) 4 times, pull up a loop in sp **before** each of next 2 sts, YO and draw through all 3 loops on hook, ch 1, skip next 2 dc, (sc in sp **before** next dc, ch 1, skip next 2 dc) 4 times, 3 sc in next ch-1 sp; repeat from ★ across to last 11 sts, (ch 1, skip next 2 dc, sc in sp **before** next st) 5 times, leave remaining st unworked; finish off.

To decrease (uses 2 ch-1 sps and one st), † YO, insert hook in next ch-1 sp, YO and pull up a loop, YO and draw through 2 loops on hook †, YO, insert hook in next st, YO and pull up a loop, YO and draw through 2 loops on hook, repeat from † to † once, YO and draw through all 4 loops on hook.

Row 3: With **right** side facing, join MC with slip st in unworked dc one row **before** previous row; ch 3, dc in next ch-1 sp on previous row, 2 dc in each of next 4 ch-1 sps, skip next sc, (2 dc, ch 1, 2 dc) in next sc, 2 dc in each of next 4 ch-1 sps, ★ decrease, 2 dc in each of next 4 ch-1 sps, skip next sc, (2 dc, ch 1, 2 dc) in next sc, 2 dc in each of next 4 ch-1 sps; repeat from ★ across to last ch-1 sp, YO, insert hook in last ch-1 sp, YO and pull up a loop, YO and draw through 2 loops on hook, YO, insert hook in unworked st one row **before** previous row, YO and pull up a loop, YO and draw through 2 loops on hook, YO and draw through all 3 loops on hook; finish off.

Repeat Rows 2 and 3 for pattern, working in stripe sequence.

69 ORIENT DELIGHT

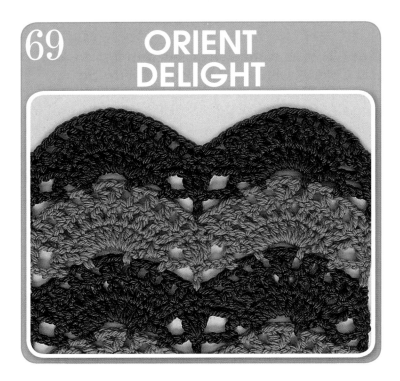

Note: Uses MC and CC in the following sequence: ★ 4 Rows **each** MC, CC; repeat from ★ for stripe sequence.

With MC, chain a multiple of 18 + 2 chs.

Row 1: Sc in second ch from hook, ch 3, skip next 2 chs, sc in next ch, (ch 5, skip next 3 chs, sc in next ch) 3 times, ★ (ch 3, skip next 2 chs, sc in next ch) twice, (ch 5, skip next 3 chs, sc in next ch) 3 times; repeat from ★ across to last 3 chs, ch 3, skip next 2 chs, sc in last ch.

Row 2 (Right side)**:** Ch 3 **(counts as first dc)**, turn; dc in first st, ch 3, skip next ch-3 sp, sc in next ch-5 sp, 9 dc in next ch-5 sp, sc in next ch-5 sp, ch 3, ★ skip next ch-3 sp, 3 dc in next st, ch 3, skip next ch-3 sp, sc in next ch-5 sp, 9 dc in next ch-5 sp, sc in next ch-5 sp, ch 3; repeat from ★ across to last ch-3 sp, skip last ch-3 sp, 2 dc in last st.

Note: Loop a short piece of yarn around any stitch to mark Row 2 as **right** side.

Row 3: Ch 1, turn; sc in first 2 dc, ch 1, skip next ch-3 sp and next sc, (dc in next dc, ch 1) 9 times, ★ skip next ch-3 sp, sc in next 3 dc, ch 1, skip next ch-3 sp and next sc, (dc in next dc, ch 1) 9 times; repeat from ★ across to last ch-3 sp, skip last ch-3 sp, sc in last 2 dc.

Row 4: Ch 1, turn; sc in first sc, ★ skip next ch-1 sp, (dc in next dc, ch 1) 4 times, (dc, ch 1) twice in next dc, dc in next dc, (ch 1, dc in next dc) 3 times, skip next sc, sc in next sc; repeat from ★ across; finish off.

Row 5: With **wrong** side facing, join CC with slip st in first sc; ch 6 **(counts as first dc plus ch 3)**, skip next 2 dc, sc in next dc, (ch 5, skip next ch-1 sp, sc in next ch-1 sp) twice, ch 5, skip next ch-1 sp, sc in next dc, ch 3, skip next 2 dc, dc in next sc, ★ ch 3, skip next 2 dc, sc in next dc, (ch 5, skip next ch-1 sp, sc in next ch-1 sp) twice, ch 5, skip next ch-1 sp, sc in next dc, ch 3, skip next 2 dc, dc in next sc; repeat from ★ across.

Repeat Rows 2-5 for pattern, working in stripe sequence.

70 ROLLING CHEVRON

71 GRANDMA'S FAVORITE

Chain a multiple of 10 + 3 chs.

To decrease (uses next 3 sts), ★ YO, insert hook in **next** st, YO and pull up a loop, YO and draw through 2 loops on hook; repeat from ★ 2 times **more**, YO and draw through all 4 loops on hook **(counts as one dc)**.

Row 1 (Right side)**:** Dc in third ch from hook and in next 3 chs, decrease, dc in next 3 chs, ★ 3 dc in next ch, dc in next 3 chs, decrease, dc in next 3 chs; repeat from ★ across to last ch, 2 dc in last ch.

Note: Loop a short piece of yarn around any stitch to mark Row 1 as **right** side.

Row 2: Ch 3 **(counts as first dc)**, turn; dc in same st and in next 3 dc, decrease, dc in next 3 dc, ★ 3 dc in next dc, dc in next 3 dc, decrease, dc in next 3 dc; repeat from ★ across to last dc, 2 dc in last dc.

Repeat Row 2 for pattern.

Note: Uses Colors A, B, and C in the following sequence: ★ 2 Rows **each** Color A, Color B, Color C; repeat from ★ for stripe sequence.

With Color A, chain a multiple of 11 + 2 chs.

Row 1 (Right side)**:** 2 Sc in second ch from hook, sc in next next 4 chs, skip next 2 chs, sc in next 4 chs, ★ 3 sc in next ch, sc in next 4 chs, skip next 2 chs, sc in next 4 chs; repeat from ★ across to last ch, 2 sc in last ch.

Note: Loop a short piece of yarn around any stitch to mark Row 1 as **right** side.

Row 2: Ch 1, turn; 2 sc in first sc, sc in next 4 sc, skip next 2 sc, sc in next 4 sc, ★ 3 sc in next sc, sc in next 4 sc, skip next 2 sc, sc in next 4 sc; repeat from ★ across to last sc, 2 sc in last sc; finish off.

Row 3: With **right** side facing, join Color B with sc in first sc **(see Joining With Sc, page 158)**; sc in same st as joining and in next 4 sc, skip next 2 sc, sc in next 4 sc, ★ 3 sc in next sc, sc in next 4 sc, skip next 2 sc, sc in next 4 sc; repeat from ★ across to last sc, 2 sc in last sc.

Repeat Rows 2 and 3 for pattern, working in stripe sequence.

72 VINTAGE LACE

Note: Uses MC and CC in the following sequence: ★ 4 Rows **each** MC, CC; repeat from ★ for stripe sequence.

With MC, chain a multiple of 18 + 2 chs.

Row 1: Sc in second ch from hook, ch 2, skip next 2 chs, sc in next ch, (ch 3, skip next 3 chs, sc in next ch) 3 times, ★ (ch 2, skip next 2 chs, sc in next ch) twice, (ch 3, skip next 3 chs, sc in next ch) 3 times; repeat from ★ across to last 3 chs, ch 2, skip next 2 chs, sc in last ch.

Row 2 (Right side)**:** Ch 1, turn; (sc, ch 3, dc) in first sc, skip next ch-2 sp, sc in next ch-3 sp, 6 dc in next ch-3 sp, sc in next ch-3 sp, skip next ch-2 sp, dc in next sc, ★ (ch 3, sc, ch 3, dc) in same st, skip next ch-2 sp, sc in next ch-3 sp, 6 dc in next ch-3 sp, sc in next ch-3 sp, skip next ch-2 sp, dc in next sc; repeat from ★ across, ch 3, sc in same st.

Note: Loop a short piece of yarn around any stitch to mark Row 2 as **right** side.

Row 3: Ch 5 **(counts as first dc plus ch 2, now and throughout)**, turn; sc in next ch-3 sp, ch 1, skip next 2 sts, (dc in next dc, ch 1) 6 times, sc in next ch-3 sp, ch 2, dc in next sc, ★ ch 2, sc in next ch-3 sp, ch 1, skip next 2 sts, (dc in next dc, ch 1) 6 times, sc in next ch-3 sp, ch 2, dc in next sc; repeat from ★ across.

Row 4: Ch 1, turn; sc in first dc, ★ skip next sc, dc in next dc and in next ch-1 sp, (2 dc in next dc, dc in next ch-1 sp) 4 times, dc in next dc, skip next sc, sc in next dc; repeat from ★ across; finish off.

Row 5: With **wrong** side facing, join CC with slip st in first sc; ch 5, skip next 2 dc, sc in next dc, ch 3, skip next 3 dc, sc in next dc, ch 3, skip next dc, sc in next dc, ch 3, skip next 3 dc, sc in next dc, ch 2, skip next 2 dc, dc in next sc, ★ ch 2, skip next 2 dc, sc in next dc, ch 3, skip next 3 dc, sc in next dc, ch 3, skip next dc, sc in next dc, ch 3, skip next 3 dc, sc in next dc, ch 2, skip next 2 dc, dc in next sc; repeat from ★ across.

Repeat Rows 2-5 for pattern, working in stripe sequence.

73 BLISS

Note: Uses Colors A, B, C, and D in the following sequence: ★ 1 Row **each** Color A, Color B, Color C, Color D; repeat from ★ for stripe sequence.

With Color A, chain a multiple of 13 + 4 chs.

To decrease (uses next 2 sts), ★ YO, insert hook in **next** st, YO and pull up a loop, YO and draw through 2 loops on hook; repeat from ★ once **more**, YO and draw through all 3 loops on hook **(counts as one dc)**.

Row 1 (Right side)**:** Dc in fourth ch from hook **(3 skipped chs count as first dc)** and in next 3 chs, decrease 3 times, dc in next 3 chs, ★ 3 dc in next ch, dc in next 3 chs, decrease 3 times, dc in next 3 chs; repeat from ★ across to last ch, 2 dc in last ch; finish off.

Note: Loop a short piece of yarn around any stitch to mark Row 1 as **right** side.

Row 2: With **wrong** side facing, join Color B with slip st in first dc; ch 3 **(counts as first dc, now and throughout)**, 2 dc in same st as joining, ch 2, skip next 3 dc, sc in next dc, ch 4, skip next 3 dc, sc in next dc, ch 2, ★ skip next 3 dc, 5 dc in next dc, ch 2, skip next 3 dc, sc in next dc, ch 4, skip next 3 dc, sc in next dc, ch 2; repeat from ★ across to last 4 dc, skip next 3 dc, 3 dc in last dc; finish off.

Row 3: With **right** side facing, join Color C with slip st in first dc; ch 3, dc in same st as joining, 2 dc in next dc, dc in next dc, ch 2, skip next ch-2 sp, sc in next ch-4 sp, ch 2, skip next ch-2 sp, dc in next dc, ★ 2 dc in next dc, 3 dc in next dc, 2 dc in next dc, dc in next dc, ch 2, skip next ch-2 sp, sc in next ch-4 sp, ch 2, skip next ch-2 sp, dc in next dc; repeat from ★ across to last 2 dc, 2 dc in each of last 2 dc; finish off.

Row 4: With **wrong** side facing, join Color D with slip st in first dc; ch 3, (2 dc in next dc, dc in next dc) twice, skip next 2 ch-2 sps, dc in next dc, ★ (2 dc in next dc, dc in next dc) 4 times, skip next 2 ch-2 sps, dc in next dc; repeat from ★ across to last 4 dc, (2 dc in next dc, dc in next dc) twice; finish off.

Row 5: With **right** side facing, join Color A with slip st in first dc; ch 3, dc in same st as joining and in next 3 dc, decrease 3 times, dc in next 3 dc, ★ 3 dc in next dc, dc in next 3 dc, decrease 3 times, dc in next 3 dc; repeat from ★ across to last dc, 2 dc in last dc; finish off.

Repeat Rows 2-5 for pattern.

TUMBLING BOXES

Note: Uses MC and CC in the follow sequence: 2 Rows MC, ★ 6 rows **each** CC, MC; repeat from ★ for stripe sequence.

With MC, chain a multiple of 16 chs.

Row 1 (Right side)**:** Working in back ridges of beginning ch *(Fig. 1, page 159)*, sc in second ch from hook and in next 6 chs, 3 sc in next ch, sc in next 7 chs, ★ skip next ch, sc in next 7 chs, 3 sc in next ch, sc in next 7 chs; repeat from ★ across; finish off.

Note: Loop a short piece of yarn around any stitch to mark Row 1 as **right** side.

Rows 2: With **right** side facing, join MC with sc in first sc *(see Joining With Sc, page 158)*; skip next sc, sc in next 6 sc, 3 sc in next sc, ★ sc in next 7 sc, skip next 2 sc, sc in next 7 sc, 3 sc in next sc; repeat from ★ across to last 8 sc, sc in next 6 sc, skip next sc, sc in last sc; finish off.

To work Front Post double crochet *(abbreviated FPdc)*, YO, insert hook from **front** to **back** around post of st indicated *(Fig. 4, page 159)*, YO and pull up a loop (3 loops on hook), (YO and draw through 2 loops on hook) twice. Skip st **behind** FPdc just made.

Row 3: With **right** side facing, join CC with sc in first sc; skip next sc, sc in next 5 sc, work FPdc around sc one row **below** next sc (first sc of 3-sc group), 3 sc in next sc, work FPdc around sc one row **below** next sc (third sc of 3-sc group), ★ sc in next 6 sc, skip next 2 sc, sc in next 6 sc, work FPdc around sc one row **below** next sc (first sc of 3-sc group), 3 sc in next sc, work FPdc around sc one row **below** next sc (third sc of 3-sc group); repeat from ★ across to last 7 sc, sc in next 5 sc, skip next sc, sc in last sc; finish off.

Row 4: With **right** side facing, join CC with sc in first sc; skip next sc, sc in next 4 sc, work FPdc around next FPdc, sc in next sc, 3 sc in next sc, sc in next sc, work FPdc around next FPdc, ★ sc in next 5 sc, skip next 2 sc, sc in next 5 sc, work FPdc around next FPdc, sc in next sc, 3 sc in next sc, sc in next sc, work FPdc around next FPdc; repeat from ★ across to last 6 sc, sc in next 4 sc, skip next sc, sc in last sc; finish off.

Row 5: With **right** side facing, join CC with sc in first sc; skip next sc, sc in next 3 sc, work FPdc around next FPdc, sc in next 2 sc, 3 sc in next sc, sc in next 2 sc, work FPdc around next FPdc, ★ sc in next 4 sc, skip next 2 sc, sc in next 4 sc, work FPdc around next FPdc, sc in next 2 sc, 3 sc in next sc, sc in next 2 sc, work FPdc around next FPdc; repeat from ★ across to last 5 sc, sc in next 3 sc, skip next sc, sc in last sc; finish off.

Row 6: With **right** side facing, join CC with sc in first sc; skip next sc, sc in next 2 sc, work FPdc around next FPdc, sc in next 3 sc, 3 sc in next sc, sc in next 3 sc, work FPdc around next FPdc, ★ sc in next 3 sc, skip next 2 sc, sc in next 3 sc, work FPdc around next FPdc, sc in next 3 sc, 3 sc in next sc, sc in next 3 sc, work FPdc around next FPdc; repeat from ★ across to last 4 sc, sc in next 2 sc, skip next sc, sc in last sc; finish off.

Row 7: With **right** side facing, join CC with sc in first sc; skip next sc, sc in next sc, work FPdc around next FPdc, sc in next 4 sc, 3 sc in next sc, sc in next 4 sc, work FPdc around next FPdc, ★ sc in next 2 sc, skip next 2 sc, sc in next 2 sc, work FPdc around next FPdc, sc in next 4 sc, 3 sc in next sc, sc in next 4 sc, work FPdc around next FPdc; repeat from ★ across to last 3 sc, sc in next sc, skip next sc, sc in last sc; finish off.

Row 8: With **right** side facing, join CC with sc in first sc; skip next sc, FPdc around next FPdc, sc in next 5 sc, 3 sc in next sc, sc in next 5 sc, work FPdc around next FPdc, ★ sc in next sc, skip next 2 sc, sc in next sc, work FPdc around next FPdc, sc in next 5 sc, 3 sc in next sc, sc in next 5 sc, work FPdc around next FPdc; repeat from ★ across to last 2 sc, skip next sc, sc in last sc; finish off.

Rows 9-14: With **right** side facing, join MC with sc in first sc; skip next st, sc in next 6 sts, 3 sc in next sc, ★ sc in next 7 sts, skip next 2 sc, sc in next 7 sts, 3 sc in next sc; repeat from ★ across to last 8 sts, sc in next 6 sc, skip next st, sc in last sc; finish off.

Repeat Rows 3-14 for pattern.

75 ALTERNATING WAVES

Note: Uses MC and CC in the following sequence: ★ 2 Rows **each** MC, CC; repeat from ★ for stripe sequence.

With MC, chain a multiple of 8 + 2 chs.

Row 1 (Right side)**:** Sc in second ch from hook and in next ch, hdc in next ch, dc in next 3 chs, hdc in next ch, ★ sc in next 3 chs, hdc in next ch, dc in next 3 chs, hdc in next ch; repeat from ★ across to last 2 chs, sc in last 2 chs.

Note: Loop a short piece of yarn around any stitch to mark Row 1 as **right** side.

Row 2: Ch 1, turn; sc in each st across; finish off.

Row 3: With **right** side facing, join CC with slip st in first sc; ch 3 **(counts as first dc)**, dc in next sc, hdc in next sc, sc in next 3 sc, hdc in next sc, ★ dc in next 3 sc, hdc in next sc, sc in next 3 sc, hdc in next sc; repeat from ★ across to last 2 sc, dc in last 2 sc.

Row 4: Ch 1, turn; sc in each st across; finish off.

Row 5: With **right** side facing, join MC with sc in first sc *(see Joining With Sc, page 158)*; sc in next sc, hdc in next sc, dc in next 3 sc, hdc in next sc, ★ sc in next 3 sc, hdc in next sc, dc in next 3 sc, hdc in next sc; repeat from ★ across to last 2 sc, sc in last 2 sc.

Repeat Rows 2-5 for pattern.

76 RELAXATION

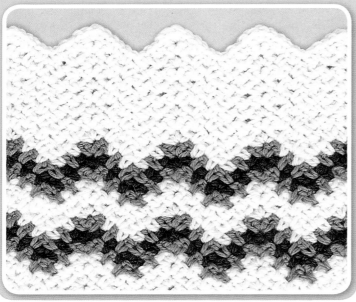

Note: Uses MC and Colors A and B in the following sequence: ★ 9 Rows MC, 1 row **each** Color A, Color B, Color A, 3 rows MC, 1 row **each** Color A, Color B, Color A; repeat from ★ for stripe sequence.

With MC, chain a multiple of 11 + 2 chs.

Row 1 (Right side): Working in back ridges of beginning ch *(Fig. 1, page 159)*, 2 sc in second ch from hook, (ch 1, skip next ch, sc in next ch) twice, skip next 2 chs, (sc in next ch, ch 1, skip next ch) twice, ★ 3 sc in next ch, (ch 1, skip next ch, sc in next ch) twice, skip next 2 chs, (sc in next ch, ch 1, skip next ch) twice; repeat from ★ across to last ch, 2 sc in last ch.

Note: Loop a short piece of yarn around any stitch to mark Row 1 as **right** side.

Rows 2-9: Ch 1, turn; 2 sc in first sc, (ch 1, sc in next ch-1 sp) twice, skip next 2 sc, (sc in next ch-1 sp, ch 1) twice, ★ skip next sc, 3 sc in next sc, (ch 1, sc in next ch-1 sp) twice, skip next 2 sc, (sc in next ch-1 sp, ch 1) twice; repeat from ★ across to last 2 sc, skip next sc, 2 sc in last sc; at end of last row, finish off.

Row 10: With **wrong** side facing, join Color A with sc in first sc *(see Joining With Sc, page 158)*; sc in same st as joining, (ch 1, sc in next ch-1 sp) twice, skip next 2 sc, (sc in next ch-1 sp, ch 1) twice, ★ skip next sc, 3 sc in next sc, (ch 1, sc in next ch-1 sp) twice, skip next 2 sc, (sc in next ch-1 sp, ch 1) twice; repeat from ★ across to last 2 sc, skip next sc, 2 sc in last sc; finish off.

Row 11: With **right** side facing, join Color B with sc in first sc; sc in same st as joining, (ch 1, sc in next ch-1 sp) twice, skip next 2 sc, (sc in next ch-1 sp, ch 1) twice, ★ skip next sc, 3 sc in next sc, (ch 1, sc in next ch-1 sp) twice, skip next 2 sc, (sc in next ch-1 sp, ch 1) twice; repeat from ★ across to last 2 sc, skip next sc, 2 sc in last sc; finish off.

Row 12: With **wrong** side facing, join Color A with sc in first sc; sc in same st as joining, (ch 1, sc in next ch-1 sp) twice, skip next 2 sc, (sc in next ch-1 sp, ch 1) twice, ★ skip next sc, 3 sc in next sc, (ch 1, sc in next ch-1 sp) twice, skip next 2 sc, (sc in next ch-1 sp, ch 1) twice; repeat from ★ across to last 2 sc, skip next sc, 2 sc in last sc; finish off.

Row 13: With **right** side facing, join MC with sc in first sc; sc in same st as joining, (ch 1, sc in next ch-1 sp) twice, skip next 2 sc, (sc in next ch-1 sp, ch 1) twice, ★ skip next sc, 3 sc in next sc, (ch 1, sc in next ch-1 sp) twice, skip next 2 sc, (sc in next ch-1 sp, ch 1) twice; repeat from ★ across to last 2 sc, skip next sc, 2 sc in last sc.

Rows 14 and 15: Ch 1, turn; 2 sc in first sc, (ch 1, sc in next ch-1 sp) twice, skip next 2 sc, (sc in next ch-1 sp, ch 1) twice, ★ skip next sc, 3 sc in next sc, (ch 1, sc in next ch-1 sp) twice, skip next 2 sc, (sc in next ch-1 sp, ch 1) twice; repeat from ★ across to last 2 sc, skip next sc, 2 sc in last sc; at end of last row, finish off.

Rows 16-18: Repeat Rows 10-12.

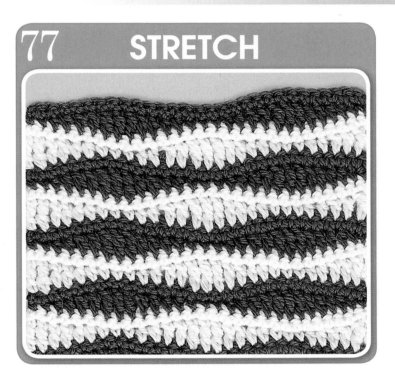

Note: Uses MC and CC in the following sequence: ★ 2 Rows **each** MC, CC; repeat from ★ for stripe sequence.

With MC, chain a multiple of 14 + 2 chs.

To treble crochet *(abbreviated tr)*, YO twice, insert hook in st indicated, YO and pull up a loop (4 loops on hook), (YO and draw through 2 loops on hook) 3 times.

Row 19: With **right** side facing, join MC with sc in first sc; sc in same st as joining, (ch 1, sc in next ch-1 sp) twice, skip next 2 sc, (sc in next ch-1 sp, ch 1) twice, ★ skip next sc, 3 sc in next sc, (ch 1, sc in next ch-1 sp) twice, skip next 2 sc, (sc in next ch-1 sp, ch 1) twice; repeat from ★ across to last 2 sc, skip next sc, 2 sc in last sc.

Repeat Rows 2-19 for pattern.

Row 1 (Right side)**:** Sc in second ch from hook and in next ch, hdc in next 2 chs, dc in next 2 chs, tr in next 3 chs, dc in next 2 chs, hdc in next 2 chs, ★ sc in next 3 chs, hdc in next 2 chs, dc in next 2 chs, tr in next 3 chs, dc in next 2 chs, hdc in next 2 chs; repeat from ★ across to last 2 chs, sc in last 2 chs.

Note: Loop a short piece of yarn around any stitch to mark Row 1 as **right** side.

Row 2: Ch 1, turn; sc in each st across; finish off.

Row 3: With **right** side facing, join CC with slip st in first sc; ch 4 **(counts as first tr)**, tr in next sc, dc in next 2 sc, hdc in next 2 sc, sc in next 3 sc, hdc in next 2 sc, dc in next 2 sc, ★ tr in next 3 sc, dc in next 2 sc, hdc in next 2 sc, sc in next 3 sc, hdc in next 2 sc, dc in next 2 sc; repeat from ★ across to last 2 sc, tr in last 2 sc.

Row 4: Ch 1, turn; sc in each st across; finish off.

Row 5: With **right** side facing, join MC with sc in first sc *(see Joining With Sc, page 158)*; sc in next sc, hdc in next 2 sc, dc in next 2 sc, tr in next 3 sc, dc in next 2 sc, hdc in next 2 sc, ★ sc in next 3 sc, hdc in next 2 sc, dc in next 2 sc, tr in next 3 sc, dc in next 2 sc, hdc in next 2 sc; repeat from ★ across to last 2 sc, sc in last 2 sc.

Repeat Rows 2-5 for pattern.

HAPPY HORIZONS

Chain a multiple of 38 + 2 chs.

To decrease (uses next 2 sts), ★ YO, insert hook in **next** st, YO and pull up a loop, YO and draw through 2 loops on hook; repeat from ★ once **more**, YO and draw through all 3 loops on hook **(counts as one dc)**.

To double crochet 5 together (abbreviated *dc5tog*), ★ YO, insert hook in **next** st, YO and pull up a loop, YO and draw through 2 loops on hook; repeat from ★ 4 times **more**, YO and draw through all 6 loops on hook **(counts as one dc)**.

Row 1 (Right side)**:** Dc in third ch from hook and in next 9 chs, ch 2, skip next 2 chs, dc in next 3 chs, ch 1, skip next 3 chs, (3 dc, ch 3, 3 dc) in next ch, ch 1, skip next 3 chs, dc in next 3 chs, ★ ch 2, skip next 2 chs, dc in next 8 chs, dc5tog, dc in next 8 chs, ch 2, skip next 2 chs, dc in next 3 chs, ch 1, skip next 3 chs, (3 dc, ch 3, 3 dc) in next ch, ch 1, skip next 3 chs, dc in next 3 chs; repeat from ★ across to last 13 chs, ch 2, skip next 2 chs, dc in next 9 chs, decrease.

Note: Loop a short piece of yarn around any stitch to mark Row 1 as **right** side.

To treble crochet (abbreviated *tr*), YO twice, insert hook in st or sp indicated, YO and pull up a loop (4 loops on hook), (YO and draw through 2 loops on hook) 3 times.

To double decrease (uses next 3 sts), ★ YO, insert hook in **next** st, YO and pull up a loop, YO and draw through 2 loops on hook; repeat from ★ 2 times **more**, YO and draw through all 4 loops on hook **(counts as one dc)**.

Row 2: Ch 2, turn; decrease, dc in next 7 dc, 2 dc in next ch-2 sp, ch 2, skip next 2 dc, dc in next dc, working **behind** next ch *(Fig. 6, page 159)*, tr in center skipped ch one row **below**, dc in next dc, ch 1, (3 dc, ch 3, 3 dc) in next ch-3 sp, ch 1, skip next 2 dc, dc in next dc, working **behind** next ch, tr in center skipped ch one row **below**, dc in next dc, ch 2, 2 dc in next ch-2 sp, ★ dc in next 6 dc, dc5tog, dc in next 6 dc, 2 dc in next ch-2 sp, ch 2, skip next 2 dc, dc in next dc, working **behind** next ch, tr in center skipped ch one row **below**, dc in next dc, ch 1, (3 dc, ch 3, 3 dc) in next ch-3 sp, ch 1, skip next 2 dc, dc in next dc, working **behind** next ch, tr in center skipped ch one row **below**, dc in next dc, ch 2, 2 dc in next ch-2 sp; repeat from ★ across to last 10 dc, dc in next 7 dc, double decrease.

To Front Post treble crochet (abbreviated *FPtr*), YO twice, working in **front** of previous row, insert hook from **front** to **back** around post of st indicated *(Fig. 4, page 159)*, YO and pull up a loop (4 loops on hook), (YO and draw through 2 loops on hook) 3 times.

Row 3: Ch 2, turn; decrease, dc in next 7 dc, 2 dc in next ch-2 sp, ch 2, skip next 2 sts, dc in next dc, work FPtr around center dc of 3-dc group one row **below** next ch, dc in next dc, ch 1, (3 dc, ch 3, 3 dc) in next ch-3 sp, ch 1, skip next 2 dc, dc in next dc, work FPtr around center dc of 3-dc group one row **below** next ch, dc in next dc, ch 2, 2 dc in next ch-2 sp, ★ dc in next 6 dc, dc5tog, dc in next 6 dc, 2 dc in next ch-2 sp, ch 2, skip next 2 sts, dc in next dc, work FPtr around center dc of 3-dc group one row **below** next ch, dc in next dc, ch 1, (3 dc, ch 3, 3 dc) in next ch-3 sp, ch 1, skip next 2 dc, dc in next dc, work FPtr around center dc of 3-dc group one row **below** next ch, dc in next dc, ch 2, 2 dc in next ch-2 sp; repeat from ★ across to last 10 dc, dc in next 7 dc, double decrease.

To Back Post treble crochet (abbreviated *BPtr*), YO twice, working **behind** previous row, insert hook from **back** to **front** around post of st indicated *(Fig. 4, page 159)*, YO and pull up a loop (4 loops on hook), (YO and draw through 2 loops on hook) 3 times.

Row 4: Ch 2, turn; decrease, dc in next 7 dc, 2 dc in next ch-2 sp, ch 2, skip next 2 sts, dc in next dc, work BPtr around center dc of 3-dc group one row **below** next ch, dc in next dc, ch 1, (3 dc, ch 3, 3 dc) in next ch-3 sp, ch 1, skip next 2 dc, dc in next dc, work BPtr around center dc of 3-dc group one row **below** next ch, dc in next dc, ch 2, 2 dc in next ch-2 sp, ★ dc in next 6 dc, dc5tog, dc in next 6 dc, 2 dc in next ch-2 sp, ch 2, skip next 2 sts, dc in next dc, work BPtr around center dc of 3-dc group one row **below** next ch, dc in next dc, ch 1, (3 dc, ch 3, 3 dc) in next ch-3 sp, ch 1, skip next 2 dc, dc in next dc, work BPtr around center dc of 3-dc group one row **below** next ch, dc in next dc, ch 2, 2 dc in next ch-2 sp; repeat from ★ across to last 10 dc, dc in next 7 dc, double decrease.

Repeat Rows 3 and 4 for pattern.

CHILD'S PLAY

Note: Uses Colors A, B, and C in the following sequence: ★ 1 Row **each** Color A, Color B, Color C; repeat from ★ for stripe sequence.

With Color A, chain a multiple of 6 + 4 chs.

To treble crochet *(abbreviated tr)*, YO twice, insert hook in st indicated, YO and pull up a loop (4 loops on hook), (YO and draw through 2 loops on hook) 3 times.

Row 1 (Right side)**:** Dc in fifth ch from hook **(4 skipped chs count as first tr)**, hdc in next ch, sc in next ch, hdc in next ch, dc in next ch, tr in next ch, ★ dc in next ch, hdc in next ch, sc in next ch, hdc in next ch, dc in next ch, tr in next ch; repeat from ★ across; finish off.

Note: Loop a short piece of yarn around any stitch to mark Row 1 as **right** side.

Row 2: With **wrong** side facing, join Color B with sc in first tr ***(see Joining With Sc, page 158)***; ★ hdc in next dc, dc in next hdc, tr in next sc, dc in next hdc, hdc in next dc, sc in next tr; repeat from ★ across; finish off.

Row 3: With **right** side facing, join Color C with slip st in first sc; ch 4 **(counts as first tr)**, ★ dc in next hdc, hdc in next dc, sc in next tr, hdc in next dc, dc in next hdc, tr in next sc; repeat from ★ across; finish off.

Repeat Rows 2 and 3 for pattern, working in stripe sequence.

80 QUICK & EASY CHEVRONS

81 DEEP CHEVRONS

Chain a multiple of 8 + 3 chs.

To decrease (uses next 2 sts), ★ YO, insert hook in **next** st, YO and pull up a loop, YO and draw through 2 loops on hook; repeat from ★ once **more**, YO and draw through all 3 loops on hook.

Row 1 (Right side)**:** Dc in fourth ch from hook **(3 skipped chs count as first dc)** and in next ch, decrease twice, dc in next ch, ★ 2 dc in each of next 2 chs, dc in next ch, decrease twice, dc in next ch; repeat from ★ across to last ch, 2 dc in last ch.

Note: Loop a short piece of yarn around any stitch to mark Row 1 as **right** side.

Row 2: Ch 3 **(counts as first dc)**, turn; dc in first 2 dc, decrease twice, dc in next dc, ★ 2 dc in each of next 2 dc, dc in next dc, decrease twice, dc in next dc; repeat from ★ across to last dc, 2 dc in last dc.

Repeat Row 2 for pattern.

Chain a multiple of 14 + 3 chs.

To decrease (uses next 3 sts), ★ YO, insert hook in **next** st, YO and pull up a loop, YO and draw through 2 loops on hook; repeat from ★ 2 times **more**, YO and draw through all 4 loops on hook.

Row 1 (Right side)**:** 2 Dc in fourth ch from hook **(3 skipped chs count as first dc)**, dc in next 3 chs, decrease twice, dc in next 3 chs, ★ 3 dc in each of next 2 chs, dc in next 3 chs, decrease twice, dc in next 3 chs; repeat from ★ across to last ch, 3 dc in last ch.

Note: Loop a short piece of yarn around any stitch to mark Row 1 as **right** side.

Row 2: Ch 3 **(counts as first dc)**, turn; 2 dc in first dc, dc in next 3 dc, decrease twice, dc in next 3 dc, ★ 3 dc in each of next 2 dc, dc in next 3 dc, decrease twice, dc in next 3 dc; repeat from ★ across to last dc, 3 dc in last dc.

Repeat Row 2 for pattern.

82 SPACED POPCORNS CHEVRON

Note: Uses MC and Colors A and B in the following sequence: ★ 3 Rows MC, 2 rows Color A, 1 row Color B, 1 row Color A, 1 row Color B, 2 rows Color A; repeat from ★ for stripe sequence.

With MC, chain a multiple of 9 + 3 chs.

Row 1 (Right side)**:** Sc in second ch from hook and in next 4 chs, 3 sc in next ch, ★ sc in next 3 chs, skip next 2 chs, sc in next 3 chs, 3 sc in next ch; repeat from ★ across to last 5 chs, sc in last 5 chs.

Note: Loop a short piece of yarn around any stitch to mark Row 1 as **right** side.

Rows 2 and 3: Ch 1, turn; sc in first sc, skip next sc, sc in next 4 sc, 3 sc in next sc, ★ sc in next 3 sc, skip next 2 sc, sc in next 3 sc, 3 sc in next sc; repeat from ★ across to last 6 sc, sc in next 4 sc, skip next sc, sc in last sc; at end of last row, finish off.

Row 4: With **wrong** side facing, join Color A with sc in first sc *(see Joining With Sc, page 158)*; skip next sc, sc in next 4 sc, 3 sc in next sc, ★ sc in next 3 sc, skip next 2 sc, sc in next 3 sc, 3 sc in next sc; repeat from ★ across to last 6 sc, sc in next 4 sc, skip next sc, sc in last sc.

Row 5: Ch 1, turn; sc in first sc, skip next sc, sc in next 4 sc, 3 sc in next sc, ★ sc in next 3 sc, skip next 2 sc, sc in next 3 sc, 3 sc in next sc; repeat from ★ across to last 6 sc, sc in next 4 sc, skip next sc, sc in last sc; finish off.

Row 6: With **wrong** side facing, join Color B with sc in first sc; skip next sc, sc in next 4 sc, 3 sc in next sc, ★ sc in next 3 sc, skip next 2 sc, sc in next 3 sc, 3 sc in next sc; repeat from ★ across to last 6 sc, sc in next 4 sc, skip next sc, sc in last sc; finish off.

To work Popcorn (uses one st), 4 dc in st indicated, drop loop from hook, insert hook from **front** to **back** in first dc of 4-dc group, hook dropped loop and draw through st.

To decrease (uses next 2 sc), ★ YO, insert hook in **next** sc, YO and pull up a loop, YO and draw through 2 loops on hook; repeat from ★ once **more**, YO and draw through all 3 loops on hook **(counts as one dc)**.

To double crochet 4 together (abbreviated dc4tog), ★ YO, insert hook in **next** sc, YO and pull up a loop, YO and draw through 2 loops on hook; repeat from ★ 3 times **more**, YO and draw through all 5 loops on hook **(counts as one dc)**.

Row 7: With **right** side facing, join Color A with slip st in first sc; ch 2, dc in next sc, decrease, work Popcorn in next sc, dc in next sc, 3 dc in next sc, dc in next sc, work Popcorn in next sc, ★ dc4tog, work Popcorn in next sc, dc in next sc, 3 dc in next sc, dc in next sc, work Popcorn in next sc; repeat from ★ across to last 4 sc, decrease twice; finish off.

Row 8: With **wrong** side facing, join Color B with sc in first dc; sc in next 4 sts, 3 sc in next dc, ★ sc in next 3 sts, skip next dc, sc in next 3 sts, 3 sc in next dc; repeat from ★ across to last 5 sts, sc in last 5 sts; finish off.

Row 9: With **right** side facing, join Color A with sc in first sc; skip next sc, sc in next 4 sc, 3 sc in next sc, ★ sc in next 3 sc, skip next 2 sc, sc in next 3 sc, 3 sc in next sc; repeat from ★ across to last 6 sc, sc in next 4 sc, skip next sc, sc in last sc.

Row 10: Ch 1, turn; sc in first sc, skip next sc, sc in next 4 sc, 3 sc in next sc, ★ sc in next 3 sc, skip next 2 sc, sc in next 3 sc, 3 sc in next sc; repeat from ★ across to last 6 sc, sc in next 4 sc, skip next sc, sc in last sc; finish off.

Row 11: With **right** side facing, join MC with sc in first sc; skip next sc, sc in next 4 sc, 3 sc in next sc, ★ sc in next 3 sc, skip next 2 sc, sc in next 3 sc, 3 sc in next sc; repeat from ★ across to last 6 sc, sc in next 4 sc, skip next sc, sc in last sc.

Repeat Rows 2-11 for pattern.

83 ELATION

Note: Uses MC and CC in the following sequence: 1 Row MC, ★ 4 rows **each** CC, MC; repeat from ★ for stripe sequence.

With MC, chain a multiple of 8 + 4 chs.

Row 1 (Right side)**:** 3 Dc in fourth ch from hook **(3 skipped chs count as first dc)**, skip next 3 chs, sc in next ch, ★ skip next 3 chs, 7 dc in next ch, skip next 3 chs, sc in next ch; repeat from ★ across to last 4 chs, skip next 3 chs, 4 dc in last ch; finish off.

Note: Loop a short piece of yarn around any stitch to mark Row 1 as **right** side.

Row 2: With **wrong** side facing, join CC with sc in first dc *(see Joining With Sc, page 158)*; ★ ch 3, skip next 3 dc, dc in next sc, ch 3, skip next 3 dc, sc in next dc; repeat from ★ across.

Rows 3 and 4: Ch 1, turn; sc in first sc, ★ ch 3, skip next 3 chs, sc in next st; repeat from ★ across.

Row 5: Ch 1, turn; sc in first sc, ★ skip next 3 chs, 7 dc in next sc, skip next 3 chs, sc in next sc; repeat from ★ across; finish off.

Row 6: With **wrong** side facing, join MC with slip st in first sc; ch 6 **(counts as first dc plus ch 3)**, skip next 3 dc, sc in next dc, ch 3, skip next 3 dc, dc in next sc, ★ ch 3, skip next 3 dc, sc in next dc, ch 3, skip next 3 dc, dc in next sc; repeat from ★ across.

Rows 7 and 8: Ch 1, turn; sc in first sc, ★ ch 3, skip next 3 chs, sc in next st; repeat from ★ across.

Row 9: Ch 3 **(counts as first dc)**, turn; 3 dc in first sc, skip next 3 chs, sc in next sc, ★ skip next 3 chs, 7 dc in next sc, skip next 3 chs, sc in next sc; repeat from ★ across to last 4 sts, skip next 3 chs, 4 dc in last sc; finish off.

Repeat Rows 2-9 for pattern.

84 REGAL WAVES

Note: Uses MC and CC in the following sequence: ★ 3 Rows **each** MC, CC; repeat from ★ for stripe sequence.

With MC, chain a multiple of 12 + 8 chs.

Row 1 (Right side)**:** Sc in 12th ch from hook **(11 skipped chs count as first dc plus ch 5 and 3 skipped chs)**, ch 5, skip next 3 chs, sc in next ch, ch 5, skip next 3 chs, dc in next ch, ★ ch 5, skip next 3 chs, (sc in next ch, ch 5, skip next 3 chs) twice, dc in next ch; repeat from ★ across.

Note: Loop a short piece of yarn around any stitch to mark Row 1 as **right** side.

Row 2: Ch 5 **(counts as first dc plus ch 2)**, turn; sc in next ch-5 sp, 8 dc in next ch-5 sp, sc in next ch-5 sp, ★ ch 5, sc in next ch-5 sp, 8 dc in next ch-5 sp, sc in next ch-5 sp; repeat from ★ across to last dc, ch 2, dc in last dc.

To work Picot, ch 3, slip st in third ch from hook.

Row 3: Ch 1, turn; sc in first dc, skip next ch-2 sp and next sc, dc in next dc, (work Picot, dc in next dc) 7 times, ★ sc in next ch-5 sp, skip next sc, dc in next dc, (work Picot, dc in next dc) 7 times; repeat from ★ across to last ch-2 sp, skip last ch-2 sp, sc in last dc; finish off.

Row 4: With **right** side facing, join CC with slip st in first sc; ch 8 **(counts as first dc plus ch 5)**, skip next 2 Picots, sc in next Picot, ch 5, skip next Picot, sc in next Picot, ch 5, skip next 2 Picots and next dc, dc in next sc, ★ ch 5, skip next 2 Picots, sc in next Picot, ch 5, skip next Picot, sc in next Picot, ch 5, skip next 2 Picots and next dc, dc in next sc; repeat from ★ across.

Repeat Rows 2-4 for pattern, working in stripe sequence.

85 GUACAMOLE DIP

Note: Uses Colors A, B, and C in the following sequence: 5 Rows Color A, ★ 2 rows Color B, 4 rows Color C, 2 rows Color B, 4 rows Color A; repeat from ★ for stripe sequence.

With Color A, chain a multiple of 23 + 3 chs.

Row 1 (Right side)**:** Sc in second ch from hook and in each ch across.

Note: Loop a short piece of yarn around any stitch to mark Row 1 as **right** side.

To work Cluster (uses one st or sp)**,** ★ YO, insert hook in st or sp indicated, YO and pull up a loop, YO and draw through 2 loops on hook; repeat from ★ 2 times **more**, YO and draw through all 4 loops on hook.

Row 2: Ch 3 **(counts as first dc, now and throughout)**, turn; skip first 3 sc, (3 dc in next sc, skip next 2 sc) 3 times, (3 dc, ch 3, 3 dc) in next sc, ★ (skip next 2 sc, 3 dc in next sc) twice, skip next 2 sc, work Cluster in next sc, skip next 4 sc, work Cluster in next sc, skip next 2 sc, (3 dc in next sc, skip next 2 sc) twice, (3 dc, ch 3, 3 dc) in next sc; repeat from ★ across to last 12 sc, (skip next 2 sc, 3 dc in next sc) 3 times, skip next 2 sc, dc in last sc.

Rows 3-5: Ch 3, turn; **[**skip next 3 dc, 3 dc in sp **before** next dc **(Fig. 5, page 159)]** 3 times, (3 dc, ch 3, 3 dc) in next ch-3 sp, ★ (skip next 3 dc, 3 dc in sp **before** next dc) twice, skip next 3 dc, work Cluster in sp **before** next Cluster, skip next 2 Clusters, work Cluster in sp **before** next dc, (skip next 3 dc, 3 dc in sp **before** next dc) twice, (3 dc, ch 3, 3 dc) in next ch-3 sp; repeat from ★ across to last 13 dc, (skip next 3 dc, 3 dc in sp **before** next dc) 3 times, skip next 3 dc, dc in last dc; at end of last row, finish off.

To double decrease (uses next 3 dc)**,** ★ YO, insert hook in **next** dc, YO and pull up a loop, YO and draw through 2 loops on hook; repeat from ★ 2 times **more**, YO and draw through all 4 loops on hook **(counts as one dc)**.

Row 6: With **wrong** side facing, join Color B with slip st in first dc; ch 3, double decrease, dc in next 9 dc, 3 dc in next ch-3 sp, dc in next 9 dc, ★ skip next 2 Clusters, dc in next 9 dc, 3 dc in next ch-3 sp, dc in next 9 dc; repeat from ★ across to last 4 dc, double decrease, dc in last dc.

To decrease (uses next 2 dc)**,** ★ YO, insert hook in **next** dc, YO and pull up a loop, YO and draw through 2 loops on hook; repeat from ★ once **more**, YO and draw through all 3 loops on hook **(counts as one dc)**.

Row 7: Ch 3, turn; decrease, dc in next 9 dc, 3 dc in next dc, dc in next 9 dc, ★ skip next 2 dc, dc in next 9 dc, 3 dc in next dc, dc in next 9 dc; repeat from ★ across to last 3 dc, decrease, dc in last dc; finish off.

Row 8: With **wrong** side facing, join Color C with slip st in first dc; ch 3, skip next 2 dc, (3 dc in next dc, skip next 2 dc) 3 times, (3 dc, ch 3, 3 dc) in next dc, ★ skip next 2 dc, (3 dc in next dc, skip next 2 dc) twice, (work Cluster in next dc, skip next 2 dc) twice, (3 dc in next dc, skip next 2 dc) twice, (3 dc, ch 3, 3 dc) in next dc; repeat from ★ across to last 12 dc, skip next 2 dc, (3 dc in next dc, skip next 2 dc) 3 times, dc in last dc.

Repeat Rows 3-8 for pattern, working in stripe sequence.

Note: Uses MC and CC in the following sequence: ★ 1 Row **each** MC, CC; repeat from ★ for stripe sequence.

With MC, chain a multiple of 26 + 2 chs.

To treble crochet (abbreviated tr), YO twice, insert hook in st indicated, YO and pull up a loop (4 loops on hook), (YO and draw through 2 loops on hook) 3 times.

Row 1 (Right side)**:** Sc in second ch from hook, (ch 1, skip next ch, sc in next ch) 3 times, ch 1, skip next ch, hdc in next ch, ch 1, skip next ch, dc in next ch, ch 1, skip next ch, (tr, ch 1) twice in next ch, tr in next ch, ch 1, (tr, ch 1) twice in next ch, skip next ch, dc in next ch, ch 1, skip next ch, hdc in next ch, ★ (ch 1, skip next ch, sc in next ch) 7 times, ch 1, skip next ch, hdc in next ch, ch 1, skip next ch, dc in next ch, ch 1, skip next ch, (tr, ch 1) twice in next ch, tr in next ch, ch 1, (tr, ch 1) twice in next ch, skip next ch, dc in next ch, ch 1, skip next ch, hdc in next ch; repeat from ★ across to last 8 chs, (ch 1, skip next ch, sc in next ch) 4 times; finish off.

Note: Loop a short piece of yarn around any stitch to mark Row 1 as **right** side.

Row 2: With **wrong** side facing, join CC with sc in first sc *(see Joining With Sc, page 158)*; ★ ch 1, skip next ch, sc in next st; repeat from ★ across; finish off.

Row 3: With **right** side facing, join MC with slip st in first sc; ch 4 **(counts as first tr)**, (skip next ch, tr in next sc) twice, ch 1, skip next ch, dc in next sc, ch 1, skip next ch, hdc in next sc, (ch 1, skip next ch, sc in next sc) 7 times, ch 1, skip next ch, hdc in next sc, ch 1, skip next ch, dc in next sc, ch 1, ★ (skip next ch, tr in next sc) 5 times, ch 1, skip next ch, dc in next sc, ch 1, skip next ch, hdc in next sc, (ch 1, skip next ch, sc in next sc) 7 times, ch 1, skip next ch, hdc in next sc, ch 1, skip next ch, dc in next sc, ch 1; repeat from ★ across to last 6 sts, (skip next ch, tr in next sc) 3 times; finish off.

Row 4: With **wrong** side facing, join CC with sc in first tr; ★ ch 1, skip next st, sc in next st; repeat from ★ across; finish off.

Row 5: With **right** side facing, join MC with sc in first sc; (ch 1, skip next ch, sc in next sc) 3 times, ch 1, skip next ch, hdc in next sc, ch 1, skip next ch, dc in next sc, ch 1, skip next ch, tr in next sc, ch 1, (tr in next ch-1 sp, ch 1, tr in next sc, ch 1) twice, skip next ch, dc in next sc, ch 1, skip next ch, hdc in next sc, ★ (ch 1, skip next ch, sc in next sc) 7 times, ch 1, skip next ch, hdc in next sc, ch 1, skip next ch, dc in next sc, ch 1, skip next ch, tr in next sc, ch 1, (tr in next ch-1 sp, ch 1, tr in next sc, ch 1) twice, skip next ch, dc in next sc, ch 1, skip next ch, hdc in next sc; repeat from ★ across to last 8 sts, (ch 1, skip next ch, sc in next sc) 4 times; finish off.

Repeat Rows 2-5 for pattern.

87 SHARP MINI SHELL CHEVRON

Note: Uses MC and CC in the following sequence: ★ 2 Rows **each** MC, CC; repeat from ★ for stripe sequence.

With MC, chain a multiple of 34 + 2 chs.

Row 1 (Right side)**:** Sc in second ch from hook, skip next ch, [(sc, ch 2, sc) in next ch, skip next 2 chs] 5 times, (sc, ch 2, sc, ch 3, sc, ch 2, sc) in next ch, ★ skip next 2 chs, [(sc, ch 2, sc) in next ch, skip next 2 chs] 4 times, sc in next ch, skip next 3 chs, sc in next ch, skip next 2 chs, [(sc, ch 2, sc) in next ch, skip next 2 chs] 4 times, (sc, ch 2, sc, ch 3, sc, ch 2, sc) in next ch; repeat from ★ across to last 17 chs, [skip next 2 chs, (sc, ch 2, sc) in next ch] 5 times, skip next ch, dc in last ch.

Note: Loop a short piece of yarn around any stitch to mark Row 1 as **right** side.

Row 2: Ch 1, turn; sc in first dc and in next ch-2 sp, (sc, ch 2, sc) in each of next 5 ch-2 sps, (sc, ch 2, sc, ch 3, sc, ch 2, sc) in next ch-3 sp, ★ (sc, ch 2, sc) in each of next 4 ch-2 sps, sc in next ch-2 sp, skip next 4 sc, sc in next ch-2 sp, (sc, ch 2, sc) in each of next 4 ch-2 sps, (sc, ch 2, sc, ch 3, sc, ch 2, sc) in next ch-3 sp; repeat from ★ across to last 6 ch-2 sps, (sc, ch 2, sc) in each of next 5 ch-2 sps, sc in last ch-2 sp, skip next sc, dc in last sc; finish off.

Row 3: With **right** side facing, join CC with sc in first dc *(see Joining With Sc, page 158)*; sc in next ch-2 sp, (sc, ch 2, sc) in each of next 5 ch-2 sps, (sc, ch 2, sc, ch 3, sc, ch 2, sc) in next ch-3 sp, ★ (sc, ch 2, sc) in each of next 4 ch-2 sps, sc in next ch-2 sp, skip next 4 sc, sc in next ch-2 sp, (sc, ch 2, sc) in each of next 4 ch-2 sps, (sc, ch 2, sc, ch 3, sc, ch 2, sc) in next ch-3 sp; repeat from ★ across to last 6 ch-2 sps, (sc, ch 2, sc) in each of next 5 ch-2 sps, sc in last ch-2 sp, skip next 2 sc, dc in last sc.

Row 4: Ch 1, turn; sc in first dc and in next ch-2 sp, (sc, ch 2, sc) in each of next 5 ch-2 sps, (sc, ch 2, sc, ch 3, sc, ch 2, sc) in next ch-3 sp, ★ (sc, ch 2, sc) in each of next 4 ch-2 sps, sc in next ch-2 sp, skip next 4 sc, sc in next ch-2 sp, (sc, ch 2, sc) in each of next 4 ch-2 sps, (sc, ch 2, sc, ch 3, sc, ch 2, sc) in next ch-3 sp; repeat from ★ across to last 6 ch-2 sps, (sc, ch 2, sc) in each of next 5 ch-2 sps, sc in last ch-2 sp, skip next 2 sc, dc in last sc; finish off.

Repeat Rows 3 and 4 for pattern, working in stripe sequence.

88 V STITCH CHEVRON

Note: Uses MC and CC in the following sequence: ★ 2 Rows **each** MC, CC; repeat from ★ for stripe sequence.

With MC, chain a multiple of 30 + 28 chs.

Row 1 (Right side)**:** Dc in third ch from hook, [skip next 2 chs, (dc, ch 1, dc) in next ch] 3 times, skip next 2 chs, dc in next ch, (ch 1, dc in same ch) 3 times, [skip next 2 chs, (dc, ch 1, dc) in next ch] 3 times, ★ [(YO, skip **next** 2 chs, insert hook in **next** ch, YO and pull up a loop, YO and draw through 2 loops on hook) 3 times, YO and draw through all 4 loops on hook **(counts as one dc)**], [skip next 2 chs, (dc, ch 1, dc) in next ch] 3 times, skip next 2 chs, dc in next ch, (ch 1, dc in same st) 3 times, [skip next 2 chs, (dc, ch 1, dc) in next ch] 3 times; repeat from ★ across to last 4 chs, [YO, skip next 2 chs, insert hook in next ch, YO and pull up a loop, YO and draw through 2 loops on hook, YO, insert hook in last ch, YO and pull up a loop, YO and draw through 2 loops on hook, YO and draw through all 3 loops on hook **(counts as one dc)**].

Note: Loop a short piece of yarn around any stitch to mark Row 1 as **right** side.

To double decrease (uses next 2 ch-1 sps and next 3 dc), YO, insert hook in next ch-1 sp, YO and pull up a loop, YO and draw through 2 loops on hook, YO, skip next 3 dc, insert hook in next ch-1 sp, YO and pull up a loop, YO and draw through 2 loops on hook, YO and draw through all 3 loops on hook **(counts as one dc)**.

Row 2: Ch 3 **(counts as first dc, now and throughout)**, turn; [YO, insert hook in next dc, YO and pull up a loop, YO and draw through 2 loops on hook, YO, insert hook in next ch-1 sp, YO and pull up a loop, YO and draw through 2 loops on hook, YO and draw through all 3 loops on hook **(counts as one dc)**], (dc, ch 1, dc) in each of next 3 ch-1 sps, dc in next ch-1 sp, (ch 1, dc in same sp) 3 times, (dc, ch 1, dc) in each of next 3 ch-1 sps, ★ double decrease, (dc, ch 1, dc) in each of next 3 ch-1 sps, dc in next ch-1 sp, (ch 1, dc in same sp) 3 times, (dc, ch 1, dc) in each of next 3 ch-1 sps; repeat from ★ across to last ch-1 sp, [YO, insert hook in last ch-1 sp, YO and pull up a loop, YO and draw through 2 loops on hook, YO, insert hook in next dc, YO and pull up a loop, YO and draw through 2 loops on hook, YO and draw through all 3 loops on hook **(counts as one dc)**], dc in last dc; finish off.

To work beginning decrease (uses next 2 dc and next ch-1 sp), YO, insert hook in next dc, YO and pull up a loop, YO and draw through 2 loops on hook, YO, skip next dc, insert hook in next ch-1 sp, YO and pull up a loop, YO and draw through 2 loops on hook, YO and draw through all 3 loops on hook **(counts as one dc)**.

To work ending decrease (uses next ch-1 sp and next 2 dc), YO, insert hook in next ch-1 sp, YO and pull up a loop, YO and draw through 2 loops on hook, YO, skip next dc, insert hook in next dc, YO and pull up a loop, YO and draw through 2 loops on hook, YO and draw through all 3 loops on hook **(counts as one dc)**.

Row 3: With **right** side facing, join CC with slip st in first dc; ch 3, work beginning decrease, (dc, ch 1, dc) in each of next 3 ch-1 sps, dc in next ch-1 sp, (ch 1, dc in same sp) 3 times, (dc, ch 1, dc) in each of next 3 ch-1 sps, ★ double decrease, (dc, ch 1, dc) in each of next 3 ch-1 sps, dc in next ch-1 sp, (ch 1, dc in same sp) 3 times, (dc, ch 1, dc) in each of next 3 ch-1 sps; repeat from ★ across to last ch-1 sp, work ending decrease, dc in last dc.

Row 4: Ch 3, turn; work beginning decrease, (dc, ch 1, dc) in each of next 3 ch-1 sps, dc in next ch-1 sp, (ch 1, dc in same sp) 3 times, (dc, ch 1, dc) in each of next 3 ch-1 sps, ★ double decrease, (dc, ch 1, dc) in each of next 3 ch-1 sps, dc in next ch-1 sp, (ch 1, dc in same sp) 3 times, (dc, ch 1, dc) in each of next 3 ch-1 sps; repeat from ★ across to last ch-1 sp, work ending decrease, dc in last dc; finish off.

Repeat Rows 3 and 4 for pattern, working in stripe sequence.

89 SIDE STEP

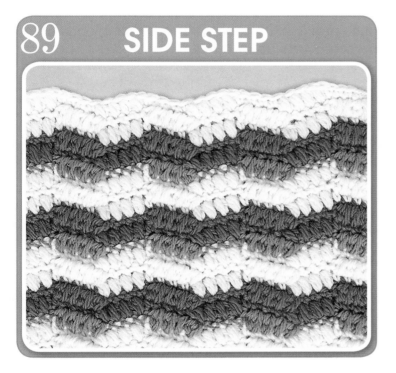

Note: Loop a short piece of yarn around any stitch to mark Row 1 as **right** side.

Rows 2 and 3: Ch 1, turn; sc in first 4 Puff Sts, work Puff St in each of next 4 sc, ★ sc in next 4 Puff Sts, work Puff St in each of next 4 sc; repeat from ★ across; at end of last row, finish off.

Row 4: With **wrong** side facing, join Color B with sc in first Puff St *(see Joining With Sc, page 159)*; sc in next 3 Puff Sts, work Puff St in each of next 4 sc, ★ sc in next 4 Puff Sts, work Puff St in each of next 4 sc; repeat from ★ across; finish off.

Row 5: With **right** side facing, join Color C with sc in first Puff St; sc in next 3 Puff Sts, work Puff St in each of next 4 sc, ★ sc in next 4 Puff Sts, work Puff St in each of next 4 sc; repeat from ★ across.

Row 6: Ch 1, turn; sc in first 4 Puff Sts, work Puff St in each of next 4 sc, ★ sc in next 4 Puff Sts, work Puff St in each of next 4 sc; repeat from ★ across; finish off.

Row 7: With **right** side facing, join Color A with sc in first Puff St; sc in next 3 Puff Sts, work Puff St in each of next 4 sc, ★ sc in next 4 Puff Sts, work Puff St in each of next 4 sc; repeat from ★ across.

Repeat Rows 2-7 for pattern.

Note: Uses Colors A, B, and C in the following sequence; ★ 3 Rows Color A, 1 row Color B, 2 rows Color C; repeat from ★ for stripe sequence.

With Color A, chain a multiple of 8 + 1 ch.

To work Puff St (uses one st), ★ YO, insert hook in st indicated, YO and pull up a loop; repeat from ★ once **more**, YO and draw through all 5 loops on hook.

Row 1 (Right side): Sc in second ch from hook and in next 3 chs, work Puff St in each of next 4 chs, ★ sc in next 4 chs, work Puff St in each of next 4 chs; repeat from ★ across.

90 DREAM LAND

Note: Uses Colors A, B, C, D, and E in the following sequence: ★ 2 Rows **each** Color A, Color B, Color C, Color D, Color E; repeat from ★ for stripe sequence.

With Color A, chain a multiple of 24 + 12 chs.

Row 1 (Right side)**:** Dc in fourth ch from hook and in next 2 chs, (dc, ch 3, dc) in next ch, ★ dc in next 3 chs, † [YO, insert hook in next ch, YO and pull up a loop, YO and draw through 2 loops on hook, YO, skip next 3 chs, insert hook in next ch, YO and pull up a loop, YO and draw through 2 loops on hook, YO and draw through all 3 loops on hook **(counts as one dc)]** †, ch 1, skip next ch, dc in next ch, ch 1, skip next ch, (dc, ch 3, dc) in next ch, ch 1, skip next ch, dc in next ch, ch 1, skip next ch, repeat from † to † once, dc in next 3 chs, (dc, ch 3, dc) in next ch; repeat from ★ across to last 5 chs, dc in next 2 chs, YO, insert hook in next ch, YO and pull up a loop, YO and draw through 2 loops on hook, YO, skip next ch, insert hook in last ch, YO and pull up a loop, YO and draw through 2 loops on hook, YO and draw through all 3 loops on hook.

Note: Loop a short piece of yarn around any stitch to mark Row 1 as **right** side.

To decrease (uses next 3 dc), YO, † insert hook in next dc, YO and pull up a loop, YO and draw through 2 loops on hook †, YO, skip next dc, repeat from † to † once, YO and draw through all 3 loops on hook **(counts as one dc)**.

To double decrease (uses next 5 sts), YO, insert hook in next dc, YO and pull up a loop, YO and draw through 2 loops on hook, ★ YO, skip **next** st, insert hook in **next** dc, YO and pull up a loop, YO and draw through 2 loops on hook; repeat from ★ once **more**, YO and draw through all 4 loops on hook **(counts as one dc)**.

Row 2: Ch 2, turn; skip first 2 sts, dc in next 2 dc, (2 dc, ch 3, 2 dc) in next ch-3 sp, ★ dc in next 2 dc, double decrease, ch 1, dc in next dc, ch 1, (dc, ch 3, dc) in next ch-3 sp, ch 1, dc in next dc, ch 1, double decrease, dc in next 2 dc, (2 dc, ch 3, 2 dc) in next ch-3 sp; repeat from ★ across to last 4 dc, dc in next dc, decrease; finish off.

Row 3: With **right** side facing, join Color B with slip st in first dc; ch 2, skip next dc, dc in next 2 dc, (2 dc, ch 3, 2 dc) in next ch-3 sp, ★ dc in next 2 dc, double decrease, ch 1, dc in next dc, ch 1, (dc, ch 3, dc) in next ch-3 sp, ch 1, dc in next dc, ch 1, double decrease, dc in next 2 dc, (2 dc, ch 3, 2 dc) in next ch-3 sp; repeat from ★ across to last 4 dc, dc in next dc, decrease.

Repeat Rows 2 and 3 for pattern, working in stripe sequence.

91 CANCUN WAVES

Note: Uses MC and CC in the following sequence: ★ 1 Row MC, 3 rows CC; repeat from ★ for stripe sequence.

With MC, chain a multiple of 12 + 3 chs.

Row 1 (Right side)**:** Dc in fourth ch from hook **(3 skipped chs count as first dc)** and in each ch across; finish off.

Note: Loop a short piece of yarn around any stitch to mark Row 1 as **right** side.

Row 2: With **wrong** side facing, join CC with slip st in first dc; ch 3 **(counts as first dc, now and throughout)**, 2 dc in same st as joining, ch 2, skip next 3 dc, sc in next dc, ch 5, skip next 3 dc, sc in next dc, ch 2, ★ skip next 3 dc, 5 dc in next dc, ch 2, skip next 3 dc, sc in next dc, ch 5, skip next 3 dc, sc in next dc, ch 2; repeat from ★ across to last 4 dc, skip next 3 dc, 3 dc in last dc.

Row 3: Ch 4 **(counts as first dc plus ch 1)**, turn; dc in next dc, ch 1, dc in next dc, ch 2, skip next ch-2 sp, sc in next ch-5 sp, ch 2, skip next ch-2 sp, dc in next dc, ★ (ch 1, dc in next dc) 4 times, ch 2, skip next ch-2 sp, sc in next ch-5 sp, ch 2, skip next ch-2 sp, dc in next dc; repeat from ★ across to last 2 dc, (ch 1, dc in next dc) twice.

Row 4: Ch 5 **(counts as first dc plus ch 2)**, turn; dc in next dc, ch 2, dc in next dc, skip next 2 ch-2 sps, dc in next dc, ★ (ch 2, dc in next dc) 4 times, skip next 2 ch-2 sps, dc in next dc; repeat from ★ across to last 2 dc, (ch 2, dc in next dc) twice; finish off.

Row 5: With **right** side facing, join MC with slip st in first dc; ch 3, 2 dc in next ch-2 sp, dc in next dc, 2 dc in next ch-2 sp, ★ skip next dc, (dc in next dc, 2 dc in next ch-2 sp) 4 times; repeat from ★ across to last 2 ch-2 sps, skip next dc, dc in next dc, (2 dc in next ch-2 sp, dc in next dc) twice; finish off.

Repeat Rows 2-5 for pattern.

92 TRIOS

To double crochet 5 together (abbreviated *dc5tog*), ★ YO, insert hook in **next** st, YO and pull up a loop, YO and draw through 2 loops on hook; repeat from ★ 4 times **more**, YO and draw through all 6 loops on hook **(counts as one dc)**.

Row 1 (Right side): Decrease beginning in fourth ch from hook, dc in next 5 chs, 4 dc in next ch, dc in next 5 chs, ★ dc5tog, dc in next 5 chs, 4 dc in next ch, dc in next 5 chs; repeat from ★ across to last 3 chs, double decrease.

Note: Loop a short piece of yarn around any stitch to mark Row 1 as **right** side.

Row 2: Ch 2, turn; skip first dc, decrease, skip next 2 dc, 5 dc in next dc, skip next 2 dc, 4 dc in sp **before** next dc *(Fig. 5, page 159)*, skip next 2 dc, 5 dc in next dc, ★ skip next 2 dc, dc5tog, skip next 2 dc, 5 dc in next dc, skip next 2 dc, 4 dc in sp **before** next dc, skip next 2 dc, 5 dc in next dc; repeat from ★ across to last 5 dc, skip next 2 dc, double decrease; finish off.

Row 3: With **right** side facing, join Color B with slip st in first dc; ch 2, decrease, skip next 2 dc, 5 dc in next dc, skip next 2 dc, 4 dc in sp **before** next dc, skip next 2 dc, 5 dc in next dc, ★ skip next 2 dc, dc5tog, skip next 2 dc, 5 dc in next dc, skip next 2 dc, 4 dc in sp **before** next dc, skip next 2 dc, 5 dc in next dc; repeat from ★ across to last 5 dc, skip next 2 dc, double decrease.

Repeat Rows 2 and 3 for pattern, working in stripe sequence.

Note: Uses Colors A, B, and C in the following sequence: ★ 2 Rows **each** Color A, Color B, Color C; repeat from ★ for stripe sequence.

With Color A, chain a multiple of 16 + 3 chs.

To decrease (uses next 2 sts), ★ YO, insert hook in **next** st, YO and pull up a loop, YO and draw through 2 loops on hook; repeat from ★ once **more**, YO and draw through all 3 loops on hook **(counts as one dc)**.

To double decrease (uses next 3 sts), ★ YO, insert hook in **next** st, YO and pull up a loop, YO and draw through 2 loops on hook; repeat from ★ 2 times **more**, YO and draw through all 4 loops on hook **(counts as one dc)**.

93 TIDAL WAVES

Row 1 (Wrong side)**:** Sc in second ch from hook and in next 2 chs, ★ skip next 3 chs, (3 tr, ch 3, sc) in next ch, ch 2, skip next 2 chs, (sc, ch 3, 3 tr) in next ch, skip next 3 chs, sc in next 3 chs; repeat from ★ across; finish off.

Note: Loop a short piece of yarn around **back** of any stitch on Row 1 to mark **right** side.

Row 2: With **right** side facing, join Color B with slip st in first sc; ch 4 **(counts as first tr)**, tr in next 2 sc, ★ dc in next tr, sc in next tr, ch 3, skip next tr and next ch-3, 2 tr in next ch-2 sp, ch 3, skip next ch-3 and next tr, sc in next tr, dc in next tr, tr in next 3 sc; repeat from ★ across; finish off.

Row 3: With **wrong** side facing, join Color C with sc in first tr *(see Joining With Sc, page 158)*; sc in next 2 tr, ★ (3 tr, ch 3, sc) in next ch-3 sp, ch 2, (sc, ch 3, 3 tr) in next ch-3 sp, skip next 2 sts, sc in next 3 tr; repeat from ★ across; finish off.

Repeat Rows 2 and 3 for pattern, working in stripe sequence.

Note: Uses Colors A, B, and C in the following sequence: ★ 1 Row **each** Color A, Color B, Color C; repeat from ★ for stripe sequence.

With Color A, chain a multiple of 13 + 4 chs.

To treble crochet *(abbreviated tr)*, YO twice, insert hook in st or sp indicated, YO and pull up a loop (4 loops on hook), (YO and draw through 2 loops on hook) 3 times.

94 MY FAIR LADY

Note: Uses MC and CC in the following sequence: ★ 3 Rows **each** MC, CC; repeat from ★ for stripe sequence.

With MC, chain a multiple of 21 + 4 chs.

Row 1 (Right side)**:** Dc in fourth ch from hook **(3 skipped chs count as first dc)**, ch 2, skip next 2 chs, sc in next ch, (ch 4, skip next 2 chs, sc in next ch) 5 times, ch 2, ★ skip next 2 chs, 4 dc in next ch, ch 2, skip next 2 chs, sc in next ch, (ch 4, skip next 2 chs, sc in next ch) 5 times, ch 2; repeat from ★ across to last 3 chs, skip next 2 chs, 2 dc in last ch.

Note: Loop a short piece of yarn around any stitch to mark Row 1 as **right** side.

Row 2: Ch 3 **(counts as first dc, now and throughout)**, turn; dc in first dc, 2 dc in next dc, ch 2, skip next ch-2 sp, sc in next ch-4 sp, (ch 4, sc in next ch-4 sp) 4 times, ch 2, ★ skip next ch-2 sp, 2 dc in each of next 4 dc, ch 2, skip next ch-2 sp, sc in next ch-4 sp, (ch 4, sc in next ch-4 sp) 4 times, ch 2; repeat from ★ across to last ch-2 sp, skip last ch-2 sp, 2 dc in each of last 2 dc.

Row 3: Ch 4 **(counts as first dc plus ch 1)**, turn; skip first dc, 2 dc in next dc, ch 1, skip next dc, 2 dc in next dc, ch 2, skip next ch-2 sp, sc in next ch-4 sp, (ch 4, sc in next ch-4 sp) 3 times, ch 2, skip next ch-2 sp, 2 dc in next dc, ch 1, ★ skip next dc, 2 dc in next dc, ch 1, dc in next 2 dc, ch 1, 2 dc in next dc, ch 1, skip next dc, 2 dc in next dc, ch 2, skip next ch-2 sp, sc in next ch-4 sp, (ch 4, sc in next ch-4 sp) 3 times, ch 2, skip next ch-2 sp, 2 dc in next dc, ch 1; repeat from ★ across to last 3 dc, skip next dc, 2 dc in next dc, ch 1, dc in last dc; finish off.

Row 4: With **wrong** side facing, join CC with slip st in first dc; ch 5 **(counts as first dc plus ch 2, now and throughout)**, (sc in next ch-1 sp, ch 4) twice, skip next ch-2 sp, sc in next ch-4 sp, ch 2, 4 dc in next ch-4 sp, ch 2, sc in next ch-4 sp, ch 4, ★ skip next ch-2 sp, (sc in next ch-1 sp, ch 4) 4 times, skip next ch-2 sp, sc in next ch-4 sp, ch 2, 4 dc in next ch-4 sp, ch 2, sc in next ch-4 sp, ch 4; repeat from ★ across to last 3 sps, skip next ch-2 sp, sc in next ch-1 sp, ch 4, sc in last ch-1 sp, ch 2, dc in last dc.

Row 5: Ch 1, turn; sc in first dc, ch 4, skip next ch-2 sp, sc in next ch-4 sp, ch 4, sc in next ch-4 sp, ch 2, skip next ch-2 sp, 2 dc in each of next 4 dc, ch 2, skip next ch-2 sp, sc in next ch-4 sp, ★ (ch 4, sc in next ch-4 sp) 4 times, ch 2, skip next ch-2 sp, 2 dc in each of next 4 dc, ch 2, skip next ch-2 sp, sc in next ch-4 sp; repeat from ★ across to last 2 sps, ch 4, sc in next ch-4 sp, ch 4, skip last ch-2 sp, sc in last dc.

Row 6: Ch 5, turn; sc in next ch-4 sp, ch 4, sc in next ch-4 sp, ch 2, skip next ch-2 sp, 2 dc in next dc, ch 1, skip next dc, 2 dc in next dc, ch 1, dc in next 2 dc, ch 1, 2 dc in next dc, ch 1, skip next dc, 2 dc in next dc, ch 2, skip next ch-2 sp, sc in next ch-4 sp, ★ (ch 4, sc in next ch-4 sp) 3 times, ch 2, skip next ch-2 sp, 2 dc in next dc, ch 1, skip next dc, 2 dc in next dc, ch 1, dc in next 2 dc, ch 1, 2 dc in next dc, ch 1, skip next dc, 2 dc in next dc, ch 2, skip next ch-2 sp, sc in next ch-4 sp; repeat from ★ across to last ch-4 sp, ch 4, sc in last ch-4 sp, ch 2, dc in last sc; finish off.

Row 7: With **right** side facing, join MC with slip st in first dc; ch 3, dc in same st as joining, ch 2, skip next ch-2 sp, sc in next ch-4 sp, ch 4, skip next ch-2 sp, (sc in next ch-1 sp, ch 4) 4 times, skip next ch-2 sp, sc in next ch-4 sp, ch 2, ★ 4 dc in next ch-4 sp, ch 2, sc in next ch-4 sp, ch 4, skip next ch-2 sp, (sc in next ch-1 sp, ch 4) 4 times, skip next ch-2 sp, sc in next ch-4 sp, ch 2; repeat from ★ across to last ch-2 sp, skip last ch-2 sp, 2 dc in last dc.

Repeat Rows 2-7 for pattern.

95 SYMMETRY

Chain a multiple of 16 + 3 chs.

To decrease (uses next 2 sts), ★ YO, insert hook in **next** st, YO and pull up a loop, YO and draw through 2 loops on hook; repeat from ★ once **more**, YO and draw through all 3 loops on hook **(counts as one dc)**.

To double decrease (uses next 3 sts), ★ YO, insert hook in **next** st, YO and pull up a loop, YO and draw through 2 loops on hook; repeat from ★ 2 times **more**, YO and draw through all 4 loops on hook **(counts as one dc)**.

To double crochet 5 together (abbreviated dc5tog), ★ YO, insert hook in **next** st, YO and pull up a loop, YO and draw through 2 loops on hook; repeat from ★ 4 times **more**, YO and draw through all 6 loops on hook **(counts as one dc)**.

Row 1 (Right side)**:** Decrease beginning in fourth ch from hook, ch 1, skip next ch, (dc in next ch, ch 1, skip next ch) twice, 5 dc in next ch, ★ ch 1, skip next ch, (dc in next ch, ch 1, skip next ch) twice, dc5tog, ch 1, skip next ch, (dc in next ch, ch 1, skip next ch) twice, 5 dc in next ch; repeat from ★ across to last 8 chs, ch 1, skip next ch, (dc in next ch, ch 1, skip next ch) twice, double decrease.

Note: Loop a short piece of yarn around any stitch to mark Row 1 as **right** side.

Row 2: Ch 1, turn; sc in each st and in each ch-1 sp across.

Row 3: Ch 2, turn; skip first sc, decrease, ch 1, skip next sc, (dc in next sc, ch 1, skip next sc) twice, 5 dc in next sc, ★ ch 1, skip next sc, (dc in next sc, ch 1, skip next sc) twice, dc5tog, ch 1, skip next sc, (dc in next sc, ch 1, skip next sc) twice, 5 dc in next sc; repeat from ★ across to last 8 sc, ch 1, skip next sc, (dc in next sc, ch 1, skip next sc) twice, double decrease.

Repeat Rows 2 and 3 for pattern.

Note: Uses MC and Colors A and B in the following sequence: ★ 2 Rows **each** MC, Color A, MC, Color B; repeat from ★ for stripe sequence.

With MC, chain a multiple of 14 + 4 chs.

To work beginning decrease (uses next 2 sts), ★ YO, insert hook in **next** st, YO and pull up a loop, YO and draw through 2 loops on hook; repeat from ★ once **more**, YO and draw through all 3 loops on hook **(counts as one dc)**.

To decrease (uses next 5 sts), YO, insert hook in next st, YO and pull up a loop, YO and draw through 2 loops on hook, ★ YO, skip **next** ch, insert hook in **next** st, YO and pull up a loop, YO and draw through 2 loops on hook; repeat from ★ once **more**, YO and draw through all 4 loops on hook **(counts as one dc)**.

To work ending decrease (uses last 3 sts), ★ YO, insert hook in **next** st, YO and pull up a loop, YO and draw through 2 loops on hook; repeat from ★ 2 times **more**, YO and draw through all 4 loops on hook **(counts as one dc)**.

Row 1 (Right side)**:** Work beginning decrease beginning in third ch from hook, ch 1, skip next 2 chs, 5 dc in next ch, ch 1, skip next 2 chs, 7 dc in next ch, ch 1, skip next 2 chs, 5 dc in next ch, ch 1, ★ skip next ch, decrease, ch 1, skip next ch, 5 dc in next ch, ch 1, skip next 2 chs, 7 dc in next ch, ch 1, skip next 2 chs, 5 dc in next ch, ch 1; repeat from ★ across to last 5 chs, skip next 2 chs, work ending decrease.

Note: Loop a short piece of yarn around any stitch to mark Row 1 as **right** side.

Row 2: Ch 2, turn; working in Back Loops Only of chs and dc **(Fig. 2, page 159)**, skip first dc, work beginning decrease, ch 1, skip next 4 dc, 5 dc in next ch, ch 1, skip next 3 dc, 7 dc in next dc, ch 1, skip next 3 dc, 5 dc in next ch, ch 1, ★ skip next 4 dc, decrease, ch 1, skip next 4 dc, 5 dc in next ch, ch 1, skip next 3 dc, 7 dc in next dc, ch 1, skip next 3 dc, 5 dc in next ch, ch 1; repeat from ★ across to last 7 sts, skip next 4 dc, work ending decrease; finish off.

Row 3: With **right** side facing and working in Back Loops Only of chs and dc, join Color A with slip st in first dc; ch 2, skip joining dc, work beginning decrease, ch 1, skip next 4 dc, 5 dc in next ch, ch 1, skip next 3 dc, 7 dc in next dc, ch 1, skip next 3 dc, 5 dc in next ch, ch 1, ★ skip next 4 dc, decrease, ch 1, skip next 4 dc, 5 dc in next ch, ch 1, skip next 3 dc, 7 dc in next dc, ch 1, skip next 3 dc, 5 dc in next ch, ch 1; repeat from ★ across to last 7 sts, skip next 4 dc, work ending decrease.

Repeat Rows 2 and 3 for pattern, working in stripe sequence.

97 BANDS OF LACE

Chain a multiple of 17 + 1 ch.

Row 1: Dc in fourth ch from hook, ch 1, skip next ch, (dc in next ch, ch 1, skip next ch) twice, (dc, ch 1) 4 times in next ch, (skip next ch, dc in next ch, ch 1) twice, ★ **[**YO, skip next ch, insert hook in next ch, YO and pull up a loop, YO and draw through 2 loops on hook, YO, skip next 4 chs, insert hook in next ch, YO and pull up a loop, YO and draw through 2 loops on hook, YO and draw through all 3 loops on hook **(counts as one dc)]**, ch 1, skip next ch, (dc in next ch, ch 1, skip next ch) twice, (dc, ch 1) 4 times in next ch, (skip next ch, dc in next ch, ch 1) twice; repeat from ★ across to last 4 chs, **[**(YO, skip next ch, insert hook in next ch, YO and pull up a loop, YO and draw through 2 loops on hook) twice, YO and draw through all 3 loops on hook **(counts as one dc)]**.

Row 2 (Right side): Ch 3 **(counts as first dc, now and throughout)**, turn; skip next ch-1 sp, (dc in next ch-1 sp, ch 1) 3 times, (dc, ch 1) 4 times in next ch-1 sp, dc in next ch-1 sp, (ch 1, dc in next ch-1 sp) twice, ★ skip next 2 ch-1 sps, (dc in next ch-1 sp, ch 1) 3 times, (dc, ch 1) 4 times in next ch-1 sp, dc in next ch-1 sp, (ch 1, dc in next ch-1 sp) twice; repeat from ★ across to last ch-1 sp, skip last ch-1 sp, dc in last dc.

Note: Loop a short piece of yarn around any stitch to mark Row 2 as **right** side.

Row 3: Ch 3, turn; skip next ch-1 sp, (dc in next ch-1 sp, ch 1) 3 times, (dc, ch 1) 4 times in next ch-1 sp, dc in next ch-1 sp, (ch 1, dc in next ch-1 sp) twice, ★ skip next 2 ch-1 sps, (dc in next ch-1 sp, ch 1) 3 times, (dc, ch 1) 4 times in next ch-1 sp, dc in next ch-1 sp, (ch 1, dc in next ch-1 sp) twice; repeat from ★ across to last ch-1 sp, skip last ch-1 sp and next dc, dc in last dc.

Row 4: Ch 3, turn; skip next ch-1 sp, dc in next dc, (dc in next ch-1 sp and in next dc) 7 times, ★ dc in next 2 ch-1 sps, dc in next dc, (dc in next ch-1 sp and in next dc) 7 times; repeat from ★ across to last ch-1 sp, skip last ch-1 sp and next dc, dc in last dc.

Row 5: Ch 3, turn; skip first 2 dc, (dc in next dc, ch 1, skip next dc) 3 times, (dc, ch 1) 4 times in next dc, skip next dc, dc in next dc, (ch 1, skip next dc, dc in next dc) twice, ★ skip next 4 dc, (dc in next dc, ch 1, skip next dc) 3 times, (dc, ch 1) 4 times in next dc, skip next dc, dc in next dc, (ch 1, skip next dc, dc in next dc) twice; repeat from ★ across to last 2 dc, skip next dc, dc in last dc.

Repeat Rows 2-5 for pattern.

98 SOLID SHELLS

Chain a multiple of 16 + 2 chs.

Row 1: Sc in second ch from hook, ★ ch 5, skip next 3 chs, sc in next ch; repeat from ★ across.

Row 2 (Right side)**:** Ch 5 **(counts as first dc plus ch 2, now and throughout)**, turn; sc in next ch-5 sp, ch 5, sc in next ch-5 sp, 4 dc in next sc, sc in next ch-5 sp, ★ (ch 5, sc in next ch-5 sp) 3 times, 4 dc in next sc, sc in next ch-5 sp; repeat from ★ across to last ch-5 sp, ch 5, sc in last ch-5 sp, ch 2, dc in last sc.

Note: Loop a short piece of yarn around any stitch to mark Row 2 as **right** side.

Row 3: Ch 1, turn; sc in first dc, ch 5, skip next ch-2 sp, sc in next ch-5 sp, 4 dc in next sc, skip next 2 dc, sc in sp **before** next dc *(Fig. 5, page 159)*, skip next 2 dc, 4 dc in next sc, sc in next ch-5 sp, ★ (ch 5, sc in next ch-5 sp) twice, 4 dc in next sc, skip next 2 dc, sc in sp **before** next dc, skip next 2 dc, 4 dc in next sc, sc in next ch-5 sp; repeat from ★ across to last ch-2 sp, ch 5, skip last ch-2 sp, sc in last dc.

Row 4: Ch 5, turn; sc in next ch-5 sp, 4 dc in next sc, skip next 2 dc, sc in sp **before** next dc, ch 5, skip next 5 sts, sc in sp **before** next dc, skip next 2 dc, 4 dc in next sc, sc in next ch-5 sp, ★ ch 5, sc in next ch-5 sp, 4 dc in next sc, skip next 2 dc, sc in sp **before** next dc, ch 5, skip next 5 sts, sc in sp **before** next dc, skip next 2 dc, 4 dc in next sc, sc in next ch-5 sp; repeat from ★ across to last sc, ch 2, dc in last sc.

Row 5: Ch 1, turn; sc in first dc, 4 dc in next sc, skip next 2 dc, sc in sp **before** next dc, ch 5, sc in next ch-5 sp, ch 5, skip next 3 sts, sc in sp **before** next dc, skip next 2 dc, 4 dc in next sc, ★ sc in next ch-5 sp, 4 dc in next sc, skip next 2 dc, sc in sp **before** next dc, ch 5, sc in next ch-5 sp, ch 5, skip next 3 sts, sc in sp **before** next dc, skip next 2 dc, 4 dc in next sc; repeat from ★ across to last dc, sc in last dc.

Row 6: Ch 3 **(counts as first dc)**, turn; 2 dc in first sc, skip next 2 dc, sc in sp **before** next dc, ch 5, sc in next ch-5 sp, 4 dc in next sc, sc in next ch-5 sp, ch 5, skip next 3 sts, sc in sp **before** next dc, ★ skip next 2 dc, 4 dc in next sc, skip next 2 dc, sc in sp **before** next dc, ch 5, sc in next ch-5 sp, 4 dc in next sc, sc in next ch-5 sp, ch 5, skip next 3 sts, sc in sp **before** next dc; repeat from ★ across to last 3 sts, skip next 2 dc, 3 dc in last sc.

Row 7: Ch 1, turn; sc in first dc, ch 5, sc in next ch-5 sp, 4 dc in next sc, skip next 2 dc, sc in sp **before** next dc, skip next 2 dc, 4 dc in next sc, sc in next ch-5 sp, ★ ch 5, skip next 3 sts, sc in sp **before** next dc, ch 5, sc in next ch-5 sp, 4 dc in next sc, skip next 2 dc, sc in sp **before** next dc, skip next 2 dc, 4 dc in next sc, sc in next ch-5 sp; repeat from ★ across to last 3 dc, ch 5, skip next 2 dc, sc in last dc.

Repeat Rows 4-7 for pattern.

99 GENTLE WAVES

Note: Uses MC and CC in the following sequence: 1 Row MC, ★ 2 rows **each** CC, MC; repeat from ★ for stripe sequence.

With MC, chain a multiple of 13 + 4 chs.

To decrease (uses next 2 sts), ★ YO, insert hook in **next** st, YO and pull up a loop, YO and draw through 2 loops on hook; repeat from ★ once **more**, YO and draw through all 3 loops on hook **(counts as one dc)**.

Row 1 (Right side)**:** Dc in fourth ch from hook **(3 skipped chs count as one dc)** and in next 3 chs, decrease 3 times, dc in next 3 chs, ★ 3 dc in next ch, dc in next 3 chs, decrease 3 times, dc in next 3 chs; repeat from ★ across to last ch, 2 dc in last ch; finish off.

Note: Loop a short piece of yarn around any stitch to mark Row 1 as **right** side.

Row 2: With **wrong** side facing, join CC with slip st in first dc; ch 3 **(counts as first dc, now and throughout)**, 2 dc in same st as joining, ch 2, skip next 3 dc, sc in next dc, ch 4, skip next 3 dc, sc in next dc, ch 2, ★ skip next 3 dc, 5 dc in next dc, ch 2, skip next 3 dc, sc in next dc, ch 4, skip next 3 dc, sc in next dc, ch 2; repeat from ★ across to last 4 dc, skip next 3 dc, 3 dc in last dc.

Row 3: Ch 3, turn; dc in first dc, 2 dc in next dc, dc in next dc, ch 2, skip next ch-2 sp, sc in next ch-4 sp, ch 2, skip next ch-2 sp, dc in next dc, ★ 2 dc in next dc, 3 dc in next dc, 2 dc in next dc, dc in next dc, ch 2, skip next ch-2 sp, sc in next ch-4 sp, ch 2, skip next ch-2 sp, dc in next dc; repeat from ★ across to last 2 dc, 2 dc in each of last 2 dc; finish off.

Row 4: With **wrong** side facing, join MC with slip st in first dc; ch 3, (2 dc in next dc, dc in next dc) twice, skip next 2 ch-2 sps, dc in next dc, ★ (2 dc in next dc, dc in next dc) 4 times, skip next 2 ch-2 sps, dc in next dc; repeat from ★ across to last 4 dc, (2 dc in next dc, dc in next dc) twice.

Row 5: Ch 3, turn; dc in first 4 dc, decrease 3 times, dc in next 3 dc, ★ 3 dc in next dc, dc in next 3 dc, decrease 3 times, dc in next 3 dc; repeat from ★ across to last dc, 2 dc in last dc; finish off.

Repeat Rows 2-5 for pattern.

100 BIG WAVES

Note: Uses Colors A, B, and C in the following sequence: ★ 2 Rows **each** Color A, Color B, Color C; repeat from ★ for stripe sequence.

With Color A, chain a multiple of 24 + 3 chs.

Row 1: Dc in sixth ch from hook **(5 skipped chs count as one dc and 2 skipped chs)** and in next 3 chs, 2 dc in next ch, (dc in next ch, 2 dc in next ch) 5 times, dc in next 4 chs, skip next 2 chs, dc in next ch, ★ skip next 2 chs, dc in next 4 chs, 2 dc in next ch, (dc in next ch, 2 dc in next ch) 5 times, dc in next 4 chs, skip next 2 chs, dc in next ch; repeat from ★ across.

To work Front Post double crochet *(abbreviated FPdc)*, YO, insert hook from **front** to **back** around post of st indicated *(Fig. 4, page 159)*, YO and pull up a loop even with loop on hook (3 loops on hook), (YO and draw through 2 loops on hook) twice. Skip st **behind** FPdc just made.

Row 2 (Right side)**:** Ch 3 **(counts as first dc, now and throughout)**, turn; working in Back Loops Only *(Fig. 2, page 159)*, skip first 4 dc, dc in next 4 dc, 2 dc in next dc, (dc in next dc, 2 dc in next dc) 5 times, dc in next 4 dc, ★ skip next 3 dc, work FPdc around next dc, skip next 3 dc, dc in next 4 dc, 2 dc in next dc, (dc in next dc, 2 dc in next dc) 5 times, dc in next 4 dc; repeat from ★ across to last 4 dc, skip next 3 dc, dc in last dc; finish off.

Note: Loop a short piece of yarn around any stitch to mark Row 2 as **right** side.

To work Back Post double crochet *(abbreviated BPdc)*, YO, insert hook from **back** to **front** around post of st indicated *(Fig. 4, page 159)*, YO and pull up a loop even with loop on hook (3 loops on hook), (YO and draw through 2 loops on hook) twice. Skip st in **front** of BPdc just made.

Row 3: With **wrong** side facing and working in Back Loops Only, join Color B with slip st in first dc; ch 3, skip next 3 dc, dc in next 4 dc, 2 dc in next dc, (dc in next dc, 2 dc in next dc) 5 times, dc in next 4 dc, ★ skip next 3 dc, work BPdc around next st, skip next 3 dc, dc in next 4 dc, 2 dc in next dc, (dc in next dc, 2 dc in next dc) 5 times, dc in next 4 dc; repeat from ★ across to last 4 dc, skip next 3 dc, dc in last dc.

Repeat Rows 2 and 3 for pattern, working in stripe sequence.

101 SOUTH OF THE BORDER

Note: Uses MC and Colors A and B in the following sequence: ★ 4 Rows MC, 1 row Color A, 1 row Color B, 1 row Color A; repeat from ★ for stripe sequence.

With MC, chain a multiple of 17 + 4 chs.

To work Cluster (uses one st or sp), ★ YO, insert hook in st or sp indicated, YO and pull up a loop, YO and draw through 2 loops on hook; repeat from ★ 2 times **more**, YO and draw through all 4 loops on hook.

Row 1 (Right side)**:** 3 Dc in sixth ch from hook **(5 skipped chs count as first dc and 2 skipped chs)**, skip next 2 chs, 3 dc in next ch, skip next 2 chs, (3 dc, ch 3, 3 dc) in next ch, ★ skip next 2 chs, 3 dc in next ch, skip next 2 chs, work Cluster in next ch, skip next 4 chs, work Cluster in next ch, skip next 2 chs, 3 dc in next ch, skip next 2 chs, (3 dc, ch 3, 3 dc) in next ch; repeat from ★ across to last 9 chs, skip next 2 chs, (3 dc in next ch, skip next 2 chs) twice, dc in last ch.

Note: Loop a short piece of yarn around any stitch to mark Row 1 as **right** side.

Rows 2-4: Ch 3 **(counts as first dc, now and throughout)**, turn; skip first 4 dc, 3 dc in sp **before** next dc *(Fig. 5, page 159)*, skip next 3 dc, 3 dc in sp **before** next dc, (3 dc, ch 3, 3 dc) in next ch-3 sp, ★ skip next 3 dc, 3 dc in sp **before** next dc, skip next 3 dc, work Cluster in sp **before** next Cluster, skip next 2 Clusters, work Cluster in sp **before** next dc, skip next 3 dc, 3 dc in sp **before** next dc, (3 dc, ch 3, 3 dc) in next ch-3 sp; repeat from ★ across to last 10 dc, skip next 3 dc, (3 dc in sp **before** next dc, skip next 3 dc) twice, dc in last dc; at end of last row, finish off.

Row 5: With **right** side facing, join Color A with sc in first dc *(see Joining With Sc, page 158)*; skip next dc, sc in next 8 dc, 3 sc in next ch-3 sp, (sc in next 14 sts, 3 sc in next ch-3 sp) across to last 10 dc, sc in next 8 dc, skip next dc, sc in last dc; finish off.

Row 6: With **wrong** side facing, join Color B with slip st in first sc; ch 3, skip next sc, dc in next 8 sc, 3 dc in next sc, ★ dc in next 7 sc, skip next 2 sc, dc in next 7 sc, 3 dc in next sc; repeat from ★ across to last 10 sc, dc in next 8 sc, skip next sc, dc in last sc; finish off.

Row 7: With **right** side facing, join Color A with sc in first dc; skip next dc, sc in next 8 dc, 3 sc in next dc, ★ sc in next 7 dc, skip next 2 dc, sc in next 7 dc, 3 sc in next dc; repeat from ★ across to last 10 dc, sc in next 8 dc, skip next dc, sc in last dc; finish off.

Row 8: With **right** side facing, join MC with slip st in first sc; ch 3, skip next 3 sc, (3 dc in next sc, skip next 2 sc) twice, (3 dc, ch 3, 3 dc) in next sc, ★ skip next 2 sc, 3 dc in next sc, skip next 2 sc, work Cluster in next sc, skip next 4 sc, work Cluster in next sc, skip next 2 sc, 3 dc in next sc, skip next 2 sc, (3 dc, ch 3, 3 dc) in next sc; repeat from ★ across to last 10 sc, (skip next 2 sc, 3 dc in next sc) twice, skip next 3 sc, dc in last sc.

Repeat Rows 2-8 for pattern.

102 INTERSECTING WAVES

Note: Uses Colors A, B, and C in the following sequence: ★ 1 Row **each** Color A, Color B, Color C, Color B; repeat from ★ for stripe sequence.

With Color A, chain a multiple of 8 + 2 chs.

Row 1 (Wrong side)**:** Hdc in third ch from hook **(2 skipped chs count as first hdc)** and in each ch across; finish off.

Note: Loop a short piece of yarn around **back** of any stitch on Row 1 to mark **right** side.

To treble crochet (abbreviated tr), YO twice, insert hook in st indicated, YO and pull up a loop (4 loops on hook), (YO and draw through 2 loops on hook) 3 times.

Row 2: With **right** side facing, join Color B with sc in first hdc **(see Joining With Sc, page 158)**; ★ hdc in next hdc, dc in next hdc, tr in next hdc, 3 tr in next hdc, tr in next hdc, dc in next hdc, hdc in next hdc, sc in next hdc; repeat from ★ across; finish off.

To dc decrease (uses next 3 sts), ★ YO, insert hook in **next** st, YO and pull up a loop, YO and draw through 2 loops on hook; repeat from ★ 2 times **more**, YO and draw through all 4 loops on hook **(counts as one dc)**.

Row 3: With **wrong** side facing, join Color C with slip st in first sc; ch 3 **(counts as first dc)**, skip next hdc, dc in next 3 sts, 3 dc in next tr, dc in next 3 sts, ★ dc decrease, dc in next 3 sts, 3 dc in next tr, dc in next 3 sts; repeat from ★ across to last 2 sts, skip next hdc, dc in last sc; finish off.

To tr decrease (uses next 3 dc), ★ YO twice, insert hook in **next** dc, YO and pull up a loop, (YO and draw through 2 loops on hook) twice; repeat from ★ 2 times **more**, YO and draw through all 4 loops on hook **(counts as one tr)**.

Row 4: With **right** side facing, join Color B with slip st in first dc; ch 4 **(counts as first tr)**, skip next dc, tr in next dc, dc in next dc, hdc in next dc, sc in next dc, hdc in next dc, dc in next dc, tr in next dc, ★ tr decrease, tr in next dc, dc in next dc, hdc in next dc, sc in next dc, hdc in next dc, dc in next dc, tr in next dc; repeat from ★ across to last 2 dc, skip next dc, tr in last dc; finish off.

Row 5: With **wrong** side facing, join Color A with slip st in first tr; ch 2 **(counts as first hdc)**, hdc in next st and in each st across; finish off.

Repeat Rows 2-5 for pattern.

103 MESH CHEVRONS

Chain a multiple of 20 + 5 chs.

To decrease (uses next 5 sts), YO, insert hook in next st, YO and pull up a loop, YO and draw through 2 loops on hook, YO, skip next 3 sts, insert hook in next st, YO and pull up a loop, YO and draw through 2 loops on hook, YO and draw through all 3 loops on hook **(counts as one dc)**.

Row 1 (Right side)**:** Dc in fifth ch from hook **(4 skipped chs count as first dc plus ch 1)**, ch 1, skip next ch, (dc in next ch, ch 1, skip next ch) 3 times, decrease, ★ ch 1, skip next ch, (dc in next ch, ch 1, skip next ch) 3 times, (dc, ch 3, dc) in next ch, ch 1, skip next ch, (dc in next ch, ch 1, skip next ch) 3 times, decrease; repeat from ★ across to last 8 chs, ch 1, skip next ch, (dc in next ch, ch 1, skip next ch) 3 times, (dc, ch 1, dc) in last ch.

Note: Loop a short piece of yarn around any stitch to mark Row 1 as **right** side.

Row 2: Ch 3 **(counts as first dc)**, turn; 2 dc in first dc, dc in next ch-1 sp, (dc in next dc and in next ch-1 sp) 3 times, decrease, ★ (dc in next ch-1 sp and in next dc) 3 times, (2 dc, ch 3, 2 dc) in next ch-3 sp, (dc in next dc and in next ch-1 sp) 3 times, decrease; repeat from ★ across to last 4 ch-1 sps, dc in next ch-1 sp, (dc in next dc and in next ch-1 sp) 3 times, 3 dc in last dc.

Row 3: Ch 4 **(counts as first dc plus ch 1)**, turn; dc in first dc, ch 1, skip next dc, (dc in next dc, ch 1, skip next dc) 3 times, decrease, ch 1, (skip next dc, dc in next dc, ch 1) 3 times, ★ (dc, ch 3, dc) in next ch-3 sp, ch 1, (dc in next dc, ch 1, skip next dc) 3 times, decrease, ch 1, (skip next dc, dc in next dc, ch 1) 3 times; repeat from ★ across to last 2 dc, skip next dc, (dc, ch 1, dc) in last dc.

Repeat Rows 2 and 3 for pattern.

104 EARLY DAWN

Note: Uses Colors A, B, and C in the following sequence: 1 Row Color A, ★ 2 rows **each** Color B, Color C, Color B, Color A; repeat from ★ for stripe sequence.

With Color A, chain a multiple of 13 + 4 chs.

To decrease (uses next 2 sts), ★ YO, insert hook in **next** st, YO and pull up a loop, YO and draw through 2 loops on hook; repeat from ★ once **more**, YO and draw through all 3 loops on hook **(counts as one dc)**.

Row 1 (Right side)**:** Dc in fourth ch from hook **(3 skipped chs count as first dc)** and in next 3 chs, decrease 3 times, dc in next 3 chs, ★ 3 dc in next ch, dc in next 3 chs, decrease 3 times, dc in next 3 chs; repeat from ★ across to last ch, 2 dc in last ch; finish off.

Note: Loop a short piece of yarn around any stitch to mark Row 1 as **right** side.

Row 2: With **wrong** side facing, join Color B with slip st in first dc; ch 3 **(counts as first dc, now and throughout)**, 2 dc in same st as joining, ch 2, skip next 3 dc, sc in next dc, ch 5, skip next 3 dc, sc in next dc, ch 2, ★ skip next 3 dc, 5 dc in next dc, ch 2, skip next 3 dc, sc in next dc, ch 5, skip next 3 dc, sc in next dc, ch 2; repeat from ★ across to last 4 dc, skip next 3 dc, 3 dc in last dc.

Row 3: Ch 3, turn; dc in first dc, 2 dc in next dc, dc in next dc, ch 2, skip next ch-2 sp, sc in next ch-5 sp, ch 2, skip next ch-2 sp, dc in next dc, ★ 2 dc in next dc, 3 dc in next dc, 2 dc in next dc, dc in next dc, ch 2, skip next ch-2 sp, sc in next ch-5 sp, ch 2, skip next ch-2 sp, dc in next dc; repeat from ★ across to last 2 dc, 2 dc in each of last 2 dc; finish off.

Row 4: With **wrong** side facing, join Color C with slip st in first dc; ch 3, (2 dc in next dc, dc in next dc) twice, skip next 2 ch-2 sps, dc in next dc, ★ (2 dc in next dc, dc in next dc) 4 times, skip next 2 ch-2 sps, dc in next dc; repeat from ★ across to last 4 dc, (2 dc in next dc, dc in next dc) twice.

Row 5: Ch 3, turn; dc in first 4 dc, decrease 3 times, dc in next 3 dc, ★ 3 dc in next dc, dc in next 3 dc, decrease 3 times, dc in next 3 dc; repeat from ★ across to last dc, 2 dc in last dc; finish off.

Repeat Rows 2-5 for pattern, working in stripe sequence.

105 SIMPLE ELEGANCE

Note: Uses Colors A, B, and C in the following sequence: ★ 4 Rows **each** Color A, Color B, Color C; repeat from ★ for stripe sequence.

With Color A, chain a multiple of 23 + 22 chs.

Row 1 (Right side)**:** Sc in second ch from hook and in next 9 chs, 3 sc in next ch, sc in next 10 chs, ★ skip next 2 chs, sc in next 10 chs, 3 sc in next ch, sc in next 10 chs; repeat from ★ across.

Note: Loop a short piece of yarn around any stitch to mark Row 1 as **right** side.

Row 2: Ch 1, turn; sc in first sc, skip next sc, sc in next 9 sc, 3 sc in next sc, ★ sc in next 10 sc, skip next 2 sc, sc in next 10 sc, 3 sc in next sc; repeat from ★ across to last 11 sc, sc in next 9 sc, skip next sc, sc in last sc.

To treble crochet (abbreviated tr), YO twice, insert hook in st indicated, YO and pull up a loop (4 loops on hook), (YO and draw through 2 loops on hook) 3 times.

To decrease (uses next 2 sc), ★ YO twice, insert hook in **next** sc, YO and pull up a loop, (YO and draw through 2 loops on hook) twice; repeat from ★ once **more**, YO and draw through all 3 loops on hook **(counts as one tr)**.

To double decrease (uses next 4 sc), YO twice, insert hook in next sc, YO and pull up a loop, (YO and draw through 2 loops on hook) twice, YO twice, skip next 2 sc, insert hook in next sc, YO and pull up a loop, (YO and draw through 2 loops on hook) twice, YO and draw through all 3 loops on hook **(counts as one tr)**.

Row 3: Ch 3, turn; skip first sc, tr in next sc, [skip next 2 sc, (tr, ch 1, tr) in next sc] twice, skip next 2 sc, tr in next sc, ch 1, (tr, ch 1) twice in next sc, tr in next sc, [skip next 2 sc, (tr, ch 1, tr) in next sc] twice, ★ skip next 2 sc, double decrease, [skip next 2 sc, (tr, ch 1, tr) in next sc] twice, skip next 2 sc, tr in next sc, ch 1, (tr, ch 1) twice in next sc, tr in next sc, [skip next 2 sc, (tr, ch 1, tr) in next sc] twice; repeat from ★ across to last 4 sc, skip next 2 sc, decrease.

Row 4: Ch 1, turn; sc in first 2 tr and in next ch-1 sp, (sc in next 2 tr and in next ch-1 sp) twice, sc in next tr, 3 sc in next ch-1 sp, ★ sc in next tr and in next ch-1 sp, (sc in next 2 tr and in next ch-1 sp) twice, sc in next tr, skip next tr, sc in next tr and in next ch-1 sp, (sc in next 2 tr and in next ch-1 sp) twice, sc in next tr, 3 sc in next ch-1 sp; repeat from ★ across to last 3 ch-1 sps, sc in next tr, (sc in next ch-1 sp and in next 2 tr) 3 times; finish off.

Row 5: With **right** side facing, join Color B with sc in first sc *(see Joining With Sc, page 158)*; skip next sc, sc in next 9 sc, 3 sc in next sc, ★ 2 sc in next sc, sc in next 8 sc, skip next 2 sc, sc in next 8 sc, 2 sc in next sc, 3 sc in next sc; repeat from ★ across to last 11 sc, sc in next 9 sc, skip next sc, sc in last sc.

Repeat Rows 2-5 for pattern, working in stripe sequence.

106 FELICITY

Chain a multiple of 25 + 4 chs.

To double crochet 4 together (abbreviated dc4tog), ★ YO, insert hook in **next** st, YO and pull up a loop, YO and draw through 2 loops on hook; repeat from ★ 3 times **more**, YO and draw through all 5 loops on hook **(counts as one dc)**.

To double crochet 5 together (abbreviated dc5tog), ★ YO, insert hook in **next** st, YO and pull up a loop, YO and draw through 2 loops on hook; repeat from ★ 4 times **more**, YO and draw through all 6 loops on hook **(counts as one dc)**.

Row 1 (Right side): Dc in fifth ch from hook **(4 skipped chs count as first dc plus one skipped ch)** and in next 10 chs, ch 3, dc in next 10 chs, ★ dc5tog, dc in next 10 chs, ch 3, dc in next 10 chs; repeat from ★ across to last 4 chs, dc4tog.

Note: Loop a short piece of yarn around any stitch to mark Row 1 as **right** side.

Row 2: Ch 3 **(counts as first dc, now and throughout)**, turn; skip first 2 dc, dc in next 3 dc, (ch 1, skip next dc, dc in next dc) 3 times, (2 dc, ch 3, 2 dc) in next ch-3 sp, (dc in next dc, ch 1, skip next dc) 3 times, dc in next 2 dc, ★ dc5tog, dc in next 2 dc, (ch 1, skip next dc, dc in next dc) 3 times, (2 dc, ch 3, 2 dc) in next ch-3 sp, (dc in next dc, ch 1, skip next dc) 3 times, dc in next 2 dc; repeat from ★ across to last 4 dc, dc4tog.

Row 3: Ch 3, turn; skip first 2 dc, dc in next dc, (dc in next ch-1 sp and in next dc) twice, ch 1, dc in next 3 dc, (2 dc, ch 3, 2 dc) in next ch-3 sp, dc in next 3 dc, ch 1, (dc in next dc and in next ch-1 sp) twice, ★ dc5tog, (dc in next ch-1 sp and in next dc) twice, ch 1, dc in next 3 dc, (2 dc, ch 3, 2 dc) in next ch-3 sp, dc in next 3 dc, ch 1, (dc in next dc and in next ch-1 sp) twice; repeat from ★ across to last 4 dc, dc4tog.

Row 4: Ch 3, turn; skip first 2 dc, dc in next 3 dc, ch 1, dc in next dc, (ch 1, skip next dc, dc in next dc) twice, (2 dc, ch 3, 2 dc) in next ch-3 sp, dc in next dc, ch 1, (skip next dc, dc in next dc, ch 1) twice, dc in next 2 dc, ★ dc5tog, dc in next 2 dc, ch 1, dc in next dc, (ch 1, skip next dc, dc in next dc) twice, (2 dc, ch 3, 2 dc) in next ch-3 sp, dc in next dc, ch 1, (skip next dc, dc in next dc, ch 1) twice, dc in next 2 dc; repeat from ★ across to last 4 dc, dc4tog.

Repeat Rows 3 and 4 for pattern.

107 ALPINE LACE

Note: Uses Colors A, B, and C in the following sequence: ★ 3 rows Color A, 1 row Color B, 3 rows Color C, 1 row Color A, 3 rows Color B, 1 row Color C; repeat from ★ for stripe sequence.

With Color A, chain a multiple of 11 + 5 chs.

Row 1 (Right side)**:** Dc in sixth ch from hook **(5 skipped chs count as first dc plus ch 2)**, (ch 1, skip next ch, dc in next ch) 3 times, skip next 3 chs, 5 dc in next ch, ★ ch 2, dc in next ch, (ch 1, skip next ch, dc in next ch) 3 times, skip next 3 chs, 5 dc in next ch; repeat from ★ across.

Note: Loop a short piece of yarn around any stitch to mark Row 1 as **right** side.

Rows 2 and 3: Ch 5 **(counts as first dc plus ch 2, now and throughout)**, turn; dc in first dc, ch 1, (skip next dc, dc in next dc, ch 1) twice, skip next ch-1 sp, dc in next ch-1 sp, ★ skip next ch-1 sp, 5 dc in next ch-2 sp, ch 2, dc in next dc, ch 1, (skip next dc, dc in next dc, ch 1) twice, skip next ch-1 sp, dc in next ch-1 sp; repeat from ★ across to last 2 sps, skip next ch-1 sp, 4 dc in last ch-2 sp, dc in last dc; at end of last row, finish off.

Row 4: With **wrong** side facing, join Color B with slip st in first dc; ch 5, dc in same st as joining, ch 1, (skip next dc, dc in next dc, ch 1) twice, skip next ch-1 sp, dc in next ch-1 sp, ★ skip next ch-1 sp, 5 dc in next ch-2 sp, ch 2, dc in next dc, ch 1, (skip next dc, dc in next dc, ch 1) twice, skip next ch-1 sp, dc in next ch-1 sp; repeat from ★ across to last 2 sps, skip next ch-1 sp, 4 dc in last ch-2 sp, dc in last dc; finish off.

Row 5: With **right** side facing, join Color C with slip st in first dc; ch 5, dc in same st as joining, ch 1, (skip next dc, dc in next dc, ch 1) twice, skip next ch-1 sp, dc in next ch-1 sp, ★ skip next ch-1 sp, 5 dc in next ch-2 sp, ch 2, dc in next dc, ch 1, (skip next dc, dc in next dc, ch 1) twice, skip next ch-1 sp, dc in next ch-1 sp; repeat from ★ across to last 2 sps, skip next ch-1 sp, 4 dc in last ch-2 sp, dc in last dc.

Repeat Rows 2-5 for pattern, working in stripe sequence.

108 POETRY

Chain a multiple of 18 + 3 chs.

Row 1: Dc in sixth ch from hook, ch 2, skip next 2 chs, dc in next ch, ch 2, skip next 2 chs, (dc, ch 5, dc) in next ch, ch 2, skip next 2 chs, dc in next ch, ★ ch 2, skip next 2 chs, [YO, insert hook in next ch, YO and pull up a loop, YO and draw through 2 loops on hook, (YO, skip **next** 2 chs, insert hook in **next** ch, YO and pull up a loop, YO and draw through 2 loops on hook) twice, YO and draw through all 4 loops on hook **(counts as one dc)]**, ch 2, skip next 2 chs, dc in next ch, ch 2, skip next 2 chs, (dc, ch 5, dc) in next ch, ch 2, skip next 2 chs, dc in next ch; repeat from ★ across to last 6 chs, ch 2, skip next 2 chs, [YO, insert hook in next ch, YO and pull up a loop, YO and draw through 2 loops on hook, YO, skip next 2 chs, insert hook in next ch, YO and pull up a loop, YO and draw through 2 loops on hook, YO and draw through all 3 loops on hook **(counts as one dc)]**.

Row 2 (Right side)**:** Ch 1, turn; sc in first dc, ★ skip next sp, (dc, ch 1, dc) in next dc, skip next sp, 11 dc in next ch-5 sp, skip next sp, (dc, ch 1, dc) in next dc, skip next sp, sc in next dc; repeat from ★ across.

Note: Loop a short piece of yarn around any stitch to mark Row 2 as **right** side.

Row 3: Ch 2, turn; dc in next ch-1 sp, skip next dc, (dc, ch 1, dc) in next dc, skip next dc, dc in next dc, (ch 1, dc in next dc) 6 times, skip next dc, (dc, ch 1, dc) in next dc, ★ [† YO, skip next dc, insert hook in next ch-1 sp, YO and pull up a loop, YO and draw through 2 loops on hook †, YO, skip next dc, insert hook in next sc, YO and pull up a loop, YO and draw through 2 loops on hook, repeat from † to † once, YO and draw through all 4 loops on hook **(counts as one dc)]**, skip next dc, (dc, ch 1, dc) in next dc, skip next dc, dc in next dc, (ch 1, dc in next dc) 6 times, skip next dc, (dc, ch 1, dc) in next dc; repeat from ★ across to last ch-1 sp, [YO, skip next dc, insert hook in next ch-1 sp, YO and pull up a loop, YO and draw through 2 loops on hook, YO, skip next dc, insert hook in next sc, YO and pull up a loop, YO and draw through 2 loops on hook, YO and draw through all 3 loops on hook **(counts as one dc)]**.

To work Picot, ch 2, slip st in top of sc just made.

Row 4: Ch 1, turn; [pull up a loop in each of first 2 sts, YO and draw through all 3 loops on hook **(counts as one sc)]**, sc in next ch-1 sp, sc in next 2 dc and in next ch-1 sp, work Picot, (sc in next dc and in next ch-1 sp, work Picot) 5 times, sc in next 2 dc and in next ch-1 sp, ★ [pull up a loop in each of next 3 sts, YO and draw through all 4 loops on hook **(counts as one sc)]**, sc in next ch-1 sp, sc in next 2 dc and in next ch-1 sp, work Picot, (sc in next dc and in next ch-1 sp, work Picot) 5 times, sc in next 2 dc and in next ch-1 sp; repeat from ★ across to last 2 dc, [pull up a loop in each of last 2 dc, YO and draw through all 3 loops on hook **(counts as one sc)]**.

Row 5: Ch 2, turn; skip first 3 sc, dc in next sc, ch 3, skip next 2 sc, dc in next sc, ch 2, skip next 2 sc, (dc, ch 5, dc) in next sc, ch 2, skip next sc, dc in next sc, ch 3, ★ skip next 3 sc, [YO, insert hook in next sc, YO and pull up a loop, YO and draw through 2 loops on hook, (YO, skip **next** 2 sc, insert hook in **next** sc, YO and pull up a loop, YO and draw through 2 loops on hook) twice, YO and draw through all 4 loops on hook **(counts as one dc)]**, ch 3, skip next 2 sc, dc in next sc, ch 2, skip next 2 sc, (dc, ch 5, dc) in next sc, ch 2, skip next sc, dc in next sc, ch 3; repeat from ★ across to last 7 sc, [YO, skip next 3 sc, insert hook in next sc, YO and pull up a loop, YO and draw through 2 loops on hook, YO, skip next 2 sc, insert hook in next sc, YO and pull up a loop, YO and draw through 2 loops on hook, YO and draw through all 3 loops on hook **(counts as one dc)]**.

Repeat Rows 2-5 for pattern.

109 BIG DIPPER

Chain a multiple of 19 + 3 chs.

To decrease (uses next 3 sts), YO, insert hook in next st, YO and pull up a loop, YO and draw through 2 loops on hook, YO, skip next st, insert hook in next st, YO and pull up a loop, YO and draw through 2 loops on hook, YO and draw through all 3 loops on hook **(counts as one dc)**.

Row 1 (Right side)**:** 5 Dc in fourth ch from hook **(3 skipped chs count as one dc)**, skip next ch, (dc in next ch, skip next ch) 3 times, decrease, (skip next ch, dc in next ch) 3 times, ★ skip next ch, 6 dc in each of next 2 chs, skip next ch, (dc in next ch, skip next ch) 3 times, decrease, (skip next ch, dc in next ch) 3 times; repeat from ★ across to last 2 chs, skip next ch, 6 dc in last ch.

Note: Loop a short piece of yarn around any stitch to mark Row 1 as **right** side.

Row 2: Ch 3 **(counts as first dc)**, turn; 5 dc in first dc, skip next dc, (dc in next dc, skip next dc) 3 times, decrease, (skip next dc, dc in next dc) 3 times, ★ skip next dc, 6 dc in each of next 2 dc, skip next dc, (dc in next dc, skip next dc) 3 times, decrease, (skip next dc, dc in next dc) 3 times; repeat from ★ across to last 2 dc, skip next dc, 6 dc in last dc.

Repeat Row 2 for pattern.

110 BUILDING BLOCKS

Note: Uses MC and Colors A and B in the following sequence: ★ 1 Row MC, 3 rows Color A, 1 row MC, 3 rows Color B; repeat from ★ for stripe sequence.

With MC, chain a multiple of 38 + 2 chs.

To dc decrease (uses next 2 sts), ★ YO, insert hook in **next** st, YO and pull up a loop, YO and draw through 2 loops on hook; repeat from ★ once **more**, YO and draw through all 3 loops on hook **(counts as one dc)**.

To double dc decrease (uses next 3 sts), ★ YO, insert hook in **next** st, YO and pull up a loop, YO and draw through 2 loops on hook; repeat from ★ 2 times **more**, YO and draw through all 4 loops on hook **(counts as one dc)**.

Row 1 (Right side)**:** Dc in third ch from hook, ch 1, (skip next 2 chs, 3 dc in next ch, ch 1) 5 times, skip next 2 chs, (3 dc, ch 3, 3 dc) in next ch, ch 1, (skip next 2 chs, 3 dc in next ch, ch 1) 5 times, ★ skip next 2 chs, double dc decrease, ch 1, (skip next 2 chs, 3 dc in next ch, ch 1) 5 times, skip next 2 chs, (3 dc, ch 3, 3 dc) in next ch, ch 1, (skip next 2 chs, 3 dc in next ch, ch 1) 5 times; repeat from ★ across to last 4 chs, skip next 2 chs, dc decrease; finish off.

Note: Loop a short piece of yarn around any stitch to mark Row 1 as **right** side.

To beginning sc decrease (uses 2 dc and one ch-1 sp), pull up a loop in first dc, in next ch-1 sp, and in next dc, YO and draw through all 4 loops on hook.

To sc decrease (uses 2 dc and one ch-1 sp), pull up a loop in next dc, in next ch-1 sp, and in next dc, YO and draw through all 4 loops on hook.

To double sc decrease (uses 2 dc and 2 ch-1 sps), pull up a loop in next dc, in each of next 2 ch-1 sps, and in next dc, YO and draw through all 5 loops on hook.

Row 2: With **right** side facing, join Color A with slip st in first dc; beginning sc decrease, (ch 3, skip next dc, sc decrease) 5 times, ch 3, skip next dc, pull up a loop in next dc and in next ch-3 sp, YO and draw through all 3 loops on hook, ch 3, pull up a loop in same ch-3 sp and in next dc, YO and draw through all 3 loops on hook, (ch 3, skip next dc, sc decrease) 5 times, ★ ch 3, skip next dc, double sc decrease, (ch 3, skip next dc, sc decrease) 5 times, ch 3, skip next dc, pull up a loop in next dc and in next ch-3 sp, YO and draw through all 3 loops on hook, ch 3, pull up a loop in same ch-3 sp and in next dc, YO and draw through all 3 loops on hook, (ch 3, skip next dc, sc decrease) 5 times; repeat from ★ across to last 3 dc, ch 3, skip next dc, pull up a loop in each of last 2 dc, YO and draw through all 3 loops on hook.

Row 3: Ch 2, turn; dc in next ch-3 sp, ch 1, (3 dc in next ch-3 sp, ch 1) 5 times, (3 dc, ch 3, 3 dc) in next ch-3 sp, ch 1, (3 dc in next ch-3 sp, ch 1) 5 times, ★ dc in next ch-3 sp, YO, insert hook in same ch-3 sp, YO and pull up a loop, YO and draw through 2 loops on hook, YO, insert hook in next ch-3 sp, YO and pull up a loop, YO and draw through 2 loops on hook, YO and draw through all 3 loops on hook, dc in same ch-3 sp, ch 1, (3 dc in next ch-3 sp, ch 1) 5 times, (3 dc, ch 3, 3 dc) in next ch-3 sp, ch 1, (3 dc in next ch-3 sp, ch 1) 5 times; repeat from ★ across to last ch-3 sp, YO, insert hook in last ch-3 sp, YO and pull up a loop, YO and draw through 2 loops on hook, YO, insert hook in last st, YO and pull up a loop, YO and draw through 2 loops on hook, YO and draw through all 3 loops on hook.

Row 4: Ch 1, turn; beginning sc decrease, (ch 3, skip next dc, sc decrease) 5 times, ch 3, skip next dc, pull up a loop in next dc and in next ch-3 sp, YO and draw through all 3 loops on hook, ch 3, pull up a loop in same ch-3 sp and in next dc, YO and draw through all 3 loops on hook,

(ch 3, skip next dc, sc decrease) 5 times, ★ ch 3, skip next dc, double sc decrease, (ch 3, skip next dc, sc decrease) 5 times, ch 3, skip next dc, pull up a loop in next dc and in next ch-3 sp, YO and draw through all 3 loops on hook, ch 3, pull up a loop in same ch-3 sp and in next dc, YO and draw through all 3 loops on hook, (ch 3, skip next dc, sc decrease) 5 times; repeat from ★ across to last 3 dc, ch 3, skip next dc, pull up a loop in each of last 2 dc, YO and draw through all 3 loops on hook; finish off.

Row 5: With **right** side facing, join MC with slip st in first st; ch 2, dc in next ch-3 sp, ch 1, (3 dc in next ch-3 sp, ch 1) 5 times, (3 dc, ch 3, 3 dc) in next ch-3 sp, ch 1, (3 dc in next ch-3 sp, ch 1) 5 times, ★ dc in next ch-3 sp, YO, insert hook in same ch-3 sp, YO and pull up a loop, YO and draw through 2 loops on hook, YO, insert hook in next ch-3 sp, YO and pull up a loop, YO and draw through 2 loops on hook, YO and draw through all 3 loops on hook, dc in same ch-3 sp, ch 1, (3 dc in next ch-3 sp, ch 1) 5 times, (3 dc, ch 3, 3 dc) in next ch-3 sp, ch 1, (3 dc in next ch-3 sp, ch 1) 5 times; repeat from ★ across to last ch-3 sp, YO, insert hook in last ch-3 sp, YO and pull up a loop, YO and draw through 2 loops on hook, YO, insert hook in last st, YO and pull up a loop, YO and draw through 2 loops on hook, YO and draw through all 3 loops on hook; finish off.

Repeat Rows 2-5 for pattern, working in stripe sequence.

111 SWEET DREAMS

Note: Uses MC and CC in the following sequence: ★ 2 Rows **each** MC, CC; repeat from ★ for stripe sequence.

With MC, chain a multiple of 28 + 2 chs.

To decrease (uses next 2 sts), ★ YO, insert hook in **next** st, YO and pull up a loop, YO and draw through 2 loops on hook; repeat from ★ once **more**, YO and draw through all 3 loops on hook **(counts as one dc).**

To double decrease (uses next 3 sts), ★ YO, insert hook in **next** st, YO and pull up a loop, YO and draw through 2 loops on hook; repeat from ★ 2 times **more**, YO and draw through all 4 loops on hook **(counts as one dc).**

Row 1 (Right side)**:** Dc in third ch from hook and in next 12 chs, 3 dc in next ch, dc in next 12 chs, ★ double decrease, dc in next 12 chs, 3 dc in next ch, dc in next 12 chs; repeat from ★ across to last 2 chs, decrease.

Note: Loop a short piece of yarn around any stitch to mark Row 1 as **right** side.

Row 2: Ch 2, turn; skip first dc, dc in next 13 dc, 3 dc in next dc, dc in next 12 dc, ★ double decrease, dc in next 12 dc, 3 dc in next dc, dc in next 12 dc; repeat from ★ across to last 2 dc, decrease; finish off.

Row 3: With **right** side facing, join CC with slip st in first dc; ch 2, (dc in next dc, skip next 2 dc, 5 dc in next dc, skip next 2 dc) twice, 2 dc in next dc, 3 dc in next dc, 2 dc in next dc, skip next 2 dc, 5 dc in next dc, skip next 2 dc, dc in next dc, skip next 2 dc, 5 dc in next dc, ★ skip next 2 dc, double decrease, skip next 2 dc, 5 dc in next dc, skip next 2 dc, dc in next dc, skip next 2 dc, 5 dc in next dc, skip next 2 dc, 2 dc in next dc, 3 dc in next dc, 2 dc in next dc, skip next 2 dc, 5 dc in next dc, skip next 2 dc, dc in next dc, skip next 2 dc, 5 dc in next dc; repeat from ★ across to last 4 dc, skip next 2 dc, decrease.

Row 4: Ch 1, turn; pull up a loop in each of first 2 dc, YO and draw through all 3 loops on hook, (ch 3, skip next dc, sc in next dc) 6 times, skip next dc, 3 dc in next dc, skip next dc, sc in next dc, (ch 3, skip next dc, sc in next dc) 5 times, ★ skip next dc, pull up a loop in each of next 3 dc, YO and draw through all 4 loops on hook, skip next dc, sc in next dc, (ch 3, skip next dc, sc in next dc) 5 times, skip next dc, 3 dc in next dc, skip next dc, sc in next dc, (ch 3, skip next dc, sc in next dc) 5 times; repeat from ★ across to last 3 dc, ch 3, skip next dc, pull up a loop in each of last 2 dc, YO and draw through all 3 loops on hook; finish off.

Row 5: With **right** side facing, join MC with slip st in first st; ch 2, dc in next ch-3 sp, 2 dc in each of next 5 ch-3 sps, skip next sc, 2 dc in next dc, 3 dc in next dc, 2 dc in next dc, 2 dc in each of next 5 ch-3 sps, ★ double decrease, 2 dc in each of next 5 ch-3 sps, skip next sc, 2 dc in next dc, 3 dc in next dc, 2 dc in next dc, 2 dc in each of next 5 ch-3 sps; repeat from ★ across to last ch-3 sp, [YO, insert hook in last ch-3 sp, YO and pull up a loop, YO and draw through 2 loops on hook, YO, insert hook in last st, YO and pull up a loop, YO and draw through 2 loops on hook, YO and draw through all 3 loops on hook **(counts as one dc)**].

Repeat Rows 2-5 for pattern.

112 WAVES OF LACE

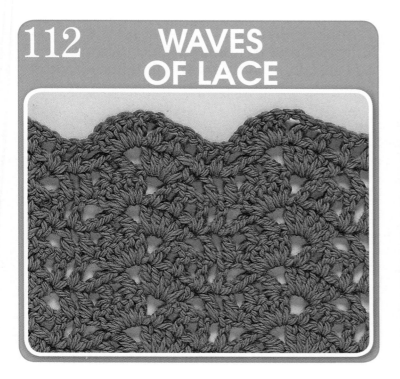

113 SIMPLICITY

Chain a multiple of 11 + 2 chs.

Row 1 (Right side)**:** Sc in second ch from hook, ★ ch 2, skip next 2 chs, dc in next 2 chs, ch 2, skip next 2 chs, sc in next 5 chs; repeat from ★ across.

Note: Loop a short piece of yarn around any stitch to mark Row 1 as **right** side.

Row 2: Ch 5 **(counts as first dc plus ch 2, now and throughout)**, turn; dc in first sc, ch 1, (skip next sc, dc in next sc, ch 1) twice, dc in next ch-2 sp, ★ 5 dc in next ch-2 sp, ch 2, dc in next sc, ch 1, (skip next sc, dc in next sc, ch 1) twice, dc in next ch-2 sp; repeat from ★ across to last ch-2 sp, 4 dc in last ch-2 sp, dc in last sc.

Row 3: Ch 5, turn; dc in first dc, ch 1, (skip next dc, dc in next dc, ch 1) twice, dc in next ch-1 sp, ★ skip next 2 ch-1 sps, 5 dc in next ch-2 sp, ch 2, dc in next dc, ch 1, (skip next dc, dc in next dc, ch 1) twice, dc in next ch-1 sp; repeat from ★ across to last 3 sps, skip next 2 ch-1 sps, 4 dc in last ch-2 sp, dc in last dc.

Repeat Row 3 for pattern.

Chain a multiple of 17 + 3 chs.

Row 1 (Right side)**:** Dc in fourth ch from hook **(3 skipped chs count as first dc)**, 2 dc in each of next 2 chs, (skip next ch, dc in next ch) 5 times, ★ skip next ch, 2 dc in each of next 6 chs, (skip next ch, dc in next ch) 5 times; repeat from ★ across to last 4 chs, skip next ch, 2 dc in each of last 3 chs.

Note: Loop a short piece of yarn around any stitch to mark Row 1 as **right** side.

Row 2: Ch 1, turn; sc in each dc across.

Row 3: Ch 3 **(counts as first dc)**, turn; dc in first sc, 2 dc in each of next 2 sc, (skip next sc, dc in next sc) 5 times, ★ skip next sc, 2 dc in each of next 6 sc, (skip next sc, dc in next sc) 5 times; repeat from ★ across to last 4 sc, skip next sc, 2 dc in each of last 3 sc.

Repeat Rows 2 and 3 for pattern.

114 TEXTURED CHEVRON

Chain a multiple of 20 + 1 ch.

To double decrease (uses next 3 sts), ★ YO, insert hook in **next** st, YO and pull up a loop, YO and draw through 2 loops on hook; repeat from ★ 2 times **more**, YO and draw through all 4 loops on hook **(counts as first dc)**.

Row 1 (Right side)**:** Dc in fourth ch from hook **(3 skipped chs count as first dc)** and in next 7 chs, 3 dc in next ch, ★ dc in next 8 chs, double decrease, dc in next 8 chs, 3 dc in next ch; repeat from ★ across to last 9 chs, dc in last 9 chs.

Note: Loop a short piece of yarn around any stitch to mark Row 1 as **right** side.

Row 2: Ch 3 **(counts as first dc, now and throughout)**, turn; skip first dc, dc in next 9 dc, 3 dc in next dc, ★ dc in next 8 dc, YO, insert hook in next dc, YO and pull up a loop, YO and draw through 2 loops on hook, YO, skip next dc, insert hook in next dc, YO and pull up a loop, YO and draw through 2 loops on hook, YO and draw through all 3 loops on hook, dc in next 8 dc, 3 dc in next dc; repeat from ★ across to last 10 dc, dc in last 10 dc.

To work Cross St (uses next 2 dc), skip next dc, dc in next dc, working **around** dc just made, dc in skipped dc.

Row 3: Ch 3, turn; working in Back Loops Only *(Fig. 2, page 159)*, skip first 2 dc, work 5 Cross Sts, ch 1, dc in next dc, working **around** dc just made, dc in same st as first dc of last Cross St, work 4 Cross Sts, ★ skip next st, work 5 Cross Sts, ch 1, dc in next dc, working **around** dc just made, dc in same st as first dc of last Cross St, work 4 Cross Sts; repeat from ★ across to last 2 dc, skip next dc, dc in last dc.

To decrease (uses next 4 sts), YO, insert hook in next dc, YO and pull up a loop, YO and draw through 2 loops on hook, YO, skip next 2 dc, insert hook in next dc, YO and pull up a loop, YO and draw through 2 loops on hook, YO and draw through all 3 loops on hook **(counts as one dc)**.

Row 4: Ch 3, turn; working in Front Loops Only *(Fig. 2, page 159)*, skip first 2 dc, dc in next 9 dc, 3 dc in next ch-1 sp, ★ dc in next 8 dc, decrease, dc in next 8 dc, 3 dc in next ch-1 sp; repeat from ★ across to last 11 dc, dc in next 9 dc, skip next dc, dc in last dc.

Row 5: Ch 3, turn; working in both loops, skip first 2 dc, dc in next 9 dc, 3 dc in next dc, ★ dc in next 8 dc, double decrease, dc in next 8 dc, 3 dc in next dc; repeat from ★ across to last 11 dc, dc in next 9 dc, skip next dc, dc in last dc.

Row 6: Ch 3, turn; working in Front Loops Only, skip first 2 dc, work 5 Cross Sts, ch 1, dc in next dc, working **around** dc just made, dc in same st as first dc of last Cross St, work 4 Cross Sts, ★ skip next dc, work 5 Cross Sts, ch 1, dc in next dc, working **around** dc just made, dc in same st as first dc of last Cross St, work 4 Cross Sts; repeat from ★ across to last 2 dc, skip next dc, dc in last dc.

Row 7: Ch 3, turn; working in Back Loops Only, skip first 2 dc, dc in next 9 dc, 3 dc in next ch-1 sp, ★ dc in next 8 dc, decrease, dc in next 8 dc, 3 dc in next ch-1 sp; repeat from ★ across to last 11 dc, dc in next 9 dc, skip next dc, dc in last dc.

Row 8: Ch 3, turn; working in both loops, skip first 2 dc, dc in next 9 dc, 3 dc in next dc, ★ dc in next 8 dc, YO, insert hook in next dc, YO and pull up a loop, YO and draw through 2 loops on hook, YO, skip next dc, insert hook in next dc, YO and pull up a loop, YO and draw through 2 loops on hook, YO and draw through all 3 loops on hook, dc in next 8 dc, 3 dc in next dc; repeat from ★ across to last 11 dc, dc in next 9 dc, skip next dc, dc in last dc.

Repeat Rows 3-8 for pattern.

115 STAGGERED SHELLS

Chain a multiple of 8 + 4 chs.

Row 1: 2 Dc in fourth ch from hook **(3 skipped chs count as first dc)**, skip next 2 chs, sc in next 3 chs, ★ skip next 2 chs, 5 dc in next ch, skip next 2 chs, sc in next 3 chs; repeat from ★ across to last 3 chs, skip next 2 chs, 3 dc in last ch.

Row 2 (Right side)**:** Ch 1, turn; working in Back Loops Only **(Fig. 2, page 159)**, sc in first 2 dc, ch 1, skip next 2 sts, (dc, ch 1) twice in next sc, ★ skip next 2 sts, sc in next 3 dc, ch 1, skip next 2 sts, (dc, ch 1) twice in next sc; repeat from ★ across to last 4 sts, skip next 2 sts, sc in last 2 dc.

Note: Loop a short piece of yarn around any stitch to mark Row 2 as **right** side.

Row 3: Ch 1, turn; working in both loops, sc in first 2 sc, skip next ch-1 sp, 5 dc in next ch-1 sp, ★ skip next ch-1 sp, sc in next 3 sc, skip next ch-1 sp, 5 dc in next ch-1 sp; repeat from ★ across to last ch-1 sp, skip last ch-1 sp, sc in last 2 sc.

Row 4: Ch 4 **(counts as first dc plus ch 1)**, turn; working in Back Loops Only, dc in first sc, ch 1, skip next 2 sts, sc in next 3 dc, ch 1, ★ skip next 2 sts, (dc, ch 1) twice in next sc, skip next 2 sts, sc in next 3 dc, ch 1; repeat from ★ across to last 3 sts, skip next 2 sts, (dc, ch 1, dc) in last sc.

Row 5: Ch 3 **(counts as first dc)**, turn; working in both loops, 2 dc in first dc, skip next 2 ch-1 sps, sc in next 3 sc, ★ skip next ch-1 sp, 5 dc in next ch-1 sp, skip next ch-1 sp, sc in next 3 sc; repeat from ★ across to last 2 ch-1 sps, skip last 2 ch-1 sps, 3 dc in last dc.

Repeat Rows 2-5 for pattern.

116 LITTLE EYELETS

Note: Uses Colors A, B, and C in the following sequence: ★ 1 Row **each** Color A, Color B, Color C; repeat from ★ for stripe sequence.

With Color A, chain a multiple of 8 + 4 chs.

To decrease (uses next 3 sts), YO, insert hook in next st, YO and pull up a loop, YO and draw through 2 loops on hook, YO, skip next st, insert hook in next st, YO and pull up a loop, YO and draw through 2 loops on hook, YO and draw through all 3 loops on hook **(counts as one dc)**.

Row 1 (Right side)**:** Dc in fourth ch from hook **(3 skipped chs count as first dc)** and in next 2 chs, decrease, dc in next 2 chs, ★ (dc, ch 1, dc) in next ch, dc in next 2 chs, decrease, dc in next 2 chs; repeat from ★ across to last ch, 2 dc in last ch; finish off.

Note: Loop a short piece of yarn around any stitch to mark Row 1 as **right** side.

Row 2: With **wrong** side facing, join Color B with slip st in first dc; ch 3 **(counts as first dc, now and throughout)**, dc in same st as joining and in next 2 dc, decrease, dc in next 2 dc, ★ (dc, ch 1, dc) in next ch-1 sp, dc in next 2 dc, decrease, dc in next 2 dc; repeat from ★ across to last dc, 2 dc in last dc; finish off.

Row 3: With **right** side facing, join Color C with slip st in first dc; ch 3, dc in same st as joining and in next 2 dc, decrease, dc in next 2 dc, ★ (dc, ch 1, dc) in next ch-1 sp, dc in next 2 dc, decrease, dc in next 2 dc; repeat from ★ across to last dc, 2 dc in last dc; finish off.

Repeat Rows 2 and 3 for pattern, working in stripe sequence.

117 TRANSITION

Note: Uses MC and Colors A and B in the following sequence: ★ 1 Row **each** MC, Color A, MC, Color B; repeat from ★ for stripe sequence.

With MC, chain a multiple of 28 + 16 chs.

To decrease (uses next 3 sts), YO, insert hook in next st, YO and pull up a loop, YO and draw through 2 loops on hook, YO, skip next st, insert hook in next st, YO and pull up a loop, YO and draw through 2 loops on hook, YO and draw through all 3 loops on hook **(counts as one dc)**.

Row 1 (Right side)**:** Dc in third ch from hook and in next 5 chs, ch 3, ★ dc in next 6 chs, skip next 2 chs, sc in next 6 chs, ch 2, sc in next 6 chs, skip next 2 chs, dc in next 6 chs, ch 3; repeat from ★ across to last 8 chs, dc in next 5 chs, decrease; finish off.

Note: Loop a short piece of yarn around any stitch to mark Row 1 as **right** side.

Row 2: With **wrong** side facing, join Color A with sc in first dc *(see Joining With Sc, page 158)*; sc in next 5 dc, (sc, ch 2, sc) in next ch-3 sp, ★ sc in next 5 dc, skip next 2 sts, dc in next 5 sc, (dc, ch 3, dc) in next ch-2 sp, dc in next 5 sc, skip next 2 sts, sc in next 5 dc, (sc, ch 2, sc) in next ch-3 sp; repeat from ★ across to last 6 dc, sc in last 6 dc; finish off.

Row 3: With **right** side facing, join MC with slip st in first sc; ch 2, skip next sc, dc in next 5 sc, (dc, ch 3, dc) in next ch-2 sp, ★ dc in next 5 sc, skip next 2 sts, sc in next 5 dc, (sc, ch 2, sc) in next ch-3 sp, sc in next 5 dc, skip next 2 sts, dc in next 5 sc, (dc, ch 3, dc) in next ch-2 sp; repeat from ★ across to last 7 sc, dc in next 4 sc, decrease; finish off.

Repeat Rows 2 and 3 for pattern, working in stripe sequence.

118 ARCHED LACE

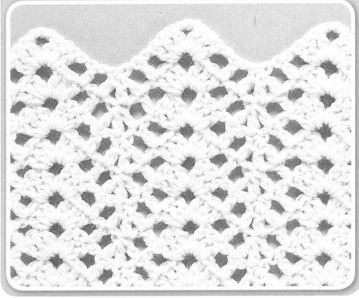

Chain a multiple of 11 + 3 chs.

Row 1 (Right side): Dc in fourth ch from hook **(3 skipped chs count as first dc)**, ch 1, skip next ch, dc in next ch, ch 1, skip next ch, 3 dc in next ch, ch 3, 3 dc in next ch, ch 1, skip next ch, dc in next ch, ch 1, ★ skip next ch, [YO, insert hook in **next** ch, YO and pull up a loop, YO and draw through 2 loops on hook] 3 times, YO and draw through all 4 loops on hook, ch 1, skip next ch, dc in next ch, ch 1, skip next ch, 3 dc in next ch, ch 3, 3 dc in next ch, ch 1, skip next ch, dc in next ch, ch 1; repeat from ★ across to last 3 chs, skip next ch, dc in last 2 chs.

Note: Loop a short piece of yarn around any stitch to mark Row 1 as **right** side.

To decrease (uses 3 sts and 2 chs), YO, insert hook in next st, YO and pull up a loop, YO and draw through 2 loops on hook, ★ YO, skip **next** ch, insert hook in **next** st, YO and pull up a loop, YO and draw through 2 loops on hook; repeat from ★ once **more**, YO and draw through all 4 loops on hook.

Row 2: Ch 3 **(counts as first dc)**, turn; dc in next dc, ch 1, skip next dc, dc in next dc, ch 1, (3 dc, ch 3, 3 dc) in next ch-3 sp, ch 1, skip next 2 dc, dc in next dc, ch 1, ★ skip next ch, decrease, ch 1, dc in next dc, ch 1, (3 dc, ch 3, 3 dc) in next ch-3 sp, ch 1, skip next 2 dc, dc in next dc, ch 1; repeat from ★ across to last 2 ch-1 sps, skip last 2 ch-1 sps, dc in last 2 dc.

Repeat Row 2 for pattern.

119 SALSA

Note: Uses MC and Colors A, B, and C in the following sequence: ★ 1 Row **each** MC, Color A, MC, Color B, MC, Color C; repeat from ★ for stripe sequence.

With MC, chain a multiple of 26 + 3 chs.

Row 1 (Right side): Dc in third ch from hook, ★ [skip next 2 chs, (dc, ch 1, dc) in next ch] 4 times, ch 3, (dc, ch 1, dc) in next ch, [skip next 2 chs, (dc, ch 1, dc) in next ch] 3 times, [YO, skip next 2 chs, insert hook in next ch, YO and pull up a loop, YO and draw through 2 loops on hook, YO, insert hook in next ch, YO and pull up a loop, YO and draw through 2 loops on hook, YO and draw through all 3 loops on hook **(counts as one dc)**]; repeat from ★ across; finish off.

Note: Loop a short piece of yarn around any stitch to mark Row 1 as **right** side.

Row 2: With **wrong** side facing, join Color A with slip st in first dc; [pull up a loop in same st as joining and in next dc, YO and draw through all 3 loops on hook **(counts as one sc)**], ch 1, (sc in next 2 dc, ch 1) 3 times, sc in next dc, (sc, ch 3, sc) in next ch-3 sp, sc in next dc, ch 1, (sc in next 2 dc, ch 1) 3 times, ★ skip next dc, sc in next dc, ch 1, skip next dc, (sc in next 2 dc, ch 1) 3 times, sc in next dc, (sc, ch 3, sc) in next ch-3 sp, sc in next dc, ch 1, (sc in next 2 dc, ch 1) 3 times; repeat from ★ across to last 2 dc, [pull up a loop in each of last 2 dc, YO and draw through all 3 loops on hook **(counts as one sc)**]; finish off.

Row 3: With **right** side facing, join MC with slip st in first sc; ch 2, dc in next ch-1 sp, (dc, ch 1, dc) in each of next 3 ch-1 sps, (dc, ch 1, dc, ch 3, dc, ch 1, dc) in next ch-3 sp, (dc, ch 1, dc) in each of next 3 ch-1 sps, ★ [(YO, insert hook in **next** ch-1 sp, YO and pull up a loop, YO and draw through 2 loops on hook) twice, YO and draw through all 3 loops on hook **(counts as one dc)**], (dc, ch 1, dc) in each of next 3 ch-1 sps, (dc, ch 1, dc, ch 3, dc, ch 1, dc) in next ch-3 sp, (dc, ch 1, dc) in each of next 3 ch-1 sps; repeat from ★ across to last ch-1 sp, [YO, insert hook in last ch-1 sp, YO and pull up a loop, YO and draw through 2 loops on hook, YO insert hook in last sc, YO and pull up a loop, YO and draw through 2 loops on hook, YO and draw through all 3 loops on hook **(counts as one dc)**]; finish off.

Repeat Rows 2 and 3 for pattern, working in stripe sequence.

120 PEEK-A-BOO SHELLS

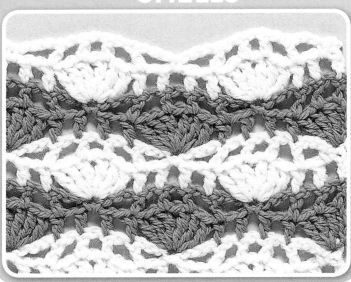

Note: Uses MC and CC in the following sequence: 1 Row MC, ★ 2 rows **each** CC, MC; repeat from ★ for stripe sequence.

With MC, chain a multiple of 12 + 6 chs.

Row 1 (Wrong side)**:** Dc in sixth ch from hook **(5 skipped chs count as first dc plus ch 1 and 1 skipped ch)**, ch 1, skip next ch, dc in next ch, ch 3, skip next 2 chs, sc in next ch, ch 3, skip next 2 chs, dc in next ch, ★ (ch 1, skip next ch, dc in next ch) 3 times, ch 3, skip next 2 chs, sc in next ch, ch 3, skip next 2 chs, dc in next ch; repeat from ★ across to last 4 chs, (ch 1, skip next ch, dc in next ch) twice; finish off.

Note: Loop a short piece of yarn around **back** of any stitch on Row 1 to mark **right** side.

To treble crochet (abbreviated tr), YO twice, insert hook in st indicated, YO and pull up a loop (4 loops on hook), (YO and draw through 2 loops on hook) 3 times.

Row 2: With **right** side facing, join CC with slip st in first dc; ch 4 **(counts as first dc plus ch 1)**, dc in next dc, ch 1, dc in next dc, (3 tr, ch 1, 3 tr) in next sc, dc in next dc, ★ (ch 1, dc in next dc) 3 times, (3 tr, ch 1, 3 tr) in next sc, dc in next dc; repeat from ★ across to last 2 dc, (ch 1, dc in next dc) twice.

Row 3: Ch 1, turn; sc in first dc and in next ch-1 sp, ★ ch 3, skip next dc, dc in next dc, ch 1, skip next 2 tr, (dc in next tr, ch 1) twice, skip next 2 tr, dc in next dc, ch 3, skip next ch-1 sp, sc in next ch-1 sp; repeat from ★ across to last dc, sc in last dc; finish off.

Row 4: With **right** side facing, join MC with slip st in first sc; ch 4 **(counts as first tr)**, 3 tr in same st as joining, skip next ch-3 sp, dc in next dc, (ch 1, dc in next dc) 3 times, ★ (3 tr, ch 1, 3 tr) in next sc, dc in next dc, (ch 1, dc in next dc) 3 times; repeat from ★ across to last 2 sc, skip next sc, 4 tr in last sc.

Row 5: Ch 4, turn; skip first 2 tr, dc in next tr, ch 1, skip next tr, dc in next dc, ch 3, skip next ch-1 sp, sc in next ch-1 sp, ch 3, skip next dc, dc in next dc, ★ ch 1, skip next 2 tr, dc in next tr, ch 1, dc in next tr, ch 1, skip next 2 tr, dc in next dc, ch 3, skip next ch-1 sp, sc in next ch-1 sp, ch 3, skip next dc, dc in next dc; repeat from ★ across to last 4 tr, (ch 1, skip next tr, dc in next tr) twice; finish off.

Repeat Rows 2-5 for pattern.

121 LOVERLY

Chain a multiple of 13 + 3 chs.

Row 1 (Right side)**:** Dc in fourth ch from hook **(3 skipped chs count as first dc)**, ch 1, skip next ch, dc in next ch, ch 1, skip next ch, 3 dc in next ch, ch 3, 3 dc in next ch, ch 1, skip next ch, dc in next ch, ch 1, ★ [YO, skip next ch, insert hook in next ch, YO and pull up a loop, YO and draw through 2 loops on hook, (YO, insert hook in **next** ch, YO and pull up a loop, YO and draw through 2 loops on hook) 4 times, YO and draw through all 6 loops on hook **(counts as one dc)]**, ch 1, skip next ch, dc in next ch, ch 1, skip next ch, 3 dc in next ch, ch 3, 3 dc in next ch, ch 1, skip next ch, dc in next ch, ch 1; repeat from ★ across to last 5 chs, YO, skip next ch, insert hook in next ch, YO and pull up a loop, YO and draw through 2 loops on hook, (YO, insert hook in **next** ch, YO and pull up a loop, YO and draw through 2 loops on hook) 3 times, YO and draw through all 5 loops on hook.

Note: Loop a short piece of yarn around any stitch to mark Row 1 as **right** side.

To decrease (uses 3 dc and 2 ch-1 sps), YO, insert hook in next dc, YO and pull up a loop, YO and draw through 2 loops on hook, [YO, insert hook in **next** ch-1 sp, YO and pull up a loop, YO and draw through 2 loops on hook, YO insert hook in **next** dc, YO and pull up a loop, YO and draw through 2 loops on hook] twice, YO and draw through all 6 loops on hook **(counts as one dc)**.

Row 2: Ch 3 **(counts as first dc)**, turn; skip next ch-1 sp, (dc in next dc, ch 1) twice, (3 dc, ch 3, 3 dc) in next ch-3 sp, ch 1, skip next 2 dc, dc in next dc, ch 1, ★ decrease, ch 1, dc in next dc, ch 1, (3 dc, ch 3, 3 dc) in next ch-3 sp, ch 1, skip next 2 dc, dc in next dc, ch 1; repeat from ★ across to last 3 dc, † YO, insert hook in **next** dc, YO and pull up a loop, YO and draw through 2 loops on hook †, YO, insert hook in next ch-1 sp, YO and pull up a loop, YO and draw through 2 loops on hook, repeat from † to † twice, YO and draw through all 5 loops on hook.

Repeat Row 2 for pattern.

122 FROLIC

Note: Uses MC and CC in the following sequence: ★ 2 Rows MC, 3 rows CC; repeat from ★ for stripe sequence.

With MC, chain a multiple of 27 + 1 ch.

To decrease (uses next 2 sts), ★ YO, insert hook in **next** st, YO and pull up a loop, YO and draw through 2 loops on hook; repeat from ★ once **more**, YO and draw through all 3 loops on hook **(counts as one dc)**.

To double crochet 4 together (abbreviated dc4tog), ★ YO, insert hook in **next** st, YO and pull up a loop, YO and draw through 2 loops on hook; repeat from ★ 3 times **more**, YO and draw through all 5 loops on hook **(counts as one dc)**.

Row 1 (Right side)**:** Dc in third ch from hook and in next 11 chs, 5 dc in next ch, dc in next 11 chs, ★ dc4tog, dc in next 11 chs, 5 dc in next ch, dc in next 11 chs; repeat from ★ across to last 2 chs, decrease.

Note: Loop a short piece of yarn around any stitch to mark Row 1 as **right** side.

To work Back Post Cluster (abbreviated BP Cluster)**,** ★ YO, insert hook from **back** to **front** around post of st indicated **(Fig. 4, page 159)**, YO and pull up a loop, YO and draw through 2 loops on hook; repeat from ★ once **more**, YO and draw through all 3 loops on hook.

To double decrease (uses next 3 sts), ★ YO, insert hook in **next** st, YO and pull up a loop, YO and draw through 2 loops on hook; repeat from ★ 2 times **more**, YO and draw through all 4 loops on hook **(counts as one dc)**.

Row 2: Ch 2, turn; skip first dc, dc in next dc, (work BP Cluster around next dc, dc in next dc) 6 times, work BP Cluster around next dc, dc in same dc, work BP Cluster around same dc, (dc in next dc, work BP Cluster around next dc) 6 times, ★ double decrease, (work BP Cluster around next dc, dc in next dc) 6 times, work BP Cluster around next dc, dc in same dc, work BP Cluster around same dc, (dc in next dc, work BP Cluster around next dc) 6 times; repeat from ★ across to last 2 dc, decrease; finish off.

Row 3: With **right** side facing, join CC with slip st in first dc; ch 3 **(counts as first hdc plus ch 1, now and throughout)**, (skip next 2 sts, sc in next st, ch 3) 4 times, skip next st, (sc, ch 3) twice in next dc, skip next st, sc in next st, (ch 3, skip next 2 sts, sc in next st) 3 times, ch 1, ★ skip next 2 sts, dc in next dc, ch 1, (skip next 2 sts, sc in next st, ch 3) 4 times, skip next st, (sc, ch 3) twice in next dc, skip next st, sc in next st, (ch 3, skip next 2 sts, sc in next st) 3 times, ch 1; repeat from ★ across to last 3 sts, skip next 2 sts, hdc in last dc.

Rows 4 and 5: Ch 3, turn; skip next ch-1 sp, (sc in next ch-3 sp, ch 3) 4 times, (sc, ch 3) twice in next ch-3 sp, sc in next ch-3 sp, (ch 3, sc in next ch-3 sp) 3 times, ★ ch 1, skip next ch-1 sp, dc in next dc, ch 1, skip next ch-1 sp, (sc in next ch-3 sp, ch 3) 4 times, (sc, ch 3) twice in next ch-3 sp, sc in next ch-3 sp, (ch 3, sc in next ch-3 sp) 3 times; repeat from ★ across to last ch-1 sp, ch 1, skip last ch-1 sp, hdc in last hdc; at end of last row, finish off.

Row 6: With **right** side facing, join MC with slip st in first hdc; ch 2, 3 dc in each of next 4 ch-3 sps, 5 dc in next ch-3 sp, 3 dc in each of next 3 ch-3 sps, 2 dc in next ch-3 sp, ★ [YO, insert hook in next sc, YO and pull up a loop, YO and draw through 2 loops on hook, (YO, skip next ch, insert hook in next st, YO and pull up a loop, YO and draw through 2 loops on hook) twice, YO and draw through all 4 loops on hook **(counts as one dc)]**, 2 dc in next ch-3 sp, 3 dc in each of next 3 ch-3 sps, 5 dc in next ch-3 sp, 3 dc in each of next 3 ch-3 sps, 2 dc in next ch-3 sp; repeat from ★ across to last ch-1 sp, [YO, insert hook in same ch-3 sp, YO and pull up a loop, YO and draw through 2 loops on hook, YO, skip next sc and last ch-1 sp, insert hook in last hdc, YO and pull up a loop, YO and draw through 2 loops on hook, YO and draw through all 3 loops on hook **(counts as one dc)]**.

Repeat Rows 2-6 for pattern.

123 WINTER IN THE ROCKIES

Note: Uses Colors A, B, and C in the following sequence: ★ 2 Rows **each** Color A, Color B, Color C; repeat from ★ for stripe sequence.

With Color A, chain a multiple of 16 + 3 chs.

To decrease (uses next 2 sts), ★ YO, insert hook in **next** st, YO and pull up a loop, YO and draw through 2 loops on hook; repeat from ★ once **more**, YO and draw through all 3 loops on hook **(counts as one dc)**.

To double decrease (uses next 3 sts), ★ YO, insert hook in **next** st, YO and pull up a loop, YO and draw through 2 loops on hook; repeat from ★ 2 times **more**, YO and draw through all 4 loops on hook **(counts as one dc)**.

To double crochet 5 together (abbreviated *dc5tog*), ★ YO, insert hook in **next** st, YO and pull up a loop, YO and draw through 2 loops on hook; repeat from ★ 4 times **more**, YO and draw through all 6 loops on hook **(counts as one dc)**.

Row 1 (Right side)**:** Decrease beginning in fourth ch from hook, ch 1, skip next ch, (dc in next ch, ch 1, skip next ch) twice, 5 dc in next ch, ★ ch 1, skip next ch, (dc in next ch, ch 1, skip next ch) twice, dc5tog, ch 1, skip next ch, (dc in next ch, ch 1, skip next ch) twice, 5 dc in next ch; repeat from ★ across to last 8 chs, ch 1, skip next ch, (dc in next ch, ch 1, skip next ch) twice, double decrease.

Note: Loop a short piece of yarn around any stitch to mark Row 1 as **right** side.

Row 2: Ch 1, turn; sc in each st and in each ch-1 sp across; finish off.

Row 3: With **right** side facing, join Color B with slip st in first sc; ch 2, decrease, ch 1, skip next sc, (dc in next sc, ch 1, skip next sc) twice, 5 dc in next sc, ★ ch 1, skip next sc, (dc in next sc, ch 1, skip next sc) twice, dc5tog, ch 1, skip next sc, (dc in next sc, ch 1, skip next sc) twice, 5 dc in next sc; repeat from ★ across to last 8 sc, ch 1, skip next sc, (dc in next sc, ch 1, skip next sc) twice, double decrease.

Repeat Rows 2 and 3 for pattern, following stripe sequence.

124 FRENCH LACE

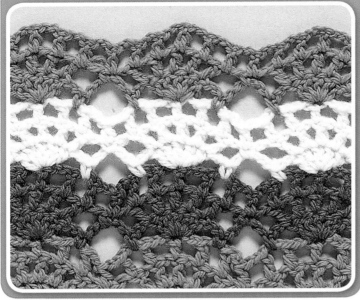

Note: Uses Colors A, B, and C in the following sequence: ★ 3 Rows **each** Color A, Color B, Color C; repeat from ★ for stripe sequence.

With Color A, chain a multiple of 12 + 7 chs.

Row 1 (Right side)**:** Sc in eighth ch from hook **(7 skipped chs count as first dc plus ch 2 and 2 skipped chs)**, ch 2, skip next 3 chs, 5 dc in next ch, ch 2, skip next 3 chs, sc in next ch, ★ ch 5, skip next 3 chs, sc in next ch, ch 2, skip next 3 chs, 5 dc in next ch, ch 2, skip next 3 chs, sc in next ch; repeat from ★ across to last 3 chs, ch 2, skip next 2 chs, dc in last ch.

Note: Loop a short piece of yarn around any stitch to mark Row 1 as **right** side.

Row 2: Ch 1, turn; sc in first dc, ch 1, skip next 2 ch-2 sps, (dc in next dc, ch 1) 5 times, ★ skip next ch-2 sp, sc in next ch-5 sp, ch 1, skip next ch-2 sp, (dc in next dc, ch 1) 5 times; repeat from ★ across to last 2 ch-2 sps, skip last 2 ch-2 sps, sc in last dc.

Row 3: Ch 5 **(counts as first dc plus ch 2, now and throughout)**, turn; skip next ch-1 sp, (dc in next dc, ch 2) 5 times, skip next ch-1 sp, dc in next sc, ★ ch 2, skip next ch-1 sp, (dc in next dc, ch 2) 5 times, skip next ch-1 sp, dc in next sc; repeat from ★ across; finish off.

Row 4: With **wrong** side facing, join Color B with slip st in first dc; ch 5, skip next ch-2 sp, sc in next ch-2 sp, ch 2, skip next ch-2 sp, 5 dc in next dc, ch 2, skip next ch-2 sp, sc in next ch-2 sp, ★ ch 5, skip next 2 ch-2 sps, sc in next ch-2 sp, ch 2, skip next ch-2 sp, 5 dc in next dc, ch 2, skip next ch-2 sp, sc in next ch-2 sp; repeat from ★ across to last ch-2 sp, ch 2, skip last ch-2 sp, dc in last dc.

Row 5: Ch 1, turn; sc in first dc, ch 1, skip next 2 ch-2 sps, (dc in next dc, ch 1) 5 times, ★ skip next ch-2 sp, sc in next ch-5 sp, ch 1, skip next ch-2 sp, (dc in next dc, ch 1) 5 times; repeat from ★ across to last 2 ch-2 sps, skip last 2 ch-2 sps, sc in last dc.

Row 6: Ch 5, turn; skip next ch-1 sp, (dc in next dc, ch 2) 5 times, skip next ch-1 sp, dc in next sc, ★ ch 2, skip next ch-1 sp, (dc in next dc, ch 2) 5 times, skip next ch-1 sp, dc in next sc; repeat from ★ across; finish off.

Row 7: With **right** side facing, join Color C with slip st in first dc; ch 5, skip next ch-2 sp, sc in next ch-2 sp, ch 2, skip next ch-2 sp, 5 dc in next dc, ch 2, skip next ch-2 sp, sc in next ch-2 sp, ★ ch 5, skip next 2 ch-2 sps, sc in next ch-2 sp, ch 2, skip next ch-2 sp, 5 dc in next dc, ch 2, skip next ch-2 sp, sc in next ch-2 sp; repeat from ★ across to last ch-2 sp, ch 2, skip last ch-2 sp, dc in last dc.

Repeat Rows 2-7 for pattern, working in stripe sequence.

125 RISING SHELLS

Note: Uses MC and CC in the following sequence: ★ 2 Rows **each** MC, CC; repeat from ★ for stripe sequence.

With MC, chain a multiple of 19 + 3 chs.

Row 1 (Right side)**:** Dc in fifth ch from hook **(4 skipped chs count as first dc and 1 skipped ch)**, (skip next ch, dc in next ch) 3 times, 5 dc in each of next 2 chs, dc in next ch, ★ (skip next ch, dc in next ch) 8 times, 5 dc in each of next 2 chs, dc in next ch; repeat from ★ across to last 8 chs, (skip next ch, dc in next ch) 4 times.

Note: Loop a short piece of yarn around any stitch to mark Row 1 as **right** side.

Row 2: Ch 3 **(counts as first dc, now and throughout)**, turn; (skip next dc, dc in next dc) 4 times, 5 dc in each of next 2 dc, dc in next dc, ★ (skip next dc, dc in next dc) 8 times, 5 dc in each of next 2 dc, dc in next dc; repeat from ★ across to last 8 dc, (skip next dc, dc in next dc) 4 times; finish off.

Row 3: With **right** side facing, join CC with slip st in first dc; ch 3, (skip next dc, dc in next dc) 4 times, 5 dc in each of next 2 dc, dc in next dc, ★ (skip next dc, dc in next dc) 8 times, 5 dc in each of next 2 dc, dc in next dc; repeat from ★ across to last 8 dc, (skip next dc, dc in next dc) 4 times.

Repeat Rows 2 and 3 for pattern, working in stripe sequence.

126 NEW WAVE

Note: Uses Colors A, B, and C in the following sequence: ★ 3 Rows **each** Color A, Color B, Color C; repeat from ★ for stripe sequence.

With Color A, chain a multiple of 12 chs.

Row 1 (Right side)**:** Dc in fourth ch from hook **(3 skipped chs count as first dc)** and in next 3 chs, ch 2, dc in next 5 chs, ★ skip next 2 chs, dc in next 5 chs, ch 2, dc in next 5 chs; repeat from ★ across.

Note: Loop a short piece of yarn around any stitch to mark Row 1 as **right** side.

To work Cluster (uses one sp), ★ YO, insert hook in sp indicated, YO and pull up a loop, YO and draw through 2 loops on hook; repeat from ★ 3 times **more**, YO and draw through all 5 loops on hook.

Row 2: Ch 3 **(counts as first dc, now and throughout)**, turn; skip first 3 dc, dc in next dc, ch 1, (dc, ch 1, work Cluster, ch 1, dc) in next ch-2 sp, ★ (ch 1, skip next dc, dc in next dc) twice, skip next 2 dc, (dc in next dc, ch 1, skip next dc) twice, (dc, ch 1, work Cluster, ch 1, dc) in next ch-2 sp; repeat from ★ across to last 5 dc, ch 1, skip next dc, dc in next dc, skip next 2 dc, dc in last dc.

Row 3: Ch 3, turn; (dc in next dc and in next ch-1 sp) twice, ch 2, (dc in next ch-1 sp and in next dc) twice, ★ dc in next 2 ch-1 sps, (dc in next dc and in next ch-1 sp) twice, ch 2, (dc in next ch-1 sp and in next dc) twice; repeat from ★ across to last dc, dc in last dc; finish off.

Row 4: With **wrong** side facing, join Color B with slip st in first dc; ch 3, skip first 3 dc, dc in next dc, ch 1, (dc, ch 1, work Cluster, ch 1, dc) in next ch-2 sp, ★ (ch 1, skip next dc, dc in next dc) twice, skip next 2 dc, (dc in next dc, ch 1, skip next dc) twice, (dc, ch 1, work Cluster, ch 1, dc) in next ch-2 sp; repeat from ★ across to last 5 dc, ch 1, skip next dc, dc in next dc, skip next 2 dc, dc in last dc.

Row 5: Ch 3, turn; (dc in next dc and in next ch-1 sp) twice, ch 2, (dc in next ch-1 sp and in next dc) twice, ★ dc in next 2 ch-1 sps, (dc in next dc and in next ch-1 sp) twice, ch 2, (dc in next ch-1 sp and in next dc) twice; repeat from ★ across to last dc, dc in last dc.

Row 6: Ch 3, turn; skip first 3 dc, dc in next dc, ch 1, (dc, ch 1, work Cluster, ch 1, dc) in next ch-2 sp, ★ (ch 1, skip next dc, dc in next dc) twice, skip next 2 dc, (dc in next dc, ch 1, skip next dc) twice, (dc, ch 1, work Cluster, ch 1, dc) in next ch-2 sp; repeat from ★ across to last 5 dc, ch 1, skip next dc, dc in next dc, skip next 2 dc, dc in last dc; finish off.

Row 7: With **right** side facing, join Color C with slip st in first dc; ch 3, (dc in next dc and in next ch-1 sp) twice, ch 2, (dc in next ch-1 sp and in next dc) twice, ★ dc in next 2 ch-1 sps, (dc in next dc and in next ch-1 sp) twice, ch 2, (dc in next ch-1 sp and in next dc) twice; repeat from ★ across to last dc, dc in last dc.

Repeat Rows 2-7 for pattern, working in stripe sequence.

127 WIDE WAVES

128 OPEN SPACES

Chain a multiple of 14 + 4 chs.

Row 1 (Right side): 3 Dc in fourth ch from hook **(3 skipped chs count as one dc)**, skip next 3 chs, sc in next 7 chs, ★ skip next 3 chs, 7 dc in next ch, skip next 3 chs, sc in next 7 chs; repeat from ★ across to last 4 chs, skip next 3 chs, 4 dc in last ch.

Note: Loop a short piece of yarn around any stitch to mark Row 1 as **right** side.

Row 2: Ch 1, turn; sc in each st across.

Row 3: Ch 1, turn; sc in first 4 sc, skip next 3 sc, 7 dc in next sc, ★ skip next 3 sc, sc in next 7 sc, skip next 3 sc, 7 dc in next sc; repeat from ★ across to last 7 sc, skip next 3 sc, sc in last 4 sc.

Row 4: Ch 1, turn; sc in each st across.

Row 5: Ch 3 **(counts as first dc)**, turn; 3 dc in first sc, skip next 3 sc, sc in next 7 sc, ★ skip next 3 sc, 7 dc in next sc, skip next 3 sc, sc in next 7 sc; repeat from ★ across to last 4 sc, skip next 3 sc, 4 dc in last sc.

Repeat Rows 2-5 for pattern.

Chain a multiple of 16 + 5 chs.

Row 1 (Right side): Dc in sixth ch from hook **(5 skipped chs count as first dc and 2 skipped chs)**, (ch 1, skip next ch, dc in next ch) 3 times, (ch 1, dc in same ch) 3 times, (ch 1, skip next ch, dc in next ch) 3 times, ★ skip next 3 chs, dc in next ch, (ch 1, skip next ch, dc in next ch) 3 times, (ch 1, dc in same ch) 3 times, (ch 1, skip next ch, dc in next ch) 3 times; repeat from ★ across to last 3 chs, skip next 2 chs, dc in last ch.

Note: Loop a short piece of yarn around any stitch to mark Row 1 as **right** side.

Row 2: Ch 3 **(counts as first dc)**, turn; skip next ch-1 sp, (dc in next ch-1 sp, ch 1) 3 times, dc in next ch-1 sp, (ch 1, dc in same sp) 3 times, (ch 1, dc in next ch-1 sp) 3 times, ★ skip next 2 ch-1 sps, (dc in next ch-1 sp, ch 1) 3 times, dc in next ch-1 sp, (ch 1, dc in same sp) 3 times, (ch 1, dc in next ch-1 sp) 3 times; repeat from ★ across to last ch-1 sp, skip last ch-1 sp and next dc, dc in last dc.

Repeat Row 2 for pattern.

129 CLASSY CLUSTERS

Note: Uses MC and CC in the following sequence: 1 Row MC, ★ 2 rows **each** CC, MC; repeat from ★ for stripe sequence.

With MC, chain a multiple of 11 chs.

To work Cluster (uses one st or sp), ★ YO, insert hook in st or sp indicated, YO and pull up a loop, YO and draw through 2 loops on hook; repeat from ★ 2 times **more**, YO and draw through all 4 loops on hook.

Row 1 (Right side)**:** Dc in fourth ch from hook, ch 1, skip next 2 chs, work (Cluster, ch 1, Cluster, ch 4, Cluster, ch 1, Cluster) in next ch, ch 1, ★ skip next 2 chs, work Cluster in next ch, ch 1, skip next 4 chs, work Cluster in next ch, ch 1, skip next 2 chs, work (Cluster, ch 1, Cluster, ch 4, Cluster, ch 1, Cluster) in next ch, ch 1; repeat from ★ across to last 4 chs, YO, skip next 2 chs, insert hook in next ch, YO and pull up a loop, YO and draw through 2 loops on hook, YO, insert hook in last ch, YO and pull up a loop, YO and draw through 2 loops on hook, YO and draw through all 3 loops on hook; finish off.

Note: Loop a short piece of yarn around any stitch to mark Row 1 as **right** side.

Row 2: With **wrong** side facing, join CC with slip st in first st; ch 1, [pull up a loop in same st as joining and in next ch-1 sp, YO and draw through all 3 loops on hook **(counts as one sc)**], ch 1, sc in next ch-1 sp, ch 1, (sc, ch 4, sc) in next ch-4 sp, ch 1, ★ (sc in next ch-1 sp, ch 1) 5 times, (sc, ch 4, sc) in next ch-4 sp, ch 1; repeat from ★ across to last 2 ch-1 sps, sc in next ch-1 sp, ch 1, [pull up a loop in last ch-1 sp and in last dc, YO and draw through all 3 loops on hook **(counts as one sc)**].

Row 3: Ch 2, turn; dc in next ch-1 sp, ch 1, skip next ch-1 sp, work (Cluster, ch 1, Cluster, ch 4, Cluster, ch 1, Cluster) in next ch-4 sp, ch 1, ★ skip next ch-1 sp, work Cluster in next ch-1 sp, ch 1, skip next 2 ch-1 sps, work Cluster in next ch-1 sp, ch 1, skip next ch-1 sp, work (Cluster, ch 1, Cluster, ch 4, Cluster, ch 1, Cluster) in next ch-4 sp, ch 1; repeat from ★ across to last 2 ch-1 sps, YO, skip next ch-1 sp, insert hook in last ch-1 sp, YO and pull up a loop, YO and draw through 2 loops on hook, YO, insert hook in last sc, YO and pull up a loop, YO and draw through 2 loops on hook, YO and draw through all 3 loops on hook; finish off.

Repeat Rows 2 and 3 for pattern, working in stripe sequence.

130 CAPRICE

Note: Uses Colors A, B, and C in the following sequence: ★ 2 Rows **each** Color A, Color B, Color C; repeat from ★ for stripe sequence.

With Color A, chain a multiple of 16 + 3 chs.

To decrease (uses next 2 sts), ★ YO, insert hook in **next** st, YO and pull up a loop, YO and draw through 2 loops on hook; repeat from ★ once **more**, YO and draw through all 3 loops on hook **(counts as one dc)**.

To double decrease (uses next 3 sts), ★ YO, insert hook in **next** st, YO and pull up a loop, YO and draw through 2 loops on hook; repeat from ★ 2 times **more**, YO and draw through all 4 loops on hook **(counts as one dc)**.

To double crochet 5 together (abbreviated dc5tog), ★ YO, insert hook in **next** st, YO and pull up a loop, YO and draw through 2 loops on hook; repeat from ★ 4 times **more**, YO and draw through all 6 loops on hook **(counts as one dc)**.

Row 1 (Right side)**:** Decrease beginning in fourth ch from hook, ch 1, skip next 2 chs, 5 dc in next ch, ch 1, skip next 2 chs, 7 dc in next ch, ch 1, skip next 2 chs, 5 dc in next ch, ch 1, ★ skip next 2 chs, dc5tog, ch 1, skip next 2 chs, 5 dc in next ch, ch 1, skip next 2 chs, 7 dc in next ch, ch 1, skip next 2 chs, 5 dc in next ch, ch 1; repeat from ★ across to last 5 chs, skip next 2 chs, double decrease.

Note: Loop a short piece of yarn around any stitch to mark Row 1 as **right** side.

Row 2: Ch 2, turn; working in Back Loops Only **(Fig. 2, page 159)** of dc and chs, skip first dc, decrease, ch 1, skip next 4 dc, 5 dc in next ch, ch 1, skip next 3 dc, 7 dc in next dc, ch 1, skip next 3 dc, 5 dc in next ch, ch 1, ★ skip next 4 dc, dc5tog, ch 1, skip next 4 dc, 5 dc in next ch, ch 1, skip next 3 dc, 7 dc in next dc, ch 1, skip next 3 dc, 5 dc in next ch, ch 1; repeat from ★ across to last 7 sts, skip next 4 dc, double decrease; finish off.

Row 3: With **right** side facing and working in Back Loops Only of dc and chs, join Color B with slip st in first st; ch 2, decrease, ch 1, skip next 4 dc, 5 dc in next ch, ch 1, skip next 3 dc, 7 dc in next dc, ch 1, skip next 3 dc, 5 dc in next ch, ch 1, ★ skip next 4 dc, dc5tog, ch 1, skip next 4 dc, 5 dc in next ch, ch 1, skip next 3 dc, 7 dc in next dc, ch 1, skip next 3 dc, 5 dc in next ch, ch 1; repeat from ★ across to last 7 sts, skip next 4 dc, double decrease.

Repeat Rows 2 and 3 for pattern, working in stripe sequence.

131 SINGLES & DOUBLES

132 GENTLE RIDGED DC WAVES

Note: Uses Colors A, B, and C in the following sequence: ★ 2 Rows **each** Color A, Color B, Color C; repeat from ★ for stripe sequence.

With Color A, chain a multiple of 17 + 3 chs.

Row 1 (Right side)**:** Dc in fourth ch from hook **(3 skipped chs count as one dc)**, 2 dc in each of next 2 chs, (skip next ch, dc in next ch) 5 times, ★ skip next ch, 2 dc in each of next 6 chs, (skip next ch, dc in next ch) 5 times; repeat from ★ across to last 4 chs, skip next ch, 2 dc in each of last 3 chs.

Note: Loop a short piece of yarn around any stitch to mark Row 1 as **right** side.

Row 2: Ch 1, turn; sc in each st across; finish off.

Row 3: With **right** side facing, join Color B with slip st in first sc; ch 3 **(counts as first dc)**, dc in same st as joining, 2 dc in each of next 2 sc, (skip next sc, dc in next sc) 5 times, ★ skip next sc, 2 dc in each of next 6 sc, (skip next sc, dc in next sc) 5 times; repeat from ★ across to last 4 sc, skip next sc, 2 dc in each of last 3 sc.

Repeat Rows 2 and 3 for pattern, working in stripe sequence.

Chain a multiple of 12 + 3 chs.

To decrease (uses next 2 sts), ★ YO, insert hook in **next** st, YO and pull up a loop, YO and draw through 2 loops on hook; repeat from ★ once **more**, YO and draw through all 3 loops on hook **(counts as one dc)**.

Row 1 (Right side)**:** Dc in fourth ch from hook **(3 skipped chs count as first dc)** and in next 3 chs, decrease twice, dc in next 3 chs, ★ 2 dc in each of next 2 chs, dc in next 3 chs, decrease twice, dc in next 3 chs; repeat from ★ across to last ch, 2 dc in last ch.

Note: Loop a short piece of yarn around any stitch to mark Row 1 as **right** side.

Row 2: Ch 3 **(counts as first dc)**, turn; working in Back Loops Only *(Fig. 2, page 159)*, dc in first 4 dc, decrease twice, dc in next 3 dc, ★ 2 dc in each of next 2 dc, dc in next 3 dc, decrease twice, dc in next 3 chs; repeat from ★ across to last dc, 2 dc in last dc.

Repeat Row 2 for pattern.

133 FANNED WAVES

Chain a multiple of 12 + 2 chs.

To double crochet 3 together *(abbreviated dc3tog)*, ★ YO, insert hook in **next** st, YO and pull up a loop, YO and draw through 2 loops on hook; repeat from ★ 2 times **more**, YO and draw through all 4 loops on hook **(counts as first dc)**.

To double crochet 4 together *(abbreviated dc4tog)*, ★ YO, insert hook in **next** st, YO and pull up a loop, YO and draw through 2 loops on hook; repeat from ★ 3 times **more**, YO and draw through all 5 loops on hook **(counts as one dc)**.

To double crochet 7 together *(abbreviated dc7tog)*, ★ YO, insert hook in **next** st, YO and pull up a loop, YO and draw through 2 loops on hook; repeat from ★ 6 times **more**, YO and draw through all 8 loops on hook **(counts as one dc)**.

Row 1 (Right side)**:** Dc3tog beginning in third ch from hook, ch 1, (dc in next ch, ch 1) twice, (dc, ch 1) twice in next ch, (dc in next ch, ch 1) twice, ★ dc7tog, ch 1, (dc in next ch, ch 1) twice, (dc, ch 1) twice in next ch, (dc in next ch, ch 1) twice; repeat from ★ across to last 4 chs, dc4tog.

Note: Loop a short piece of yarn around any stitch to mark Row 1 as **right** side.

To decrease (uses next 2 ch-1 sps), ★ YO, insert hook in **next** ch-1 sp, YO and pull up a loop, YO and draw through 2 loops on hook; repeat from ★ once **more**, YO and draw through all 3 loops on hook **(counts as one dc)**.

To work ending decrease (uses last ch-1 sp and last dc), YO, insert hook in last ch-1 sp, YO and pull up a loop, YO and draw through 2 loops on hook, YO, insert hook in last dc, YO and pull up a loop, YO and draw through 2 loops on hook, YO and draw through all 3 loops on hook **(counts as one dc)**.

Row 2: Ch 2, turn; (dc in next ch-1 sp and in next dc) 6 times, ★ decrease, dc in next dc, (dc in next ch-1 sp and in next dc) 5 times; repeat from ★ across to last ch-1 sp, work ending decrease.

Row 3: Ch 2, turn; skip first dc, dc3tog, ch 1, (dc in next dc, ch 1) twice, (dc, ch 1) twice in next dc, (dc in next dc, ch 1) twice, ★ dc7tog, ch 1, (dc in next dc, ch 1) twice, (dc, ch 1) twice in next dc, (dc in next dc, ch 1) twice; repeat from ★ across to last 4 dc, dc4tog.

Repeat Rows 2 and 3 for pattern.

134 ROMANCE

Note: Uses MC and CC in the following sequence: 3 Rows MC, ★ 2 rows **each** CC, MC; repeat from ★ for stripe sequence.

With MC, chain a multiple of 12 + 2 chs.

Row 1 (Right side)**:** Sc in second ch from hook and in next 4 chs, ch 5, ★ skip next 3 chs, sc in next 9 chs, ch 5; repeat from ★ across to last 8 chs, skip next 3 chs, sc in last 5 chs.

Note: Loop a short piece of yarn around any stitch to mark Row 1 as **right** side.

To work Half Cluster (uses one st), ★ YO, insert hook in st indicated, YO and pull up a loop, YO and draw through 2 loops on hook; repeat from ★ once **more**, YO and draw through all 3 loops on hook.

To work Cluster (uses one st), ★ YO, insert hook in st indicated, YO and pull up a loop, YO and draw through 2 loops on hook; repeat from ★ 2 times **more**, YO and draw through all 4 loops on hook.

Row 2: Ch 2, turn; (dc, ch 3, work Cluster) in first sc, ch 2, sc in next ch-5 sp, ch 2, ★ skip next 4 sc, work Cluster in next sc, (ch 3, work Cluster in same st) twice, ch 2, sc in next ch-5 sp, ch 2; repeat from ★ across to last 5 sc, skip next 4 sc, work (Cluster, ch 3, Half Cluster) in last sc.

Row 3: Ch 3 **(counts as first dc, now and throughout)**, turn; dc in first Half Cluster, 3 dc in next ch-3 sp, 2 dc in next ch-2 sp, dc in next sc, 2 dc in next ch-2 sp, 3 dc in next ch-3 sp, ★ 3 dc in next Cluster and in next ch-3 sp, 2 dc in next ch-2 sp, dc in next sc, 2 dc in next ch-2 sp, 3 dc in next ch-3 sp; repeat from ★ across to last dc, 2 dc in last dc; finish off.

Row 4: With **wrong** side facing, join CC with sc in first dc *(see Joining With Sc, page 158)*; ★ ch 2, skip next 6 dc, work Cluster in next dc, (ch 3, work Cluster in same st) twice, ch 2, skip next 6 dc, sc in next dc; repeat from ★ across.

Row 5: Ch 3, turn; ★ 2 dc in next ch-2 sp, 3 dc in next ch-3 sp, 3 dc in next Cluster and in next ch-3 sp, 2 dc in next ch-2 sp, dc in next sc; repeat from ★ across; finish off.

Row 6: With **wrong** side facing, join MC with slip st in first dc; ch 2, (dc, ch 3, work Cluster) in same st as joining, ch 2, skip next 6 dc, sc in next dc, ch 2, skip next 6 dc, work Cluster in next dc, ★ (ch 3, work Cluster in same st) twice, ch 2, skip next 6 dc, sc in next dc, ch 2, skip next 6 dc, work Cluster in next dc; repeat from ★ across, ch 3, work Half Cluster in same st.

Repeat Rows 3-6 for pattern.

135 MYSTERY RIPPLE

Note: Uses Colors A, B, and C in the following sequence: ★ 4 Rows **each** Color A, Color B, Color C; repeat from ★ for stripe sequence.

With Color A, chain a multiple of 10 + 2 chs.

Row 1: Sc in second ch from hook and in each ch across.

Row 2 (Right side)**:** Ch 1, turn; working in Back Loops Only *(Fig. 2, page 159)*, [pull up a loop in first 3 sc, YO and draw through all 4 loops on hook **(counts as one sc)]**, sc in next sc, (ch 1, sc in next sc) 4 times, ★ [pull up a loop in next 5 sc, YO and draw through all 6 loops on hook **(counts as one sc)]**, sc in next sc, (ch 1, sc in next sc) 4 times; repeat from ★ across to last 3 sc, [pull up a loop in last 3 sc, YO and draw through all 4 loops on hook **(counts as one sc)]**.

Note: Loop a short piece of yarn around any stitch to mark Row 2 as **right** side.

Row 3: Ch 1, turn; sc in Back Loop Only of each sc and each ch across.

Row 4: Ch 1, turn; working in Back Loops Only, [pull up a loop in first 3 sc, YO and draw through all 4 loops on hook **(counts as one sc)]**, sc in next sc, (ch 1, sc in next sc) 4 times, ★ [pull up a loop in next 5 sc, YO and draw through all 6 loops on hook **(counts as one sc)]**, sc in next sc, (ch 1, sc in next sc) 4 times; repeat from ★ across to last 3 sc, [pull up a loop in last 3 sc, YO and draw through all 4 loops on hook **(counts as one sc)]**; finish off.

Row 5: With **wrong** side facing and working in Back Loops Only, join Color B with sc in first sc *(see Joining With Sc, page 158)*; sc in each sc and in each ch across.

Repeat Rows 2-5 for pattern, working in stripe sequence.

136 FROTHY WAVES

Note: Uses MC and CC in the following sequence: 2 Rows MC, ★ 3 rows **each** CC, MC; repeat from ★ for stripe sequence.

With MC, chain a multiple of 10 + 5 chs.

Row 1 (Right side)**:** Sc in seventh ch from hook **(6 skipped chs counts as first hdc plus ch 2 and 2 skipped chs)**, ★ ch 5, skip next 4 chs, sc in next ch; repeat from ★ across to last 3 chs, ch 2, skip next 2 chs, hdc in last ch.

Note: Loop a short piece of yarn around any stitch to mark Row 1 as **right** side.

Row 2: Ch 3 **(counts as first dc, now and throughout)**, turn; 3 dc in next ch-2 sp, ch 2, sc in next ch-5 sp, ch 2, ★ (3 dc, ch 2) twice in next ch-5 sp, sc in next ch-5 sp, ch 2; repeat from ★ across to last ch-2 sp, 3 dc in last ch-2 sp, dc in last hdc; finish off.

Row 3: With **right** side facing, join CC with sc in first dc *(see Joining With Sc, page 158)*; ch 3, dc in next 3 dc, skip next 2 ch-2 sps, dc in next 3 dc, ch 3, ★ sc in next ch-2 sp, ch 3, dc in next 3 dc, skip next 2 ch-2 sps, dc in next 3 dc, ch 3; repeat from ★ across to last dc, sc in last dc.

Row 4: Ch 5 **(counts as first dc plus ch 2, now and throughout)**, turn; skip next ch-3 sp, sc in next dc, ch 5, skip next 4 dc, sc in next dc, ★ ch 5, skip next 2 ch-3 sps, sc in next dc, ch 5, skip next 4 dc, sc in next dc; repeat from ★ across to last ch-3 sp, ch 2, skip last ch-3 sp, dc in last sc.

Row 5: Ch 1, turn; sc in first dc, skip next ch-2 sp, (3 dc, ch 2, 3 dc) in next ch-5 sp, ★ ch 2, sc in next ch-5 sp, ch 2, (3 dc, ch 2, 3 dc) in next ch-5 sp; repeat from ★ across to last ch-2 sp, skip last ch-2 sp, sc in last dc; finish off.

Row 6: With **wrong** side facing, join MC with slip st in first dc; ch 3, dc in next 3 dc, ch 3, sc in next ch-2 sp, ch 3, dc in next 3 dc, ★ skip next 2 ch-2 sps, dc in next 3 dc, ch 3, sc in next ch-2 sp, ch 3, dc in next 3 dc; repeat from ★ across to last sc, dc in last sc.

Row 7: Ch 5, turn; skip first 3 dc, sc in next dc, ch 5, skip next 2 ch-3 sps, sc in next dc, ★ ch 5, skip next 4 dc, sc in next dc, ch 5, skip next 2 ch-3 sps, sc in next dc; repeat from ★ across to last 3 dc, ch 2, skip next 2 dc, dc in last dc.

Repeat Rows 2-7 for pattern.

Chain a multiple of 18 + 2 chs.

Row 1 (Right side)**:** Sc in second ch from hook, ★ skip next 2 chs, 5 dc in next ch, skip next 2 chs, sc in next ch; repeat from ★ across.

Note: Loop a short piece of yarn around any stitch to mark Row 1 as **right** side.

To work Small Cluster (uses 2 sts), YO, insert hook in same st as last st made, YO and pull up a loop, YO, insert hook in next st, YO and pull up a loop, YO and draw through all 5 loops on hook.

Row 2: Ch 3 **(counts as first dc, now and throughout)**, turn; 2 dc in first sc, skip next 2 dc, sc in next dc, ch 1, skip next 3 sts, dc in next dc, (ch 2, work Small Cluster) 4 times, ch 2, dc in same st as last Cluster, ch 1, skip next 3 sts, sc in next dc, ★ skip next 2 dc, 5 dc in next sc, skip next 2 dc, sc in next dc, ch 1, skip next 3 sts, dc in next dc, (ch 2, work Small Cluster) 4 times, ch 2, dc in same st as last Cluster, ch 1, skip next 3 sts, sc in next dc; repeat from ★ across to last 3 sts, skip next 2 dc, 3 dc in last sc.

To work Large Cluster (uses 2 sts and 1 ch-2 sp), YO, insert hook in same st as last st made, YO and pull up a loop, YO, skip next ch-2 sp, insert hook in next st, YO and pull up a loop, YO and draw through all 5 loops on hook.

Row 3: Ch 1, turn; sc in first dc, ★ skip next 2 dc and next sc, dc in next dc, (ch 2, work Large Cluster) 5 times, ch 2, dc in same st as last Cluster, skip next sc and next 2 dc, sc in next dc; repeat from ★ across.

Row 4: Ch 1, turn; sc in first sc, (sc in next st, 2 sc in next ch-2 sp) 6 times, ★ sc in next 3 sts, 2 sc in next ch-2 sp, (sc in next st, 2 sc in next ch-2 sp) 5 times; repeat from ★ across to last 2 sts, sc in last 2 sts.

Row 5: Ch 1, turn; sc in first sc, ★ skip next 3 sc, 5 dc in next sc, (skip next 2 sc, sc in next sc, skip next 2 sc, 5 dc in next sc) twice, skip next 3 sc, sc in next sc; repeat from ★ across.

Repeat Rows 2-5 for pattern.

138 SPRING FLING

Note: Uses Colors A, B, C, and D in the following sequence: ★ 1 Row Color A, 3 rows Color B, 1 row Color A, 1 row Color C, 1 row Color D, 1 row Color C; repeat from ★ for stripe sequence.

With Color A, chain a multiple of 15 + 5 chs.

To double crochet 5 together *(abbreviated dc5tog)*, ★ YO, insert hook in **next** st, YO and pull up a loop, YO and draw through 2 loops on hook; repeat from ★ 4 times **more**, YO and draw through all 6 loops on hook **(counts as one dc)**.

Row 1 (Right side)**:** Dc in fifth ch from hook **(4 skipped chs count as first dc and 1 skipped ch)** and in next 5 chs, 2 dc in next ch, ch 3, 2 dc in next ch, ★ dc in next 4 chs, dc5tog, dc in next 4 chs, 2 dc in next ch, ch 3, 2 dc in next ch; repeat from ★ across to last 8 chs, dc in next 6 chs, skip next ch, dc in last ch; finish off.

Note: Loop a short piece of yarn around any stitch to mark Row 1 as **right** side.

To decrease *(uses next 3 dc)*, ★ YO, insert hook in **next** dc, YO and pull up a loop, YO and draw through 2 loops on hook; repeat from ★ 2 times **more**, YO and draw through all 4 loops on hook **(counts as one dc)**.

Row 2: With **wrong** side facing and working in both loops, join Color B with slip st in first dc; ch 3 **(counts as first dc, now and throughout)**, skip first 3 dc, (dc in next dc, ch 1, skip next dc) 3 times, (dc, ch 3, dc) in next ch-3 sp, ★ ch 1, (skip next dc, dc in next dc, ch 1) twice, skip next dc, decrease, ch 1, skip next dc, (dc in next dc, ch 1, skip next dc) twice, (dc, ch 3, dc) in next ch-3 sp; repeat from ★ across to last 9 dc, (ch 1, skip next dc, dc in next dc) 3 times, skip next 2 dc, dc in last dc.

To double decrease *(uses 3 dc and 2 chs)*, YO, insert hook in next dc, YO and pull up a loop, YO and draw through 2 loops on hook, ★ YO, skip **next** ch, insert hook in **next** dc, YO and pull up a loop, YO and draw through 2 loops on hook; repeat from ★ once **more**, YO and draw through all 4 loops on hook **(counts as one dc)**.

Row 3: Ch 3, turn; (dc in next ch-1 sp and in next dc) 3 times, (2 dc, ch 3, 2 dc) in next ch-3 sp, ★ (dc in next dc and in next ch-1 sp) twice, double decrease, (dc in next ch-1 sp and in next dc) twice, (2 dc, ch 3, 2 dc) in next ch-3 sp; repeat from ★ across to last 5 dc, (dc in next dc and in next ch-1 sp) 3 times, skip next dc, dc in last dc.

Row 4: Ch 3, turn; skip first 3 dc, (dc in next dc, ch 1, skip next dc) 3 times, (dc, ch 3, dc) in next ch-3 sp, ★ ch 1, (skip next dc, dc in next dc, ch 1) twice, skip next dc, decrease, ch 1, skip next dc, (dc in next dc, ch 1, skip next dc) twice, (dc, ch 3, dc) in next ch-3 sp; repeat from ★ across to last 9 dc, (ch 1, skip next dc, dc in next dc) 3 times, skip next 2 dc, dc in last dc; finish off.

Row 5: With **right** side facing, join Color A with slip st in first dc; ch 3, (dc in next ch-1 sp and in next dc) 3 times, (2 dc, ch 3, 2 dc) in next ch-3 sp, ★ (dc in next dc and in next ch-1 sp) twice, double decrease, (dc in next ch-1 sp and in next dc) twice, (2 dc, ch 3, 2 dc) in next ch-3 sp; repeat from ★ across to last 5 dc, (dc in next dc and in next ch-1 sp) 3 times, skip next dc, dc in last dc; finish off.

Row 6: With **wrong** side facing, join Color C with slip st in first dc; ch 3, working in Back Loops Only **(Fig. 2, page 159)**, skip first 3 dc, dc in next 6 dc, (2 dc, ch 3, 2 dc) in next ch-3 sp, ★ dc in next 4 dc, dc5tog, dc in next 4 dc, (2 dc, ch 3, 2 dc) in next ch-3 sp; repeat from ★ across to last 9 dc, dc in next 6 dc, skip next 2 dc, dc in last dc; finish off.

Row 7: With **right** side facing, join Color D with slip st in first dc; ch 3, working in Back Loops Only, skip first 3 dc, dc in next 6 dc, (2 dc, ch 3, 2 dc) in next ch-3 sp, ★ dc in next 4 dc, dc5tog, dc in next 4 dc, (2 dc, ch 3, 2 dc) in next ch-3 sp; repeat from ★ across to last 9 dc, dc in next 6 dc, skip next 2 dc, dc in last dc; finish off.

Row 8: With **wrong** side facing, join Color C with slip st in first dc; ch 3, working in Back Loops Only, skip first 3 dc, dc in next 6 dc, (2 dc, ch 3, 2 dc) in next ch-3 sp, ★ dc in next 4 dc, dc5tog, dc in next 4 dc, (2 dc, ch 3, 2 dc) in next ch-3 sp; repeat from ★ across to last 9 dc, dc in next 6 dc, skip next 2 dc, dc in last dc; finish off.

Row 9: With **right** side facing, join Color A with slip st in first dc; ch 3, working in Back Loops Only, skip first 3 dc, dc in next 6 dc, (2 dc, ch 3, 2 dc) in next ch-3 sp, ★ dc in next 4 dc, dc5tog, dc in next 4 dc, (2 dc, ch 3, 2 dc) in next ch-3 sp; repeat from ★ across to last 9 dc, dc in next 6 dc, skip next 2 dc, dc in last dc; finish off.

Repeat Rows 2-9 for pattern.

139 RIDGED HDC CHEVRON

Note: Uses Colors A, B, and C in the following sequence: ★ 1 Row **each** Color A, Color B, Color C; repeat from ★ for stripe sequence.

With Color A, chain a multiple of 14 + 12 chs.

Row 1 (Right side)**:** Hdc in third ch from hook **(2 skipped chs count as first hdc)** and in next 3 chs, 3 hdc in next ch, hdc in next 5 chs, ★ skip next ch, hdc in next ch, skip next ch, hdc in next 5 chs, 3 hdc in next ch, hdc in next 5 chs; repeat from ★ across; finish off.

Note: Loop a short piece of yarn around any stitch to mark Row 1 as **right** side.

Row 2: With **wrong** side facing and working in Front Loops Only **(Fig. 2, page 159)**, join Color B with slip st in first hdc; ch 2 **(counts as first hdc, now and throughout)**, skip first 2 hdc, hdc in next 4 hdc, 3 hdc in next hdc, ★ hdc in next 5 hdc, skip next hdc, hdc in next hdc, skip next hdc, hdc in next 5 hdc, 3 hdc in next hdc; repeat from ★ across to last 6 hdc, hdc in next 4 hdc, skip next hdc, hdc in last hdc; finish off.

Row 3: With **right** side facing and working in Back Loops Only **(Fig. 2, page 159)**, join Color C with slip st in first hdc; ch 2, skip first 2 hdc, hdc in next 4 hdc, 3 hdc in next hdc, ★ hdc in next 5 hdc, skip next hdc, hdc in next hdc, skip next hdc, hdc in next 5 hdc, 3 hdc in next hdc; repeat from ★ across to last 6 hdc, hdc in next 4 hdc, skip next hdc, hdc in last hdc; finish off.

Repeat Rows 2 and 3 for pattern, working in stripe sequence.

140 ARAN CHEVRON

Chain a multiple of 16 + 3 chs.

To decrease (uses next 2 sts), ★ YO, insert hook in **next** st, YO and pull up a loop, YO and draw through 2 loops on hook; repeat from ★ once **more**, YO and draw through all 3 loops on hook **(counts as one dc)**.

To double decrease (uses next 3 sts), ★ YO, insert hook in **next** st, YO and pull up a loop, YO and draw through 2 loops on hook; repeat from ★ 2 times **more**, YO and draw through all 4 loops on hook **(counts as one dc)**.

To double crochet 5 together (abbreviated dc5tog), ★ YO, insert hook in **next** st, YO and pull up a loop, YO and draw through 2 loops on hook; repeat from ★ 4 times **more**, YO and draw through all 6 loops on hook **(counts as one dc)**.

Row 1 (Right side)**:** Decrease beginning in fourth ch from hook, dc in next 5 chs, (2 dc, ch 1, 2 dc) in next ch, dc in next 5 chs, ★ dc5tog, dc in next 5 chs, (2 dc, ch 1, 2 dc) in next ch, dc in next 5 chs; repeat from ★ across to last 3 chs, double decrease.

Note: Loop a short piece of yarn around any stitch to mark Row 1 as **right** side.

To work Front Post double crochet (abbreviated FPdc), YO, insert hook from **front** to **back** around post of next st *(Fig. 4, page 159)*, YO and pull up a loop (3 loops on hook), (YO and draw through 2 loops on hook) twice.

To work Back Post decrease (abbreviated BP decrease) (uses next 2 sts), ★ YO, insert hook from **back** to **front** around post of **next** st *(Fig. 4, page 159)*, YO and pull up a loop, YO and draw through 2 loops on hook; repeat from ★ once **more**, YO and draw through all 3 loops on hook.

To work double Back Post decrease (abbreviated double BP decrease) (uses last 3 sts), ★ YO, insert hook from **back** to **front** around post of **next** st, YO and pull up a loop, YO and draw through 2 loops on hook; repeat from ★ 2 times **more**, YO and draw through all 4 loops on hook.

To Back Post double crochet 5 together (abbreviated BPdc5tog), ★ YO, insert hook from **back** to **front** around post of **next** st, YO and pull up a loop, YO and draw through 2 loops on hook; repeat from ★ 4 times **more**, YO and draw through all 6 loops on hook.

Row 2: Ch 2, turn; skip first st, work BP decrease, work FPdc around each of next 5 sts, (2 dc, ch 1, 2 dc) in next ch-1 sp, work FPdc around each of next 5 sts, ★ BPdc5tog, work FPdc around each of next 5 sts, (2 dc, ch 1, 2 dc) in next ch-1 sp, work FPdc around each of next 5 sts; repeat from ★ across to last 3 sts, work double BP decrease.

To work Back Post double crochet (abbreviated BPdc), YO, insert hook from **back** to **front** around post of next st, YO and pull up a loop (3 loops on hook), (YO and draw through 2 loops on hook) twice.

To work Front Post decrease (abbreviated FP decrease) (uses next 2 sts), ★ YO, insert hook from **front** to **back** around post of **next** st, YO and pull up a loop, YO and draw through 2 loops on hook; repeat from ★ once **more**, YO and draw through all 3 loops on hook.

To work double Front Post decrease (abbreviated double FP decrease) (uses last 3 sts), ★ YO, insert hook from **front** to **back** around post of **next** st, YO and pull up a loop, YO and draw through 2 loops on hook; repeat from ★ 2 times **more**, YO and draw through all 4 loops on hook.

To Front Post double crochet 5 together (abbreviated FPdc5tog), ★ YO, insert hook from **front** to **back** around post of **next** st, YO and pull up a loop, YO and draw through 2 loops on hook; repeat from ★ 4 times **more**, YO and draw through all 6 loops on hook.

Row 3: Ch 2, turn; skip first st, work FP decrease, work BPdc around each of next 5 sts, (2 dc, ch 1, 2 dc) in next ch-1 sp, work BPdc around each of next 5 sts, ★ FPdc5tog, work BPdc around each of next 5 sts, (2 dc, ch 1, 2 dc) in next ch-1 sp, work BPdc around each of next 5 sts; repeat from ★ across to last 3 sts, work double FP decrease.

Repeat Rows 2 and 3 for pattern.

141 PROVINCIAL

Note: Uses Colors A, B, and C in the following sequence: 5 Rows Color A, ★ 4 rows **each** Color B, Color C, Color A; repeat from ★ for stripe sequence.

With Color A, chain a multiple of 21 + 1 ch.

To double decrease (uses next 3 sts), pull up a loop in next st, skip next st, pull up a loop in next st, YO and draw through all 3 loops on hook **(counts as one sc)**.

Row 1: 2 Sc in second ch from hook, sc in next 8 chs, double decrease, ★ sc in next 9 chs, ch 2, sc in next 9 chs, double decrease; repeat from ★ across to last 9 chs, sc in next 8 chs, 2 sc in last ch.

Row 2 (Right side)**:** Ch 1, turn; working in Back Loops Only *(Fig. 2, page 159)*, 2 sc in first sc, sc in next 8 sc, double decrease, ★ sc in next 8 sc and in next ch, ch 2, sc in next ch and in next 8 sc, double decrease; repeat from ★ across to last 9 sc, sc in next 8 sc, 2 sc in last sc.

Note: Loop a short piece of yarn around any stitch to mark Row 2 as **right** side.

To double crochet 5 together (abbreviated *dc5tog*), ★ YO, insert hook in **next** st, YO and pull up a loop, YO and draw through 2 loops on hook; repeat from ★ 4 times **more**, YO and draw through all 6 loops on hook **(counts as one dc)**.

Row 3: Ch 3 **(counts as first dc)**, turn; working in both loops, 2 dc in first sc, ch 1, skip next sc, (dc in next sc, ch 1, skip next sc) 3 times, dc5tog, ★ ch 1, skip next sc, (dc in next sc, ch 1, skip next sc) 3 times, 5 dc in next ch-2 sp, ch 1, skip next sc, (dc in next sc, ch 1, skip next sc) 3 times, dc5tog; repeat from ★ across to last 8 sc, ch 1, skip next sc, (dc in next sc, ch 1, skip next sc) 3 times, 3 dc in last sc.

Row 4: Ch 1, turn; sc in first 3 dc and in next ch, (sc in next dc and in next ch) 3 times, skip next dc, sc in next ch, (sc in next dc and in next ch) 3 times, ★ sc in next 5 dc and in next ch, (sc in next dc and in next ch) 3 times, skip next dc, sc in next ch, (sc in next dc and in next ch) 3 times; repeat from ★ across to last 3 dc, sc in last 3 dc.

To decrease, pull up a loop in each of next 2 sc, YO and draw through all 3 loops on hook **(counts as one sc)**.

Row 5: Ch 1, turn; working in Front Loops Only *(Fig. 2, page 159)*, 2 sc in first sc, sc in next 8 sc, decrease, sc in next 8 sc, ★ (sc, ch 2, sc) in next sc, sc in next 8 sc, decrease, sc in next 8 sc; repeat from ★ across to last sc, 2 sc in last sc; finish off.

Row 6: With **right** side facing and working in Back Loops Only, join Color B with sc in first sc *(see Joining With Sc, page 158)*; sc in same st as joining and in next 8 sc, double decrease, ★ sc in next 8 sc and in next ch, ch 2, sc in next ch and in next 8 sc, double decrease; repeat from ★ across to last 9 sc, sc in next 8 sc, 2 sc in last sc.

Repeat Rows 3-6 for pattern, working in stripe sequence.

142 LADDER CHEVRON

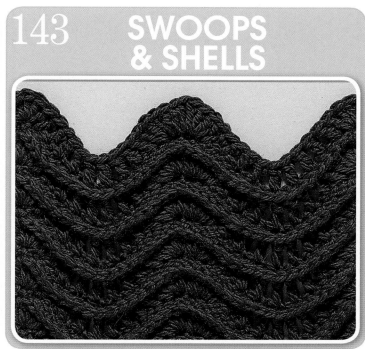

143 SWOOPS & SHELLS

Chain a multiple of 17 + 15 chs.

Row 1 (Right side)**:** Working in back ridges of beginning ch *(Fig. 1, page 159)*, 2 sc in second ch from hook, sc in next 5 chs, skip next 2 chs, sc in next 5 chs, 2 sc in next ch, ★ ch 3, skip next 3 chs, 2 sc in next ch, sc in next 5 chs, skip next 2 chs, sc in next 5 chs, 2 sc in next ch; repeat from ★ across.

Note: Loop a short piece of yarn around any stitch to mark Row 1 as **right** side.

Row 2: Ch 1, turn; working in Back Loops Only *(Fig. 2, page 159)*, 2 sc in first sc, sc in next 5 sc, skip next 2 sc, sc in next 5 sc, 2 sc in next sc, ★ ch 3, 2 sc in next sc, sc in next 5 sc, skip next 2 sc, sc in next 5 sc, 2 sc in next sc; repeat from ★ across.

Repeat Row 2 for pattern.

Chain a multiple of 19 + 3 chs.

Row 1 (Right side)**:** 4 Dc in fourth ch from hook **(3 skipped chs count as first dc)**, dc in next ch, (skip next ch, dc in next ch) 8 times, ★ 5 dc in each of next 2 chs, dc in next ch, (skip next ch, dc in next ch) 8 times; repeat from ★ across to last ch, 5 dc in last ch.

Note: Loop a short piece of yarn around any stitch to mark Row 1 as **right** side.

To work Front Post single crochet *(abbreviated FPsc)*, insert hook from **front** to **back** around post of dc indicated *(Fig. 4, page 159)*, YO and pull up a loop, YO and draw through both loops on hook.

Row 2: Ch 1, turn; sc in first dc, work FPsc around next dc and around each dc across to last dc, sc in last dc.

Row 3: Ch 3 **(counts as first dc)**, turn; 4 dc in first sc, dc in next FPsc, (skip next FPsc, dc in next FPsc) 8 times, ★ 5 dc in each of next 2 FPsc, dc in next FPsc, (skip next FPsc, dc in next FPsc) 8 times; repeat from ★ across to last sc, 5 dc in last sc.

Repeat Rows 2 and 3 for pattern.

144 SNOWBALL CHEVRONS

Note: Uses Colors A, B, and C in the following sequence: ★ 4 Rows Color A, 2 rows Color B, 4 rows Color C, 2 rows Color B; repeat from ★ for stripe sequence.

With Color A, chain a multiple of 9 + 3 chs.

Row 1: Sc in second ch from hook and in next 4 chs, 3 sc in next ch, ★ sc in next 3 chs, skip next 2 chs, sc in next 3 chs, 3 sc in next ch; repeat from ★ across to last 5 chs, sc in last 5 chs.

To work beginning decrease, pull up a loop in each of first 2 sc, YO and draw through all 3 loops on hook **(counts as one sc)**.

To work ending decrease, pull up a loop in each of last 2 sc, YO and draw through all 3 loops on hook **(counts as one sc)**.

Row 2 (Right side)**:** Ch 1, turn; working in Back Loops Only *(Fig. 2, page 159)*, work beginning decrease, sc in next 4 sc, 3 sc in next sc, ★ sc in next 3 sc, skip next 2 sc, sc in next 3 sc, 3 sc in next sc; repeat from ★ across to last 6 sc, sc in next 4 sc, work ending decrease.

Note: Loop a short piece of yarn around any stitch to mark Row 2 as **right** side.

Rows 3 and 4: Ch 1, turn; working in Back Loops Only, work beginning decrease, sc in next 4 sc, 3 sc in next sc, ★ sc in next 3 sc, skip next 2 sc, sc in next 3 sc, 3 sc in next sc; repeat from ★ across to last 6 sc, sc in next 4 sc, work ending decrease; at end of last row, finish off.

Row 5: With **wrong** side facing and working in Back Loops Only, join Color B with slip st in first sc; ch 1, work beginning decrease, sc in next 4 sc, 3 sc in next sc, ★ sc in next 3 sc, skip next 2 sc, sc in next 3 sc, 3 sc in next sc; repeat from ★ across to last 6 sc, sc in next 4 sc, work ending decrease.

Row 6: Ch 1, turn; working in Back Loops Only, work beginning decrease, sc in next 4 sc, 3 sc in next sc, ★ sc in next 3 sc, skip next 2 sc, sc in next 3 sc, 3 sc in next sc; repeat from ★ across to last 6 sc, sc in next 4 sc, work ending decrease; finish off.

To treble crochet (abbreviated tr), YO twice, insert hook in st indicated, YO and pull up a loop (4 loops on hook), (YO and draw through 2 loops on hook) 3 times.

Row 7: With **wrong** side facing and working in both loops, join Color C with slip st in first sc; ch 1, work beginning decrease, sc in next 4 sc, (tr, sc, tr) in next sc, ★ sc in next 3 sc, skip next 2 sc, sc in next 3 sc, (tr, sc, tr) in next sc; repeat from ★ across to last 6 sc, sc in next 4 sc, work ending decrease.

Row 8: Ch 1, turn; work beginning decrease, sc in next 4 sts, 3 sc in next sc, ★ sc in next 3 sts, skip next 2 sc, sc in next 3 sts, 3 sc in next sc; repeat from ★ across to last 6 sts, sc in next 4 sts, work ending decrease.

Row 9: Ch 1, turn; work beginning decrease, sc in next 2 sc, tr in next sc, sc in next sc, (tr, sc, tr) in next sc, sc in next sc, tr in next sc, ★ sc in next sc, skip next 2 sc, sc in next sc, tr in next sc, sc in next sc, (tr, sc, tr) in next sc, sc in next sc, tr in next sc; repeat from ★ across to last 4 sc, sc in next 2 sc, work ending decrease.

Row 10: Ch 1, turn; work beginning decrease, sc in next 4 sts, 3 sc in next sc, ★ sc in next 3 sts, skip next 2 sc, sc in next 3 sts, 3 sc in next sc; repeat from ★ across to last 6 sts, sc in next 4 sts, work ending decrease; finish off.

Rows 11 and 12: Repeat Rows 5 and 6.

Row 13: With **wrong** side facing and working in Back Loops Only, join Color A with slip st in first sc; ch 1, work beginning decrease, sc in next 4 sc, 3 sc in next sc, ★ sc in next 3 sc, skip next 2 sc, sc in next 3 sc, 3 sc in next sc; repeat from ★ across to last 6 sc, sc in next 4 sc, work ending decrease.

Repeat Rows 2-13 for pattern.

145 SHELLS & CHEVRONS

Chain a multiple of 14 + 4 chs.

Row 1 (Right side): Dc in fourth ch from hook **(3 skipped chs count as first dc)** and in next 3 chs, skip next 3 chs, dc in next ch, (ch 1, dc in same st) 4 times, skip next 3 chs, dc in next 3 chs, ★ 3 dc in next ch, dc in next 3 chs, skip next 3 chs, dc in next ch, (ch 1, dc in same st) 4 times, skip next 3 chs, dc in next 3 chs; repeat from ★ across to last ch, 2 dc in last ch.

Note: Loop a short piece of yarn around any stitch to mark Row 1 as **right** side.

Row 2: Ch 3 **(counts as first dc, now and throughout)**, turn; dc in first 4 dc, sc in next ch-1 sp, (ch 3, sc in next ch-1 sp) 3 times, skip next 2 dc, dc in next 3 dc, ★ 3 dc in next dc, dc in next 3 dc, sc in next ch-1 sp, (ch 3, sc in next ch-1 sp) 3 times, skip next 2 dc, dc in next 3 dc; repeat from ★ across to last dc, 2 dc in last dc.

Row 3: Ch 3, turn; dc in first 4 dc, skip next ch-3 sp, dc in next ch-3 sp, (ch 1, dc in same sp) 4 times, skip next ch-3 sp and next 2 sts, dc in next 3 dc, ★ 3 dc in next dc, dc in next 3 dc, skip next ch-3 sp, dc in next ch-3 sp, (ch 1, dc in same sp) 4 times, skip next ch-3 sp and next 2 sts, dc in next 3 dc; repeat from ★ across to last dc, 2 dc in last dc.

Repeat Rows 2 and 3 for pattern.

146 ACUTE POST STITCH

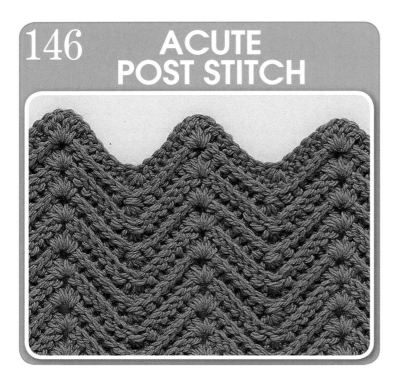

Chain a multiple of 16 + 3 chs.

Row 1 (Right side)**:** YO, insert hook in fourth ch from hook, YO and pull up a loop, YO and draw through 2 loops on hook, YO, insert hook in next ch, YO and pull up a loop, YO and draw through 2 loops on hook, YO and draw through all 3 loops on hook, dc in next 5 chs, (2 dc, ch 1, 2 dc) in next ch, dc in next 5 chs, ★ [YO, insert hook in **next** ch, YO and pull up a loop, YO and draw through 2 loops on hook] 5 times, YO and draw through all 6 loops on hook, dc in next 5 chs, (2 dc, ch 1, 2 dc) in next ch, dc in next 5 chs; repeat from ★ across to last 3 chs, [YO, insert hook in **next** ch, YO and pull up a loop, YO and draw through 2 loops on hook] 3 times, YO and draw through all 4 loops on hook.

Note: Loop a short piece of yarn around any stitch to mark Row 1 as **right** side.

To work Front Post double crochet (abbreviated FPdc), YO, insert hook from **front** to **back** around post of next st *(Fig. 4, page 159)*, YO and pull up a loop (3 loops on hook), (YO and draw through 2 loops on hook) twice.

To work Front Post decrease (abbreviated FP decrease) (uses next 2 sts), ★ YO, insert hook from **front** to **back** around post of **next** st, YO and pull up a loop, YO and draw through 2 loops on hook; repeat from ★ once **more**, YO and draw through all 3 loops on hook.

To work double Front Post decrease (abbreviated double FP decrease) (uses last 3 sts), ★ YO, insert hook from **front** to **back** around post of **next** st, YO and pull up a loop, YO and draw through 2 loops on hook; repeat from ★ 2 times **more**, YO and draw through all 4 loops on hook.

To Front Post double crochet 5 together (abbreviated FPdc5tog), ★ YO, insert hook from **front** to **back** around post of **next** st, YO and pull up a loop, YO and draw through 2 loops on hook; repeat from ★ 4 times **more**, YO and draw through all 6 loops on hook.

Row 2: Ch 3, turn; skip first st, work FP decrease, work FPdc around each of next 5 sts, (2 dc, ch 1, 2 dc) in next ch-1 sp, work FPdc around each of next 5 sts, ★ FPdc5tog, work FPdc around each of next 5 sts, (2 dc, ch 1, 2 dc) in next ch-1 sp, work FPdc around each of next 5 sts; repeat from ★ across to last 3 sts, work double FP decrease.

To work Back Post double crochet (abbreviated BPdc), YO, insert hook from **back** to **front** around post of next st *(Fig. 4, page 159)*, YO and pull up a loop (3 loops on hook), (YO and draw through 2 loops on hook) twice.

To work Back Post decrease (abbreviated BP decrease) (uses next 2 sts), ★ YO, insert hook from **back** to **front** around post of **next** st, YO and pull up a loop, YO and draw through 2 loops on hook; repeat from ★ once **more**, YO and draw through all 3 loops on hook.

To work double Back Post decrease (abbreviated double BP decrease) (uses last 3 sts), ★ YO, insert hook from **back** to **front** around post of **next** st, YO and pull up a loop, YO and draw through 2 loops on hook; repeat from ★ 2 times **more**, YO and draw through all 4 loops on hook.

To Back Post double crochet 5 together (*abbreviated BPdc5tog*), ★ YO, insert hook from **back** to **front** around post of **next** st, YO and pull up a loop, YO and draw through 2 loops on hook; repeat from ★ 4 times **more**, YO and draw through all 6 loops on hook.

Row 3: Ch 3, turn; skip first st, work BP decrease, work BPdc around each of next 5 sts, (2 dc, ch 1, 2 dc) in next ch-1 sp, work BPdc around each of next 5 sts, ★ BPdc5tog, work BPdc around each of next 5 sts, (2 dc, ch 1, 2 dc) in next ch-1 sp, work BPdc around each of next 5 sts; repeat from ★ across to last 3 sts, work double BP decrease.

Repeat Rows 2 and 3 for pattern.

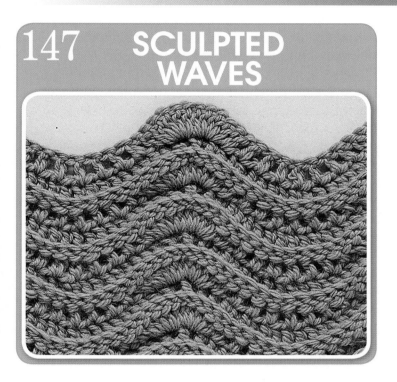

147 SCULPTED WAVES

To work Back Post double crochet (*abbreviated BPdc*), YO, insert hook from **back** to **front** around post of next st *(Fig. 4, page 159)*, YO and pull up a loop (3 loops on hook), (YO and draw through 2 loops on hook) twice.

Row 2 (Right side)**:** Ch 1, turn; sc in first dc, work BPdc around next dc and around each dc across to last dc, sc in last dc.

Note: Loop a short piece of yarn around any stitch to mark Row 2 as **right** side.

Row 3: Ch 3 **(counts as first dc)**, turn; 4 dc in first sc, dc in next st, (skip next st, dc in next st) 8 times, ★ 5 dc in each of next 2 sts, dc in next st, (skip next st, dc in next st) 8 times; repeat from ★ across to last sc, 5 dc in last sc.

Repeat Rows 2 and 3 for pattern.

Chain a multiple of 19 + 3 chs.

Row 1: 4 Dc in fourth ch from hook **(3 skipped chs count as first dc)**, dc in next ch, (skip next ch, dc in next ch) 8 times, ★ 5 dc in each of next 2 chs, dc in next ch, (skip next ch, dc in next ch) 8 times; repeat from ★ across to last ch, 5 dc in last ch.

148 INTERMITTENT CHEVRON

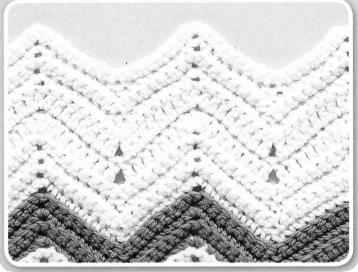

Note: Uses MC and Colors A and B in the following sequence: ★ 10 Rows MC, 2 rows Color A, 2 rows Color B; repeat from ★ for stripe sequence.

With MC, chain a multiple of 17 + 16 chs.

Row 1 (Right side)**:** Sc in second ch from hook and in next 6 chs, 3 sc in next ch, sc in next 7 chs, ★ skip next 2 chs, sc in next 7 chs, 3 sc in next ch, sc in next 7 chs; repeat from ★ across.

Note: Loop a short piece of yarn around any stitch to mark Row 1 as **right** side.

Rows 2-4: Ch 1, turn; working in Back Loops Only *(Fig. 2, page 159)*, sc in first sc, skip next sc, sc in next 6 sc, 3 sc in next sc, ★ sc in next 7 sc, skip next 2 sc, sc in next 7 sc, 3 sc in next sc; repeat from ★ across to last 8 sc, sc in next 6 sc, skip next sc, sc in last sc.

Rows 5 and 6: Ch 3 **(counts as first dc)**, turn; working in Back Loops Only, skip first 2 sts, dc in next 6 sts, 3 dc in next st, ★ dc in next 7 sts, skip next 2 sts, dc in next 7 sts, 3 dc in next st; repeat from ★ across to last 8 sts, dc in next 6 sts, skip next st, dc in last st.

Rows 7-10: Ch 1, turn; working in Back Loops Only, sc in first st, skip next st, sc in next 6 sts, 3 sc in next st, ★ sc in next 7 sts, skip next 2 sts, sc in next 7 sts, 3 sc in next st; repeat from ★ across to last 8 sts, sc in next 6 sts, skip next st, sc in last st; at end of last row, finish off.

Row 11: With **right** side facing and working in Back Loops Only, join Color A with sc in first sc *(see Joining With Sc, page 158)*; skip next sc, sc in next 6 sc, 3 sc in next sc, ★ sc in next 7 sc, skip next 2 sc, sc in next 7 sc, 3 sc in next sc; repeat from ★ across to last 8 sc, sc in next 6 sc, skip next sc, sc in last sc.

Row 12: Ch 1, turn; working in Back Loops Only, sc in first sc, skip next sc, sc in next 6 sc, 3 sc in next sc, ★ sc in next 7 sc, skip next 2 sc, sc in next 7 sc, 3 sc in next sc; repeat from ★ across to last 8 sc, sc in next 6 sc, skip next sc, sc in last sc; finish off.

Rows 13 and 14: With Color B, repeat Rows 11 and 12.

Row 15: With **right** side facing and working in Back Loops Only, join MC with sc in first sc; skip next sc, sc in next 6 sc, 3 sc in next sc, ★ sc in next 7 sc, skip next 2 sc, sc in next 7 sc, 3 sc in next sc; repeat from ★ across to last 8 sc, sc in next 6 sc, skip next sc, sc in last sc.

Repeat Rows 2-15 for pattern.

149 STAINED GLASS

Note: Uses MC and Colors A, B, and C in the following sequence: ★ 2 Rows **each** MC, Color A, MC, Color B, MC, Color C; repeat from ★ for stripe sequence.

With MC, chain a multiple of 4 chs.

Row 1 (Right side)**:** 2 Dc in fourth ch from hook **(3 skipped chs count as first dc)**, ★ skip next 3 chs, (sc, ch 3, 3 dc) in next ch; repeat from ★ across to last 4 chs, skip next 3 chs, sc in last ch.

Note: Loop a short piece of yarn around any stitch to mark Row 1 as **right** side.

Row 2: Ch 3 **(counts as first dc, now and throughout)**, turn; 2 dc in first sc, skip next 3 dc, sc in next ch, ch 3, 3 dc around ch-3, ★ skip next 4 sts, sc in next ch, ch 3, 3 dc around ch-3; repeat from ★ across to last 4 sts, skip next 3 sts, sc in last dc; finish off.

Row 3: With **right** side facing, join Color A with slip st in first sc; ch 3, 2 dc in same st as joining, skip next 3 dc, sc in next ch, ch 3, 3 dc around ch-3, ★ skip next 4 sts, sc in next ch, ch 3, 3 dc around ch-3; repeat from ★ across to last 4 sts, skip next 3 sts, sc in last dc.

Repeat Rows 2 and 3 for pattern, working in stripe sequence.

150 WIDE RIDGED CHEVRONS

Chain a multiple of 14 + 4 chs.

To decrease (uses next 3 sts), ★ YO insert hook in **next** st, YO and pull up a loop, YO and draw through 2 loops on hook; repeat from ★ 2 times **more**, YO and draw through all 4 loops on hook **(counts as one dc)**.

Row 1 (Right side): Dc in fourth ch from hook **(3 skipped chs count as first dc)** and in next 5 chs, decrease, dc in next 5 chs, ★ (dc, ch 1, dc) in next ch, dc in next 5 chs, decrease, dc in next 5 chs; repeat from ★ across to last ch, 2 dc in last ch.

Note: Loop a short piece of yarn around any stitch to mark Row 1 as **right** side.

Row 2: Ch 3 **(counts as first dc, now and throughout)**, turn; working in Front Loops Only **(Fig. 2, page 159)**, dc in first 6 dc, decrease, dc in next 5 dc, ★ (dc, ch 1, dc) in next ch-1 sp, dc in next 5 dc, decrease, dc in next 5 dc; repeat from ★ across to last dc, 2 dc in last dc.

Row 3: Ch 3, turn; working in Back Loops Only **(Fig. 2, page 159)**, dc in first 6 dc, decrease, dc in next 5 dc, ★ (dc, ch 1, dc) in next ch-1 sp, dc in next 5 dc, decrease, dc in next 5 dc; repeat from ★ across to last dc, 2 dc in last dc.

Repeat Rows 2 and 3 for pattern.

151 EYELET CHEVRON

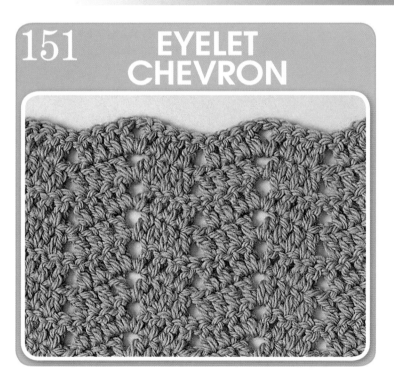

Chain a multiple of 10 + 3 chs.

Row 1 (Right side): Dc in fourth ch from hook **(3 skipped chs count as first dc)** and in next 3 chs, ★ skip next 2 chs, dc in next 4 chs, ch 2, dc in next 4 chs; repeat from ★ across to last 6 chs, skip next 2 chs, dc in next 3 chs, 2 dc in last ch.

Note: Loop a short piece of yarn around any stitch to mark Row 1 as **right** side.

Row 2: Ch 3 **(counts as first dc)**, turn; dc in first 4 dc, skip next 2 dc, dc in next 3 dc, ★ (dc, ch 2, dc) in next ch-2 sp, dc in next 3 dc, skip next 2 dc, dc in next 3 dc; repeat from ★ across to last dc, 2 dc in last dc.

Repeat Row 2 for pattern.

152 GRANNY CHEVRON

Note: Uses Colors A, B, C, and D in the following sequence: ★ 2 Rows **each** Color A, Color B, Color C, Color D; repeat from ★ for stripe sequence.

With Color A, chain a multiple of 23 + 4 chs.

To work Cluster (uses one st or sp), ★ YO, insert hook in st or sp indicated, YO and pull up a loop, YO and draw through 2 loops on hook; repeat from ★ 2 times **more**, YO and draw through all 4 loops on hook.

Row 1 (Right side)**:** 3 Dc in sixth ch from hook **(5 skipped chs count as first dc and 2 skipped chs)**, skip next 2 chs, (3 dc in next ch, skip next 2 chs) twice, (3 dc, ch 3, 3 dc) in next ch, ★ skip next 2 chs, (3 dc in next ch, skip next 2 chs) twice, work Cluster in next ch, skip next 4 chs, work Cluster in next ch, skip next 2 chs, (3 dc in next ch, skip next 2 chs) twice, (3 dc, ch 3, 3 dc) in next ch; repeat from ★ across to last 12 chs, skip next 2 chs, (3 dc in next ch, skip next 2 chs) 3 times, dc in last ch.

Note: Loop a short piece of yarn around any stitch to mark Row 1 as **right** side.

Row 2: Ch 3 **(counts as first dc, now and throughout)**, turn; skip first 4 dc, 3 dc in sp **before** next dc *(Fig. 5, page 159)*, (skip next 3 dc, 3 dc in sp **before** next dc) twice, (3 dc, ch 3, 3 dc) in next ch-3 sp, ★ skip next 3 dc, (3 dc in sp **before** next dc, skip next 3 dc) twice, work Cluster in sp **before** next Cluster, skip next 2 Clusters, work Cluster in sp **before** next dc, (skip next 3 dc, 3 dc in sp **before** next dc) twice, (3 dc, ch 3, 3 dc) in next ch-3 sp; repeat from ★ across to last 13 dc, skip next 3 dc, (3 dc in sp **before** next dc, skip next 3 dc) 3 times, dc in last dc; finish off.

Row 3: With **right** side facing, join Color B with slip st in first dc; ch 3, skip next 3 dc, 3 dc in sp **before** next dc, (skip next 3 dc, 3 dc in sp **before** next dc) twice, (3 dc, ch 3, 3 dc) in next ch-3 sp, ★ skip next 3 dc, (3 dc in sp **before** next dc, skip next 3 dc) twice, work Cluster in sp **before** next Cluster, skip next 2 Clusters, work Cluster in sp **before** next dc, (skip next 3 dc, 3 dc in sp **before** next dc) twice, (3 dc, ch 3, 3 dc) in next ch-3 sp; repeat from ★ across to last 13 dc, skip next 3 dc, (3 dc in sp **before** next dc, skip next 3 dc) 3 times, dc in last dc.

Repeat Rows 2 and 3 for pattern, working in stripe sequence.

153 UNDULATION

Note: Uses Colors A, B, C, D, and E in the following sequence: ★ 2 Rows Color A, 4 rows Color B, 2 rows Color C, 2 rows Color D, 4 rows Color E; repeat from ★ for stripe sequence.

With Color A, chain a multiple of 31 + 21 chs.

Row 1 (Right side)**:** Sc in second ch from hook and in next 4 chs, 2 sc in next ch, sc in next 3 chs, skip next 2 chs, sc in next 3 chs, 2 sc in next ch, ★ sc in next 6 chs, skip next ch, sc in next 3 chs, (sc, ch 1, sc) in next ch, sc in next 3 chs, skip next ch, sc in next 6 chs, 2 sc in next ch, sc in next 3 chs, skip next 2 chs, sc in next 3 chs, 2 sc in next ch; repeat from ★ across to last 5 chs, sc in last 5 chs.

Note: Loop a short piece of yarn around any stitch to mark Row 1 as **right** side.

Row 2: Ch 1, turn; working in Back Loops Only *(Fig. 2, page 159)*, sc in first 5 sc, 2 sc in next sc, sc in next 3 sc, skip next 2 sc, sc in next 3 sc, 2 sc in next sc, ★ sc in next 6 sc, skip next sc, sc in next 3 sc, (sc, ch 1, sc) in next ch-1 sp, sc in next 3 sc, skip next sc, sc in next 6 sc, 2 sc in next sc, sc in next 3 sc, skip next 2 sc, sc in next 3 sc, 2 sc in next sc; repeat from ★ across to last 5 sc, sc in last 5 sc; finish off.

Row 3: With **right** side facing and working in Back Loops Only, join Color B with sc in first sc *(see Joining With Sc, page 158)*; sc in next 4 sc, 2 sc in next sc, sc in next 3 sc, skip next 2 sc, sc in next 3 sc, 2 sc in next sc, ★ sc in next 6 sc, skip next sc, sc in next 3 sc, (sc, ch 1, sc) in next ch-1 sp, sc in next 3 sc, skip next sc, sc in next 6 sc, 2 sc in next sc, sc in next 3 sc, skip next 2 sc, sc in next 3 sc, 2 sc in next sc; repeat from ★ across to last 5 sc, sc in last 5 sc.

Rows 4-6: Ch 1, turn; working in Back Loops Only, sc in first 5 sc, 2 sc in next sc, sc in next 3 sc, skip next 2 sc, sc in next 3 sc, 2 sc in next sc, ★ sc in next 6 sc, skip next sc, sc in next 3 sc, (sc, ch 1, sc) in next ch-1 sp, sc in next 3 sc, skip next sc, sc in next 6 sc, 2 sc in next sc, sc in next 3 sc, skip next 2 sc, sc in next 3 sc, 2 sc in next sc; repeat from ★ across to last 5 sc, sc in last 5 sc; at end of last row, finish off.

Row 7: With **right** side facing and working in Back Loops Only, join Color C with sc in first sc; sc in next 4 sc, 2 sc in next sc, sc in next 3 sc, skip next 2 sc, sc in next 3 sc, 2 sc in next sc, ★ sc in next 6 sc, skip next sc, sc in next 3 sc, (sc, ch 1, sc) in next ch-1 sp, sc in next 3 sc, skip next sc, sc in next 6 sc, 2 sc in next sc, sc in next 3 sc, skip next 2 sc, sc in next 3 sc, 2 sc in next sc; repeat from ★ across to last 5 sc, sc in last 5 sc.

Row 8: Ch 1, turn; working in Back Loops Only, sc in first 5 sc, 2 sc in next sc, sc in next 3 sc, skip next 2 sc, sc in next 3 sc, 2 sc in next sc, ★ sc in next 6 sc, skip next sc, sc in next 3 sc, (sc, ch 1, sc) in next ch-1 sp, sc in next 3 sc, skip next sc, sc in next 6 sc, 2 sc in next sc, sc in next 3 sc, skip next 2 sc, sc in next 3 sc, 2 sc in next sc; repeat from ★ across to last 5 sc, sc in last 5 sc; finish off.

Rows 9 and 10: With Color D, repeat Rows 7 and 8.

Rows 11-14: With Color E, repeat Rows 3-6.

Row 15: With **right** side facing and working in Back Loops Only, join Color A with sc in first sc *(see Joining With Sc, page 158)*; sc in next 4 sc, 2 sc in next sc, sc in next 3 sc, skip next 2 sc, sc in next 3 sc, 2 sc in next sc, ★ sc in next 6 sc, skip next sc, sc in next 3 sc, (sc, ch 1, sc) in next ch-1 sp, sc in next 3 sc, skip next sc, sc in next 6 sc, 2 sc in next sc, sc in next 3 sc, skip next 2 sc, sc in next 3 sc, 2 sc in next sc; repeat from ★ across to last 5 sc, sc in last 5 sc.

Repeat Rows 2-15 for pattern.

154 COLUMNS OF PUFF STITCHES

Chain a multiple of 17 + 1 ch.

To decrease (uses next 2 sts), ★ YO, insert hook in **next** st, YO and pull up a loop, YO and draw through 2 loops on hook; repeat from ★ once **more**, YO and draw through all 3 loops on hook **(counts as one dc)**.

To work Puff St (uses one st), ★ YO, insert hook in st indicated, YO and pull up a loop; repeat from ★ 2 times **more**, YO and draw through all 7 loops on hook.

Row 1 (Right side)**:** Dc in third ch from hook, decrease twice, ch 1, (work Puff St in next ch, ch 1) 5 times, ★ decrease 6 times, ch 1, (work Puff St in next ch, ch 1) 5 times; repeat from ★ across to last 6 chs, decrease 3 times.

Note: Loop a short piece of yarn around any stitch to mark Row 1 as **right** side.

Row 2: Ch 1, turn; sc in each st and in each ch across.

Row 3: Ch 2, turn; skip first sc, dc in next sc, decrease twice, ch 1, (work Puff St in next sc, ch 1) 5 times, ★ decrease 6 times, ch 1, (work Puff St in next sc, ch 1) 5 times; repeat from ★ across to last 6 sc, decrease 3 times.

Repeat Rows 2 and 3 for pattern.

GENERAL INSTRUCTIONS

ABBREVIATIONS

BP	Back Post
BPdc	Back Post double crochet(s)
BPdc5tog	Back Post double crochet 5 together
BPtr	Back Post treble crochet(s)
CC	Contrasting Color
ch(s)	chain(s)
cm	centimeters
dc	double crochet(s)
dc3tog	double crochet 3 together
dc4tog	double crochet 4 together
dc5tog	double crochet 5 together
dc7tog	double crochet 7 together
dtr	double treble crochet(s)
FP	Front Post
FPdc	Front Post double crochet(s)
FPdc5tog	Front Post double crochet 5 together
FPdtr	Front Post double treble crochet(s)
FPhdc	Front Post half double crochet(s)
FPsc	Front Post single crochet(s)
FPtr	Front Post treble crochet(s)
hdc	half double crochet(s)
LDC	Long double crochet(s)
LFPtr	Long Front Post treble crochet(s)
LSC	Long single crochet(s)
MC	Main Color
mm	millimeters
sc	single crochet(s)
sc5tog	single crochet 5 together
sp(s)	space(s)
st(s)	stitch(es)
tog	together
tr	treble crochet(s)
YO	yarn over

★ — work instructions following ★ as many **more** times as indicated in addition to the first time.

† to † — work all instructions from first † to second † **as many** times as specified.

( ) or [ ] — work enclosed instructions **as many** times as specified by the number immediately following **or** work all enclosed instructions in the stitch or space indicated **or** contains explanatory remarks.

MULTIPLES

Multiples are the number of stitches required to work a pattern. A very simple pattern could be worked by making a chain using just the numbers given at the beginning of the instructions. However, most patterns need twice the number of stitches given in order for all the rows to work. For example, #154 Columns of Puff Stitches, on page 157, lists a multiple of 17 stitches plus 1 chain. If you chained 18, you will only be able to work the instructions for the stitches before and after a star (★) repeat. But, if you chained 35 (17 x 2 = 34 + 1 ch), you will be able to work across an entire row.

JOINING WITH SC

When instructed to join with sc, begin with a slip knot on hook. Insert hook in stitch or space indicated, YO and pull up a loop, YO and draw through both loops on hook.

CROCHET TERMINOLOGY		
UNITED STATES		**INTERNATIONAL**
slip stitch (slip st)	=	single crochet (sc)
single crochet (sc)	=	double crochet (dc)
half double crochet (hdc)	=	half treble crochet (htr)
double crochet (dc)	=	treble crochet (tr)
treble crochet (tr)	=	double treble crochet (dtr)
double treble crochet (dtr)	=	triple treble crochet (ttr)
triple treble crochet (tr tr)	=	quadruple treble crochet (qtr)
skip	=	miss

CROCHET HOOKS													
U.S.	B-1	C-2	D-3	E-4	F-5	G-6	H-8	I-9	J-10	K-10½	N	P	Q
Metric - mm	2.25	2.75	3.25	3.5	3.75	4	5	5.5	6	6.5	9	10	15